Field Guide to Child Welfare

Volume II

Judith S. Rycus & Ronald C. Hughes

CWLA Press
Washington, DC

Institute for Human Services
Columbus, OH

CWLA Press is an imprint of the Child Welfare League of America. The Child Welfare League of America (CWLA) is a privately supported, nonprofit, membership-based organization committed to preserving, protecting, and promoting the well-being of all children and their families. Believing that children are our most valuable resource, CWLA, through its membership, advocates for high standards, sound public policies, and quality services for children in need and their families.

CHILD WELFARE LEAGUE OF AMERICA, INC.
440 First Street, NW, Third Floor, Washington, DC 20001-2085
Email: books@cwla.org

CURRENT PRINTING (last digit)
10 9 8 7 6 5 4 3

Cover and text design by James Graham
Photographs by Jeffrey A. Rycus

Printed in the United States of America

ISBN # 0–87868-618-5

Rycus, Judith S.
       Field guide to child welfare / Judith S. Rycus & Ronald C. Hughes.
           p.   cm.
       Includes bibliographical references and index.
           ISBN 0-87868-617-7 (v. 1). -- ISBN 0-87868-618-5 (v. 2). - - ISBN
       0-87868-619-3 (v. 3). -- ISBN 0-87868-620-7 (v. 4)
           1. Child welfare--United States.   2. Social case work with
       children--United States.   3. Family social work--United States.
       I. Hughes, Ronald C.   II. Title
       HV741.R94   1998   98-4701
       362.7'0973--dc21   CIP

CONTENTS

Volume II

CASE PLANNING AND FAMILY–CENTERED CASEWORK

IV. Case Planning and Family–Centered Casework

A. Integrating Casework and Protective Authority

B. The Casework Relationship: The Foundation of Family-Centered Child Welfare

C. Conducting the Family Assessment

D. Developing the Case Plan

E. Case Closure and Recidivism

F. The Casework Interview: Implementing the Helping Process

G. Case Recording

A. INTEGRATING CASEWORK AND PROTECTIVE AUTHORITY

1. Conceptual Framework

2. Application

3. Case Example

Conceptual Framework

There are inherent social work practice dilemmas within the field of child welfare. One of the most significant is the need to balance the dissonant and conflicting responsibilities of being both an intrusive protective authority, and an empowering and collaborative advocate.

Child welfare workers must always intervene to assure that children are protected from maltreatment by their parents or caregivers. However, whenever possible, we must simultaneously prevent the serious trauma associated with separation and placement. This is best accomplished by strengthening and enabling families to protect and nurture their children in their own homes. When we succeed, children can remain permanently with their families, and still be safe from harm.

To strengthen and empower families, the caseworker must be an agent for positive developmental change, and a professional problem solver who can educate, motivate, and support parents in their efforts to change their parenting behaviors to meet their children's needs. People will only make significant and lasting changes if they believe those changes to be both valuable and achievable. Child welfare interventions must, therefore, include strategies that promote a family's investment in the change process.

Engaging families to be collaborators in a change process is not difficult when the parents or caregivers recognize that their children are at risk of harm, and they seek help to become better parents. However, very few families served by child welfare agencies ask for help voluntarily. Most enter the system because of allegations from others that their children have been harmed, or are at risk of being harmed. A percentage of maltreating families will deny the allegations and refuse involvement in any voluntary change process. In situations where children are at high risk of harm, and their families refuse to make the changes necessary to assure their children's safety, protecting the child will require the utilization of intrusive protective authority. Thus, child welfare workers must be invested with the responsibility and the legal authority to intervene to protect children at serious risk of harm.

Herein lies the dilemma. The caseworker must have the authority to intervene without parental consent, if this is necessary to protect children. Yet, the exercise of this authority can interfere with the development of a collaborative relationship, and the establishment of an effective change process.

The definition of a child welfare caseworker as a "helping person" who, nonetheless, has the authority and responsibility to enforce certain standards of parenting, not only creates confusion for workers regarding their role, but sends a contradictory "double message" to families. The dynamics of this dilemma are easy to understand. Most people resent intrusive authority. Characteristic emotional responses range from caution and ambivalence to anger and resistance. As such, the authority vested in the child welfare worker's position is likely to create suspicion, and increase resistance by family members.

Conversely, most people accept requests for social cooperation and collaboration. Such requests imply respect for individual autonomy and self–determination, and communicate a belief in the value of collaborative decision making. Approaching family members from a position of collaborative advocacy generally increases their comfort with, motivation for, and involvement in change.

Most people experience emotional dissonance when the same person is viewed both as having intrusive authority over them, and as also being empathetic and supportive. This is one reason why it is so difficult for us to appreciate the goodwill of the state highway patrol officer when he wishes us a good trip and reminds us to drive safely, after having given us a speeding ticket.

Many families we serve do not trust that people in positions of authority will always act in their best interests. This is not paranoia. Even within the most healthy perspective, powerful strangers can pose a very real threat. Therefore, caseworkers' vested authority is often perceived by families as a potential threat, and implies a loss of control. Thus, protective defenses are generated that include avoidance and resistance. This natural cautiousness is heightened when family members have previously had negative experiences with persons in positions of authority. Families from minority groups, particularly, have often experienced discrimination from people in positions with prescribed authority. For these reasons, the caseworker's position of authority may interfere in attempts to engage parents in a process of positive change.

Yet, the safety of the child is paramount. When a child is at high risk of harm, and cannot be protected unless the caseworker utilizes intrusive authority to assure timely protective intervention, the caseworker must do so, regardless of the negative consequences on the casework relationship. This critical point differentiates family–centered child welfare from other social work and human service interventions, in which the client always retains the right to self–determination and autonomy. Family–centered child protective services is the balanced integration of these dual responsibilities of a protective authority and facilitating advocacy. Good practice is knowing when, and how, to utilize the appropriate intervention approach.

COMPARING MODELS

The family–centered casework approach, and the use of prescribed authority, can be viewed as different points on a continuum of interventions. Both approaches have a common goal of protecting children from maltreatment, and both can be legitimate interventions, depending upon the circumstances. However, the underlying assumptions, methods, strategies, and potential outcomes of the two approaches are quite different. The chart on the next page compares and contrasts the components of the casework model and the protective authority model as they are applied to child protective services, and summarizes the potential outcomes of both.

CASEWORK PRACTICE

Focus of Intervention: The family is viewed as a unit, and is the primary focus of involvement and services.

PROTECTIVE AUTHORITY

Focus of Intervention: The child and the abusing or neglectful parent are each viewed individually as the focus of intervention.

Intervention Method: The family is involved in a *mutual case assessment* that includes both the causal and contributing factors to maltreatment, and inherent family strengths and resources.

Intervention Method: The *agency determines* the scope and nature of the family's problems, often in terms of visible problem behaviors only.

Case goals and case plans are developed *with* the family. The plan is a *contract* that outlines all parties' agreed–upon roles, respon-sibilities, and activities.

Case goals and case plans are developed *for* the family. The plan is a written set of *agency expectations* for the family.

Potential Outcomes: A family that is *involved* in the assessment of its own strengths and problems is *more likely to perceive benefit* to being involved with the caseworker and the agency.

Potential Outcomes: A family that is *not involved* in the assessment of its own strengths and problems is *not likely to perceive benefit,* nor make connections between their own behavior and the agency's expectations.

Family members are *empowered* to act in productive ways on their own behalf. This reduces resistance. The goal is *collaboration* to promote change.

Family members are *forced* to act in ways that meet the requirements of the agency. This increases their resistance. The agency relies on the family's *fear of retaliation* to generate change.

Changes may be *integrated* into the family's lifestyle and sustained beyond the agency's involvement.

Changes are likely to be *abandoned* if external supervision and monitoring are withdrawn, since there generally was no investment by the family to begin with.

Casework intervention *may not be sufficient to assure protection of the child* in a high risk situation, when the family is initially resistant, or is unable or unwilling to engage in activities to protect their child.

Worker has *unilateral ability to assure protection of the child* in a high risk situation, even when the family is initially resistant, or is unable or unwilling to engage in activities to protect their child.

In a protective authority model, the caseworker is essentially an enforcer. The components of this approach are as follows:

- The child welfare agency establishes standards regarding what children need for healthy development; knows what particular conditions place children at high risk of harm; and knows how parents must typically behave to meet their children's needs. Basic standards of child care are set by the community, and enforced by the agency. This provides a minimal standard of care to be met by all families.

- In each family situation, the caseworker determines the conditions that have increased risk of harm, and determines the specific changes that must occur in the family to assure protection of the children.

- The caseworker instructs family members regarding what must be done to provide safe care for their children. The case plan document is the tool that formally communicates agency expectations for family members and that directs their activities. Success is dictated by the degree to which family members comply with case plan expectations.

- The caseworker links the family to relevant services, and may directly provide assistance or direction; however, the worker's most salient role is monitoring the family's achievement of expectations, and administering sanctions for noncompliance, often by developing an alternative placement plan for the children.

- The caseworker's authority may be further strengthened by an action of the juvenile court.

- The strength of the protective authority model is that it allows workers to intervene immediately to protect children at high risk of harm, when other less intrusive methods cannot.

In the casework model, the role of the caseworker is that of an enabler. The model integrates social work and family–centered practice values. The underlying assumptions of this model are as follows:

- Family members are respected as individuals with inherent dignity, worth and value, and who have the capacity to participate as equal members in a collaborative change process. Family members retain the right to make important decisions about their own lives, including decisions about the best ways to protect their children from harm.

- Family members are viewed as unique persons within family, community, and cultural contexts, with unique experiences that have shaped their lives, and with inherent strengths and capabilities that can be mobilized to achieve productive change.

The casework method is based upon these assumptions. Its primary characteristics are:

- Casework consists of a series of well–defined steps that help family members identify and make important changes to improve their life situation and the care of their children.

- Casework requires the joint involvement of the caseworker and family members in all aspects of the change process. This includes the case assessment, case planning, problem solving, the delivery of services, and evaluating outcomes. The caseworker's role is that of expert facilitator or enabler, who assists the family in these activities.

- The caseworker provides guidance, support, encouragement, and reinforcement for efforts toward positive change, and gives constructive feedback that guides family members in trying new strategies and solutions.

- The caseworker may give advice and recommend solutions, but every effort is made to empower family members to generate their own solutions through their active participation in the development and implementation of the activities in the case plan.

- The caseworker approaches each family in a manner that is consistent with the family's cultural background and values.

- The liability of casework is that its success depends upon establishment of a collaborative relationship with family members. This usually takes time, even though a skilled worker can often engage a family sufficiently in a first contact to develop a safety plan that protects the children at home. However, casework alone is often not sufficient to protect children at high risk of harm when their parents are unable or unwilling to engage in strategies that reduce the risk to their children.

Application

The ideal approach to child protection is a service model which emphasizes the primary utilization of family–centered casework, without compromising the appropriate use of authority when necessary. This requires a flexible and individualized integration of strategies that can respond to changing situations, and that can be responsive to the needs and strengths of each family member. Examples of these strategies would include:

- The caseworker initially uses the casework method to "engage the family," or establish a supportive and collaborative relationship with family members. The expectation of collaboration is clearly communicated to the family. This enables parents or caregivers to contribute to developing and implementing a safety plan to protect their children.

- Throughout the life of the case, the worker conducts activities to strengthen the casework relationship, to identify and remove barriers to family participation, and to facilitate joint planning and problem solving. The agency helps families access and utilize the services they need to enable them to protect their children.

- The parents have the choice of working collaboratively with the caseworker to reduce the risk of harm to their children; or, by failing to do so, make it necessary for the worker to exercise unilateral authority to assure protection of the child.

- Prescribed authority is used only in those situations where the provision of family supportive services and other casework interventions cannot protect the child from harm.

- The worker may need, initially, to use the prescribed power of her position to gain entry into the home and to communicate the importance and seriousness of the situation to the family, thereby validating her presence in family members' lives. Relationship development occurs simultaneously. The caseworker's authority to enforce change may also be used as leverage to motivate family members to become involved in resolving their own problems. If family members can be engaged into a mutual problem–solving process, the first step of which is assuring immediate protection of their children, the worker may never need to exercise additional authority or unilateral mandates. Family members can be empowered to make all case decisions, so long as they identify and implement legitimate strategies that assure the safety of their children.

- When attempts to engage family members are unsuccessful, and children are determined to be at high risk of harm, the worker must use protective authority and act decisively to protect the children. However, the worker will continue to work toward engaging the family, until such time as it is determined that the parents' rights should be permanently terminated, and an alternative family is found for the child.

The following case example illustrates and compares how a caseworker might respond to an allegation of child abuse, first utilizing a strictly protective authority approach, then a strictly social work approach, and finally, an appropriate and balanced family–centered child protection approach.

Case Example

🚶 Susan Forrester and Jon, age nine

Susan Forrester is a divorced, 29-year-old mother who lives alone with her two children, Jon, age nine, and Wendy, age four. She supports herself and her children through public assistance. Jon attends public school, and Wendy stays with a day care provider for three days a week, while Susan attends job training.

The school nurse called the child welfare agency to report that Jon had appeared at school with a cut and large bruise on his forehead, and the beginnings of a serious black eye. He told his teacher that he had fallen off his bike. The nurse examined Jon and identified multiple additional large bruises on his buttocks, legs, shoulders, chest, and back, some of which appeared to be almost healed. The nurse told Jon that he couldn't have gotten all those bruises from a single fall off his bike, and asked him to tell her the truth about how they happened. Jon began to cry, and said that his mom "got mad and threw the frying pan at me because she made fish, and I hate fish." He also said, "She hits me sometimes when she's mad. She says if she doesn't make me mind, I'm going to grow up just like my dad."

Worker: Pamela Protective Authority

Pamela arrived at the school within a half-hour of the referral from the school nurse. The nurse showed her Jon's bruises. Pamela concurred that the bruises appeared to have been inflicted, and she worried about their seriousness. She asked the nurse if she thought Jon was at imminent risk from the head injury. The nurse said he was showing no signs of concussion, but that he should be examined by a physician within a few hours. Pamela asked the nurse to watch Jon while she went to the Forrester home to meet with Jon's mother.

Pamela arrived at the home, unannounced. She introduced herself to Ms. Forrester, explained she was from children's services, and stated that she needed to talk with Ms. Forrester about the possibility of Jon's having been abused. Ms. Forrester immediately denied any such allegation, and expressed fury at the suggestion she was a child abuser. She demanded to know who had called in the referral. Pamela said she couldn't reveal this information; it was confidential. She described the bruise on Jon's head and the multiple bruises on Jon's body. Pamela asked Ms. Forrester how they had happened. Ms. Forrester said Jon had fallen off his bike and hurt his head the evening before. As for the other bruises, she insisted she had never seen them, and stated they must have been inflicted at school to keep Jon in line, or they had happened on the playground. She stated she would go to the school and confront the teacher the very next day. Pamela said it was highly unlikely that the school personnel would have any reason to hit Jon, and that children don't get bruises all over their bodies from the playground. Ms. Forrester insisted that Jon hadn't been abused by anyone; she had seen abused children on television, and Jon didn't look like any of them. Besides, Jon had always bruised easily, and often fell down. If he had any bruises, it was a combination of these factors that had caused them.

She then asked the worker to leave, since there was no reason for children's services to be involved. Pamela stressed that the agency had a responsibility to be involved, since Jon had indicated that he had been hurt by his mother, more than once, and he was clearly at risk of being harmed again. Pamela said that Jon needed to go to the hospital for x-rays, and asked Ms. Forrester to accompany her. Ms. Forrester said Jon didn't need to go to any hospital, that she had never laid a hand on Jon, and that she would neither accompany Pamela, nor allow her to take Jon anywhere. Pamela then said she would call either the police or the court to get an order that would allow her to take Jon. And, if Ms. Forrester prevented her from getting medical care for Jon, she would place him in a foster home, at least temporarily. Pamela told Ms. Forrester that if she cooperated with the agency, John could likely come home again at some time in the future. Pamela said she would develop a case plan to protect Jon and to help Ms. Forrester, and that Ms. Forrester would likely have to attend parenting classes and counseling. Ms. Forrester insisted she wasn't crazy, didn't need counseling, certainly didn't need any classes, and would get an attorney and fight the agency immediately. Pamela made it clear that Ms. Forrester could do as she pleased, but if she didn't cooperate, the court would not look kindly upon reunification.

Worker: Scott Social Worker

Scott arrived at the school within a half-hour of the referral from the school nurse. The nurse showed him Jon's bruises. Scott concurred that the bruises appeared to have been inflicted, and he worried about their seriousness. He asked the nurse if she thought Jon were at imminent risk from the head injury. The nurse said Jon was showing no signs of concussion, but that he should be examined by a physician within a few hours. Scott asked the nurse to watch Jon while he went to the Forrester home to meet with Jon's mother.

Scott called Ms. Forrester from the school and asked if he could come talk with her. He explained he worked for an agency that helped parents with their children, and he had received a call suggesting that Ms. Forrester might benefit from help in managing Jon. Ms. Forrester said she didn't need any help. Scott suggested he needed to come visit her anyway, because Jon appeared to have been hurt, and was in need of immediate medical care. Ms. Forrester reluctantly agreed, and said she could see him in half an hour.

When Scott arrived at the home, he told Ms. Forrester his agency helped families with their children. Ms. Forrester stressed she had no problems, that her family was fine. Scott described Jon's bruises, including the bad bruise on his head, and said he needed to be seen by a doctor to make sure he didn't have a concussion. He said he had heard about the frying pan, told Ms. Forrester she must have been very angry and frustrated to have hit him, and asked Ms. Forrester to tell him about how Jon might have gotten the other bruises. Ms. Forrester angrily said she didn't know who had said anything about a frying pan, that Jon had taken a spill on his bike the night before and banged his head pretty badly. She didn't know anything about any other bruises. She said Jon had always bruised easily, and he often fell down. If he had other bruises, they were probably from roughhousing with his friends.

Scott asked Ms. Forrester to explain how she disciplined Jon. She said Jon was easy to care for, and she didn't have to discipline him often. When she did, she sent him to his room, and on occasion, spanked him once on his buttocks, through his clothes, with her hand. She then said, "You'd better not be saying I abused him!" Scott said he wasn't accusing her of anything, but understood that "children sometimes get hurt if their parents punish them a little too forcefully when they're mad. It's my job to help parents learn ways to discipline their children so they don't hurt them." Ms. Forrester said Jon was not abused; she had seen abused children on television.

Scott then said regardless of how it had happened, Jon really should be examined by a doctor. He offered to take Ms. Forrester and Jon to the emergency clinic. Ms. Forrester said that would not be necessary; she could take Jon herself when he got home from school. Scott again said he would like to go along, but Ms. Forrester stressed it wouldn't be necessary. Scott then said he would call her the next day to see what the doctor had said, and would bring some information back on parenting classes and alternative forms of discipline. He also left his phone number, explaining that he was always available to help, and he encouraged Ms. Forrester to call him if she needed him.

Worker: Carol Child Welfare Worker

Carol arrived at the school within a half-hour of the referral from the school nurse. The nurse showed her Jon's bruises. Carol agreed that the bruises were probably inflicted, and she worried about their seriousness. She asked the nurse if she thought Jon were at imminent risk from the head injury. The nurse said Jon was showing no signs of concussion, but that he should be examined by a physician within a few hours. Carol asked the nurse to watch Jon while she went to the Forrester home to meet with Jon's mother.

Carol called Ms. Forrester from the school. Carol told Ms. Forrester she was from children's services, and that she would like to talk with Ms. Forrester about Jon. Ms. Forrester told Carol she had nothing to say to her. Carol stressed that Jon had been hurt, and that she needed to talk with Ms. Forrester as soon as possible. Ms. Forrester reluctantly agreed. Carol told Ms. Forrester she would be there in 10 minutes.

When Carol arrived at the home, she thanked Ms. Forrester for meeting with her, asked her where she would like to talk, and followed her to the kitchen table. Carol explained that she had received a call about Jon, that he had a head injury and numerous bruises, and that he needed immediate medical attention.

Carol then asked Ms. Forrester what she knew about children's services. Ms. Forrester said she knew all about children's services, and she didn't need the agency's help. She didn't have any problems. She had seen abused children on television, and Jon had never been abused. She loved him, and took good care of him. She also knew that children's services took children away from their families and placed them in foster homes. Carol clarified that the agency never removed children from their families, unless the children could not be protected at home. Ms. Forrester said she always protected both her children, and she listed all the things she did for them. Carol said it certainly seemed she did many things for her children. Ms. Forrester said she certainly did, so Carol could leave now, since she didn't need help.

Carol said she couldn't leave just yet, because she wasn't sure how Jon had been hurt, and Carol asked if they could talk more about that. Ms. Forrester said she didn't know who called children's services, but Jon bruised his head when he fell off his bike. As far as she knew, he didn't have any other bruises. Even if he did, Jon often fell down, and he bruised easily. She said it was no big deal, so Carol could leave them alone now and go help families who really needed help.

Carol then said, "Ms. Forrester, I need you to understand the seriousness of the situation. I saw Jon at school, and he has a very serious bruise on his head, and multiple bruises all over his body. He needs medical attention immediately, and I was hoping you would accompany me to the hospital." Ms. Forrester responded furiously, "You have no right to go sneaking around and seeing my children at their school." Carol calmly explained that sometimes children *are* at serious risk, and the child welfare agency must act quickly, or many children would be permanently hurt or die. Ms. Forrester said caustically that Jon wasn't about to die. Carol said, "No, but I am very concerned about his head injury and his bruises. If he has a concussion, he needs special care to prevent long–term harm." Carol then gently, but matter–of–factly, explained why multiple bruises in different stages of healing, especially on soft body parts, are generally not accidental. She again asked Mrs. Forrester to go with her to take Jon to the hospital.

Ms. Forrester jumped up from the table and yelled, "I will not have you accusing me of having hurt my child, and you're not going to take him anywhere!" Carol said calmly, "I'm not accusing you, nor am I blaming you. I'm asking you to work with me, to clear up how Jon got hurt, and to get the proper help to keep it from happening again. I think you may know how it happened. You may be afraid to tell me. I'm sure you don't yet trust me. But I want you to know I understand that parenting can be very stressful, and sometimes, children get hurt. I'm concerned about Jon, but I'm equally concerned about the rest of his family. Despite what you may have heard, children's services is here to help in any way we can, and believe me, we've helped in some pretty tough situations. But right now, we need to get Jon to the hospital."

Ms. Forrester told Carol she would take Jon herself when he got home from school. Carol said it was important that she go with them. Ms. Forrester said, "You're saying I don't have a choice. Either way, you take him." Carol said, "No, you do have a choice. Here are the options. You can go with me now. You're his mother. He'll be frightened if he has to go to the hospital alone. I'd much rather you go, too. But, I'll have to take him, with or without your permission. If you don't come along, I'll need to get an order from the court, and I'd really rather not put you, or me, through that."

Ms. Forrester said, "You're threatening me." Carol said, "No, I'm helping you understand the reality of this situation. Jon has been seriously hurt, and I will do whatever I must to assure that he is protected from harm. But, if you help me do that, and we can work together, we can probably resolve this together, too."

Ms. Forrester grudgingly sat down, looked directly at Carol and asked, "Why should I trust you?" Carol shrugged, and said, "Because I believe you when you say you work hard to give Jon good care, and I believe that he should stay with you. That's why I want to help you address this problem now. I know you've only just met me, and I understand why you might not trust me. But, let's take this one step at a time. Let's go to the school to get Jon, and to the hospital from there. We can talk more later. I really would like you to go with us." She then smiled at Ms. Forrester and said, "You know, some people say I'm a pretty nice person. I'm a parent too. You might be surprised what I can understand." Ms. Forrester looked at Carol for a very long time, and then rose from the table, saying, "I'll get my coat."

SYNOPSIS

The three previous approaches had very different outcomes.

Pamela appropriately stressed the seriousness of Jon's situation. However, her lack of empathy for Ms. Forrester, her reference to "abuse" when discussing Jon's injuries, her accusations about how the abuse occurred, and her defensive responses to Ms. Forrester's anger only served to escalate hostility. Pamela had no choice but to exercise unilateral authority, which alienated Ms. Forrester even further.

Scott was sympathetic to Ms. Forrester, but he exerted no authority, and he abdicated his responsibility to protect Jon. While he was generally supportive and understanding, even about the possibility of serious abuse, he was powerless to assure Jon's protection. He did all he could do using persuasion, but he could not even assure that Ms. Forrester would actually get Jon to the hospital. Therefore, Jon remained at serious risk of further harm.

Carol engaged Ms. Forrester to work collaboratively, yet made sure she understood the seriousness of the situation. Carol explained how and when she would use her authority, and she stressed her preference that Ms. Forrester work *with* her to resolve the problem. She communicated this in a kind, matter–of–fact manner, without accusation or blame. She did not press Ms. Forrester regarding how the abuse had occurred, nor did she mention that Jon had told her about the frying pan. There would be a more appropriate time and place for these discussions. Carol did not want Jon to be punished for disclosing the abuse. She also hoped to first develop rapport, and hoped that Ms. Forrester would eventually tell her of her own accord. They would have another opportunity to discuss it further when the hospital physician confirmed the likelihood of abuse. Carol had also reinforced what positive parenting she had observed, and she stressed that Ms. Forrester's presence would be important to Jon in a frightening situation. This supported her remaining in a primary parenting role. Carol communicated that she could understand Ms. Forrester's frustration, and that she would like to earn her trust. The message to Ms. Forrester in this early interaction was that Carol was clearly going to protect Jon, but that she preferred doing so by working collaboratively with Ms. Forrester.

If Ms. Forrester had continued to refuse assistance, despite Carol's attempts to engage her, Carol would have had no choice but to return with law enforcement support, or a court order, to assure that Jon received the necessary medical care and protection. However, Carol would have continued to actively work with Ms. Forrester, and encourage her to become involved in the planning and service delivery process.

B. THE CASEWORK RELATIONSHIP: THE FOUNDATION OF FAMILY–CENTERED CHILD WELFARE

1. Conceptual Framework

2. Application

3. Case Example

Conceptual Framework

The *relationship* distinguishes casework from other problem–solving or service interventions. It has been the hallmark of the casework method since the early days of social work's development as a profession. Relationship was defined by Gordon Hamilton as follows:

> Within the democratic frame of reference, the professional relationship involves a mutual process of shared responsibilities, recognition of the other's rights, acceptance of difference, with the goal, not of isolation, but of... stimulating growth through interaction...The professional self is controlled towards the end one is serving–namely, to understand and meet the psychosocial needs of clients...[to this end] The social worker must be a person of genuine warmth...He must be willing to enter into the feeling experience of another, willing to listen to the other's view of his problem, and willing to go patiently along with him in his struggles for a solution [Hamilton 1940].

In short, the casework relationship is the vehicle of change, and is essential for constructive and collaborative family interventions. A professional relationship characterized by collaboration, trust, and honest communication is the most effective method of helping people identify their needs, and construct strategies to address them. Within a casework relationship, the worker is often an educator or teacher; an empathetic listener; a supportive advocate and ally; an honest, constructive critic; and a motivator.

If family members feel confident in the worker's sincerity and ability, they are usually more willing to accept the worker's guidance. If they respect the worker, they will model the worker's actions and consider suggestions. If they feel comfortable and collaborative, they will be more willing to confront the worker when they feel the worker is wrong, or honestly state their own thoughts and beliefs. The worker can communicate integrity and sincerity by developing an understanding of each family member, the family's culture and traditions, their beliefs, and their unique situation. Such communication can build family members' self–esteem, and increase their motivation to work on new challenges.

The development of a collaborative and honest casework relationship in the field of child protection presents considerable challenges. Honest communication in child protective services requires that families reveal and discuss highly personal and often threatening topics with a worker who is vested with considerable prescribed authority.

Most people feel threatened if called upon to reveal highly personal or sensitive information to other people. Unless we feel confident that the listener is trustworthy, accepting, and supportive, we may feel vulnerable, misunderstood or demeaned. Our self–esteem and confidence may be threatened. It is difficult enough to admit potential failings to oneself, much less to other people. We also know that unscrupulous or opportunistic listeners can use information about our weaknesses or vulnerabilities to harm us. It is important for caseworkers to understand that these are realistic fears, not paranoia. Most of us have experienced shame and distress when persons we trusted did not act in our best interests. When child protective services is involved, this normal distrust of powerful strangers often is combined with guilt. Many parents know they acted inappropriately and feel they deserve, and will receive, punishment that will deprive them of their families and their freedom.

The avoidance of relationships reduces these risks. People who have experienced only painful and unsatisfying relationships may find them too threatening, and may choose to remain emotionally insulated and withdrawn from others. Such self-imposed isolation is a dynamic often seen in parents who abuse their children.

It is easy to see why child welfare interventions are perceived as threats by many of those we are committed to helping. We are strangers, with the authority to disrupt their lives. It is normal and typical for clients to respond with caution and suspicion to such perceived threats, and their past experiences may heighten their propensity to do so. Yet, in spite of our understanding of these typical dynamics, we quickly label many families "resistive," because they evoke our own feelings of anger, resentment, and inadequacy by not responding to our efforts to be helpful.

UNDERSTANDING RESISTANCE

The term "resistance" is used globally to describe a client's apparent unwillingness to fully participate in the casework process. Resistance may be manifested in family members' verbal, behavioral, and affective (emotional) responses to the caseworker and to agency involvement. They may refuse to let the worker in the home; refuse to talk to the worker; exhibit verbal hostility and other expressions of anger; staunchly deny the existence of any problems; attribute blame for their problems to something or someone else; lie about their situation or their beliefs; consistently miss scheduled appointments; appear to be accepting of services, yet lack commitment to follow through; say one thing and do something entirely different; or openly threaten the worker or the agency with physical harm or legal action.

In child protection, initial resistance by family members is normal and expected. The unrequested intrusion into their lives by a stranger vested with considerable authority, who challenges their parenting capability and their rights to retain their children, is almost always experienced as a threat, regardless of how well-intentioned the worker. Resistance is exhibited because the family believes the caseworker and the agency are potentially harmful to them.

When we assume the perspective of a family that has been referred for alleged child maltreatment, there are some very real potential threats, as well as the more general threats of an unknown situation. First, regardless of our intent to keep families together, caseworkers do have the ability to remove and place the children. The family may believe if the caseworker learns enough about them, the caseworker may use that information as cause to remove the children from the home. This may be accurate.

The fact that a complaint has been filed and the agency is involved is often perceived by parents as a reflection of their inadequacy. This may be a significant affront to parents' identity and self-esteem. Parents may also feel that the caseworker may unfairly judge them and their situation, particularly if the worker is young, has never raised children, has never lived in poverty, is of a different cultural background, or has never experienced similar stresses and problems. At times, this may also be true.

Many families who are referred for alleged child maltreatment have previously had negative or punitive experiences with authority figures, and they may expect the same from the child welfare worker. Historical experiences with racism and other forms of discrimination by persons of minority cultures have created, for many, a generalized mistrust of persons outside their own communities, and particularly of institutional authority. Members of some cultural groups also strongly believe that sharing personal and family information with persons outside of the family is highly inappropriate. This may place families in serious conflict; they must violate their most fundamental beliefs and inappropriately divulge information to the worker, or risk losing their children. Resistance is to be expected.

Finally, change itself is inherently threatening. Many people find large-scale change difficult, even if they are unhappy in their current situation. While they often would like the pain to end, change may be perceived as potentially more painful. Even in situations when families have voluntarily requested help, they may have second thoughts when they begin to understand that they will have to change their behavior or lifestyle, or confront their limitations, in order to achieve their goals.

Resistant responses by family members are, therefore, instinctive strategies to protect themselves by effectively blocking communication, and by avoiding involvement in the casework relationship and activities. This helps reduce the perception of threat; helps family members feel in control rather than powerless and helpless; and, consequently, helps to lessen their anxiety.

Application

The relationship is the foundation of the casework process. It promotes the development of trust, fosters open and honest communication, and strives for collaborative problem solving. All are essential to effective casework. The formation of a trusting, consistent, and mutually respectful relationship between the family members and the caseworker will reduce, and sometimes eliminate resistance.

The caseworker must take the first step toward establishing a relationship with family members, and must strengthen and nurture this relationship when involved with the family. The worker's actions toward developing this relationship are called "engaging the family." Engaging strategies are designed to do the following:

1) Establish the caseworker's intent to be honest and forthright in dealings with the family, then acting on this by being honest and forthright in communications. This helps to reduce the family's fears and expectations of becoming uninformed victims of a potentially punitive authority.

2) The caseworker must clearly state the expectation that the family will be an active participant in all planning and decision making, and that the worker expects the family to take a leadership role in resolving their problems. This reduces family members' feelings of helplessness and loss of control, and is an important aspect of empowerment.

3) The caseworker must provide families with a "road map" regarding the agency's involvement, and what is likely to occur. The caseworker should clearly explain what the agency does, what assistance can be provided, and what can be expected to happen next. This helps families better understand the reasons for the worker's involvement and actions, thereby further reducing ambiguity and resulting anxiety.

4) The caseworker must deal openly with and accept the family's anger, frustration, hostility, and resistance. The worker should communicate that these are normal reactions, and that in time, the worker hopes the family will feel comfortable enough to work collaboratively. This can be communicated by encouraging them to verbally express their anger, or by voicing their likely concerns, if family members cannot. For example, the following strategies could be used to reduce tension:

    > "I know you're very angry about this. It would help me to understand what you're most upset about. Maybe I can address some of your concerns."

    > "Many families feel like someone is accusing them of a crime. I'm not here to accuse or judge you. I really believe that most parents

don't want to hurt their children. I'm here to help us both understand why this happened, and see what we can do to keep it from
happening again."

"I expect that, at first, you may not trust me. After all, you don't
know me. But, I can assure you I'll do my best to be honest and
above board with you, and to do things in a way that feels comfortable
to you. As you get to know me better, you may feel more comfortable."

5) The caseworker should act in ways that reaffirm for family members that
the worker is concerned, dependable, competent, and respectful of them.
This can be accomplished through activities such as meeting the family's
immediate needs; following through with commitments; understanding
and accessing the broader community of which the family is a part;
understanding the nuances of the client's culture; and assuring congru-
ence in communications by the worker and other staff of the agency.

6) The caseworker should demonstrate the ability to understand and
empathize with the difficulties faced by the family in their current situation.

7) The caseworker should routinely identify, support, and utilize the family's strengths. This improves self-esteem and motivation, and also
increases the likelihood of successful solutions. Families should be
empowered and encouraged to retain control in changing their own
lives, as long as their solutions can assure that their children receive
proper care and are not placed at risk.

8) The caseworker should promote the involvement of family members in
all aspects of the casework process; the assessment of problems, needs,
and strengths; the development of goals; setting priorities; and identifying resources and action plans. The caseworker should encourage the
family to take as much responsibility as possible for case plan development and implementation. Solutions that are constructed by family
members themselves are more likely to be carried out.

DEALING WITH ISSUES RELATED TO THE WORKER'S AUTHORITY

While the caseworker may want to engage the family in a collaborative relationship, the family's awareness of the caseworker's authority and power may
interfere with development of this relationship. A common concern is typically,
"After I tell you about all the problems, you'll have enough evidence to remove
my children!"

To set the stage to permit the utilization of casework as the principal intervention, and to resolve the conflicting roles of helper and protective authority,
the issue of the worker's authority must be dealt with openly and honestly. The
following strategies can help deal with this issue in a constructive manner:

1) The caseworker must openly acknowledge and describe the nature and
extent of the authority inherent in the protective service agency and in
the caseworker's position. The worker might explain the following:

"Yes, you're right. Our agency has the responsibility to insure that children are safe and unharmed, and that they receive proper care. So we have to look into it, any time we're led to believe there are children at risk of harm."

"Many children are seriously harmed, even killed at times, by their parents or caregivers. Our agency is expected, by law, to protect children from maltreatment. That's why we carefully assess any situation where we think a child is being harmed."

2) Early in the relationship, and as needed throughout case involvement, the caseworker should acknowledge the family's concerns about the agency's authority to remove children and enforce change. The caseworker must be honest about the possibility of removal of the children, and should explain clearly the conditions under which this would be considered. The caseworker should stress, however, that removal is considered only if it is felt that the child cannot be protected from abuse or neglect in the home, and that the caseworker's most important job is to work with the family to prevent placement. If placement is necessary, then rapid reunification becomes the goal.

"The court does give us the authority to remove children and place them in other families, when that is the *only* way we can assure that they will be protected from harm. But you need to understand, our first choice is always to help families care for their own children."

3) The caseworker should explain that removal of the children is only used as a last resort, when the caseworker and family cannot jointly make the necessary changes to remove the risk to the children at home. Even when a child is removed, it is expected that placement will be only as long as is necessary to assure that the child's home is safe. The worker should also explain that placement doesn't mean whisking the child away to a stranger's home, with limited access and infrequent contact with the child. Placement can be with a relative, or in a home of the parent's choosing, if that home can guarantee safety for the child.

4) The caseworker should stress that while he does have considerable vested authority, he would prefer not to have to exercise this authority, and that there are many ways to avoid having to do so. Examples would be:

"My preference is to work with you, not against you. If you are able to collaborate with me on resolving this, I won't have to do things against your will."

"Your involvement in this is extremely important. You know your family and your needs better than I do, and the solutions will be more valid if you're involved. The first step is to talk about it and see what we can agree on."

"The choice is really yours. If you want to work together, and we can work out solutions, then I won't have to force you to do anything. I'd rather that you and I could work it out together."

Casework is our intervention of choice because it is the most effective way of generating long-term changes in a family. Yet, casework depends upon the formation of a trusting and collaborative relationship with family members. The relationship building process is begun during the first contact with the family, and will continue throughout the entire life of the case.

However, some families will never become invested or engaged in the casework process, despite our best efforts. Their relationship capacity may be seriously damaged, or they may be pathologically hostile, even dangerous. In these situations, the use of authority to enforce child protection is not only permissible, but essential. The role of the caseworker, first and foremost, is to protect the child. While we prefer to do this by enabling the family to protect their children in their own homes, when this is not achievable, we must exercise our authority and act to address the best interests of the child, irrespective of the effects on the casework relationship.

CULTURAL FACTORS IN THE CASEWORK RELATIONSHIP

Cultural differences between the worker and the family can sometimes present barriers to the development of trust, empathy, and a collaborative relationship between the caseworker and the family.

Casework values stress respect for each family's individuality, the right of each family to self-determination, and mutuality in the casework relationship. Casework, therefore, provides a valuable framework within which to transcend cultural differences between the caseworker and the family, and to establish a mutual, constructive, relationship.

The following attitudes and strategies can help the caseworker engage families of different cultural backgrounds into a productive and mutual relationship. These strategies are particularly valuable during the initial stages of casework, but strengthening and maintaining a relationship across cultures is an ongoing process.

1) The caseworker should understand the values, attitudes, traditions, and beliefs of the cultural groups served by the agency. Such an understanding can prevent the caseworker from inadvertently insulting or criticizing a family member, or misinterpreting the meaning of family members' communications and behaviors. However, the worker must remember that all generalizations about a cultural group must be "checked out" to determine their applicability to any individual family, or else there is the risk of stereotyping.

2) The caseworker should become familiar with the rules of social behavior for a particular group and abide by them. It is important to tread gently until the culture is better understood. The caseworker should ask how each of the family members would like to be addressed, and what they would feel most comfortable calling the worker. The caseworker may request their guidance to help in understanding them and to avoid offending them.

3) The worker should openly acknowledge cultural differences during the early stages of the relationship, and acknowledge that there may be misunderstandings as a result. The worker might suggest that many people

find it harder to trust someone who is very different from them, and should encourage the family to point out when they identify differences, so they can better understand each other and avoid misunderstandings. If lack of cultural knowledge leads to a blunder, the caseworker should apologize and assure the family that no insult was intended. The worker should, similarly, not automatically assume that what is perceived as an insult or an affront was so intended by the family.

4) The caseworker should know the cultural norms of the family's primary reference group regarding the involvement of outside persons or agencies in family problems. These norms will affect the family's view of the caseworker and the agency. What appears to be resistance may instead reflect feelings of shame or embarrassment because family problems have become public, or a pervasive distrust of institutional authority. Such feelings are typical when a family values privacy, self-sufficiency, and independence. In some cultures, it is permissible to discuss problems within one's own family and community, but never with representatives of formal institutions. A caseworker who understands these issues can respond accordingly, and can establish a relationship that is comfortable for the family before addressing more sensitive issues. The worker might also utilize community leaders or extended family members to gain access to otherwise isolated or reluctant families. The worker's association with a person who is trusted by the family can speed up the establishment of a positive relationship. However, workers should not expect to be automatically accepted or trusted by members of the community. These relationships will also have to be developed and nurtured.

5) The caseworker should communicate interest in the family and in understanding things from their perspective. A willingness to listen and to learn from the family can help the worker identify areas of commonality, and also communicates respect for the family's strengths and uniqueness. During the early stages of the relationship, workers should do a lot of listening. Ask gentle, clarifying questions to help family members explain themselves, their views, and describe their lives. For example, "It may be harder for me to understand what you mean, since I grew up very differently, but tell me about it. I'd like to understand better."

6) The caseworker should use interviewing techniques which can clarify the subtleties of the family's communications. The caseworker should never assume what the family means, nor assume that the family understands the worker's intentions. The caseworker should clearly explain the meaning of his or her own responses and behaviors, and ask for feedback from family members to assure their understanding.

7) We cannot underestimate the barriers posed by language differences between workers and families. While basic communication is often possible, it requires considerable proficiency in a language to accurately express the subtleties and nuances associated with feelings, values, and beliefs. And, while it is possible for a worker to better understand a fam-

ily's culture simply by asking the proper questions and listening careful-ly, if family members must explain or represent themselves in a language they neither speak nor understand well, the risk of miscommunication and misinterpretation is high. Families should normally be assigned workers who speak their language, and trained interpreters should be used when workers are not fluent in the family's language.

(See related discussion in Chapter V, Culture and Diversity in Child Welfare Practice.)

Case Example

⚐ Establishing the Casework Relationship

This case example illustrates casework interventions that promote the development of the casework relationship, while simultaneously assuring protection of a child at high risk. The initial contacts with Jon and Ms. Forrester were described in the case example in the previous section of this text. (Refer to Section IV–A, "Integrating Casework and Protective Authority.")

This example is not designed to illustrate all activities at the intake level. The caseworker's direct contact with the mother is highlighted to illustrate the strategies and interviewing methods used by the worker to engage the mother.

The interviews with Ms. Forrester to complete the family assessment and to develop the case plan are included in subsequent sections of this book. (See Sections IV–C, "Conducting the Family Assessment," and IV–D, "Developing the Case Plan.")

Family:	Forrester, Susan, age 29
	Forrester, Jon, age nine
	Forrester, Wendy, age four
Worker:	Carol Johnson

Summary to Date:

Jon was referred to children's services by his school nurse because he came to school with a large bruise and cut on his forehead, and multiple bruises on other parts of his body. Carol Johnson was assigned the case. Her initial contact was with the school, where she verified that Jon's bruises were likely inflicted. She and the nurse also concurred that Jon needed immediate medical attention for his head injury. Carol met with Ms. Forrester, and despite Ms. Forrester's initial resistance, Carol succeeded in getting Ms. Forrester to accompany her in taking Jon to the hospital emergency clinic to be examined. (See Section IV–A, "Integrating Casework and Protective Authority.")

Goal of Current Activities: Relationship Development

Carol and Ms. Forrester drove to the school to pick up Jon. Carol explained to Ms. Forrester that they would be taking Jon to the Children's Hospital emergency room, because there were doctors and nurses there who were specialists in children's injuries, and that they would also be able to help the Forrester family. Ms. Forrester said accusingly, "You mean the abuse clinic. I know that's where we're going." Carol said, yes, some people called it that, and commented that it sounded like that bothered Ms. Forrester. Ms. Forrester remained silent. Carol continued gently, "I won't understand how you feel about it, unless you tell me, and I'd really like to know." Ms. Forrester said nothing. Carol then said, "I'd guess you may be upset because you think you're being accused of abuse." Ms. Forrester remained quiet. Carol continued, "I want to tell you again…we're not here to punish people, but to help them so children aren't harmed again. Very few parents hurt their children on purpose. We believe it's the result of a lot of different stresses, which is why we want to help." Ms. Forrester remained quiet, and Carol dropped the discussion. She believed her actions at the hospital and afterward would be more convincing than verbal reassurances.

When they reached the school, Carol told Ms. Forrester she would like her to take the lead, both at the school and at the hospital. Carol told Ms. Forrester she would support her as necessary, and asked if she were comfortable with this. Ms. Forrester said she was. Carol wanted to encourage Ms. Forrester to take as much responsibility as possible for her son's care. She also wanted to communicate her confidence in Ms. Forrester as a responsible parent.

When they arrived at the school, Carol suggested that Ms. Forrester go in first, and she would follow. She suggested Ms. Forrester sign Jon out from the school nurse's office and explain she was taking Jon for medical care. In this way, Carol's behavior was consistent with her spoken intent that Ms. Forrester remain in the parent role. Carol remained several steps behind Ms. Forrester as she went to get Jon and walked him out to the car.

When she saw Jon, Carol said, "Hello again," and asked how his head was feeling. Jon said, "I guess okay." Carol said, "Well, your mom and I are taking you to the clinic to see about that cut and make sure it gets healed." Jon asked where they were going. Carol looked to Ms. Forrester expectantly, and nodded to her, suggesting that she answer Jon. Ms. Forrester said, somewhat abruptly, "To the hospital." Jon said nothing. Carol said, "You might be a little scared, but your mom and I will both be there with you the whole time."

When they arrived at the hospital, Carol again directed Ms. Forrester to take the lead in approaching the outpatient nurse in the emergency room. Ms. Forrester told the nurse her son had hurt his head, and the social worker thought he should be seen. The nurse directed Ms. Forrester to the proper clinic. While they waited to see the doctor, Carol engaged Ms. Forrester in casual conversation about her family, her daughter Wendy, and her interests. Carol learned about Ms. Forrester's job training program, and asked her to talk more about it. For the first time since meeting Carol, Ms. Forrester talked openly. She told Carol about the training program, how she was learning to use computers, and how she hoped to get a good job and get off public assistance. Carol agreed that knowing how to operate a computer would make her much more employable. Ms. Forrester asked Carol if she knew how to use one. Carol said she did, but learning it hadn't been easy. Ms. Forrester agreed, and said emphatically that it was a real challenge. Carol asked Ms. Forrester if she were concerned about succeeding. She said not really, she thought she could do it. Carol reassured her that it was harder in the beginning, but once you got the basics down, it got easier.

Through this conversation, Carol was trying to take pressure off Ms. Forrester, and help her relax in Carol's presence. Carol expressed her interest in Ms. Forrester's activities, supported Ms. Forrester's attempts to develop herself, and empathized with the stress involved in learning something new. In doing so,

Carol communicated that she was interested in Ms. Forrester as a whole person, not just "an abusing parent." Her nonverbal message was that she could listen, could understand how Ms. Forrester felt, and could be nonjudgmental and supportive of her. Jon continued to listen intently to the conversation, while trying to look as if he weren't at all interested. Carol felt it important that Jon see her as a helpful and supportive person who wouldn't hurt his mom.

When they were called into the clinic, Carol again let Ms. Forrester take the lead. Ms. Forrester appeared nervous. Carol said, "I'm here to help you, if you need me." The clinic pediatrician first examined and talked with Jon. She then asked Ms. Forrester questions about how the injury had occurred. Ms. Forrester again said Jon had fallen off his bike. She could not explain the other bruises. The doctor then said while Jon was not exhibiting signs of brain injury, because of the location and severity of the head injury, she felt Jon should have a CAT Scan. The doctor explained the procedure, and sent Jon and his mother with the nurse to the radiology lab. The doctor asked Carol to come with her for a minute to her office. Carol followed. The doctor reiterated her suspicion of abuse, and Carol concurred. Carol also told the doctor about Jon's having disclosed to her at school that he had been hit with a frying pan. The doctor said the placement and extent of the injuries were more consistent with a severe blow with a hard object than with a bike accident. The doctor also said Jon's other bruises were very suspicious of inflicted injury. Carol suggested that the doctor tell Ms. Forrester her findings directly. She agreed she would, after Jon's CAT scan had been completed.

Carol joined Ms. Forrester outside the radiology lab and told her the doctor had some preliminary conclusions about Jon's injuries, and would talk with them both as soon as the CAT scan was completed. Carol wanted to communicate that there would be no secrets, and that the doctor would talk directly with Ms. Forrester. This was an attempt to reduce Ms. Forrester's suspiciousness. Ms. Forrester said, "Why don't you tell me what she said?" Carol responded, "She's the doctor, I'm not... and I think you'd get better information if you heard it directly from her." Ms. Forrester said nothing, and was very quiet while they waited for the CAT scan. Carol did not pursue conversation, but sat quietly with her. Carol felt Ms. Forrester was probably worried about what she would be told and how she would respond. Carol did not reassure her. She felt Ms. Forrester's heightened anxiety might help break through her defensiveness about the injuries. Carol's hope was, when confronted with clear evidence of inflicted injury, Ms. Forrester would at least partially disclose what had happened, giving Carol the opportunity to reinforce and support Ms. Forrester's honesty, and help her to understand the next step was help for her, not punishment.

The meeting with the doctor occurred as planned. Carol listened while the doctor talked directly to Ms. Forrester. The doctor clearly, but gently, explained that Jon's bruises had almost certainly been inflicted, and that it was important that Ms. Forrester accept this fact. Jon's head injury could have blinded him in one eye, or even led to serious and permanent brain damage, if it had been just a little more serious, or in a slightly different location. The doctor also said that bruises on Jon's chest and abdomen reflected blows that could have resulted in permanent organ damage. She wanted to keep Jon in the hospital overnight for observation because she was still worried about concussion, and she wouldn't have the results of the CAT scan for several hours.

The doctor concluded by saying that Jon was probably a very lucky boy, but that he definitely needed to be protected. She then asked Ms. Forrester to respond. Ms. Forrester was quiet, then began to cry softly. She turned away, as if embarrassed. The doctor handed her a box of tissues, and Carol said, "I know this is probably one of the hardest things you've ever done. But if you tell us the truth, we'll be better able to help you and Jon." Ms. Forrester swallowed, and then said quietly, "I never meant to hurt him bad. I never did. I love my son." Carol asked her, "How does it happen?" Ms. Forrester said, "He makes me mad. I only want to make him mind me. But he never does. I don't mean to hurt him." While Carol believed there might be more to the explanation, she felt Ms. Forrester's acknowledgment was sufficient to help finalize her assessment of risk, and begin to develop a safety plan for Jon.

Carol thanked the doctor for her help. The doctor asked Carol to take Ms. Forrester to the proper department to fill out the forms to admit Jon overnight. Carol asked what provisions could be made for Ms. Forrester to stay with Jon. The doctor said she would arrange special visiting hours, and felt if all went well during the night, Jon could be released the following day. If not, they would talk again tomorrow.

After the doctor left, Carol sat with Ms. Forrester and said nothing, letting her cry. Ms. Forrester finally said, "You're going to take him away from me now, aren't you?" Carol said, "I hope not." Ms. Forrester looked at Carol strangely and said, "What do you mean, you hope not?" Carol said, "A lot will depend on you. Remember, I told you earlier that I wanted to work with you, not against you? Well, now's the time to begin. Right now, we have to decide on a safety plan for Jon so we can be sure he won't be hurt again. Is there someone in your family that Jon could stay with for the weekend, and you and I will talk again on Monday and start working on these problems?" Ms. Forrester began to cry again. "I promise I won't hurt him. Let him stay at home." Carol said gently, "I know you mean that sincerely. But you also said you didn't mean to hurt him before. From what you said, it sounds like things may get out of control pretty quickly, and you may react more forcefully than you intend. Until we can understand what happens, and help you learn to control it, I think that it could happen again, even though you don't mean for it to."

Ms. Forrester remained silent for several minutes, apparently thinking about what Carol had said. Finally she said, "I suppose he could stay with his cousins. He really likes them, and I think my sister would take him." Carol said she would like to meet and talk with Ms. Forrester's sister, and then work out the arrangements. Carol said, "You need to understand, if he goes to your sister's, you can't take him from there. You can visit him, as long as your sister is present. We can explain this to her when we get there." Ms. Forrester began to cry again. "How can I ever face my sister? She'll never forgive me." Carol said, "If you like, I'll help explain that whatever happened, you've admitted it, and that you'll be working to correct it, and that you need her help. How do you think she'll respond to that?" Ms. Forrester said, "I don't know." Carol said, "If you're that worried about it, would you like to think of somewhere else Jon can stay?" She said, "There is no one else." Carol said, "We can place him temporarily in a foster home, if you'd prefer that. You can visit with him in the foster home." Ms. Forrester said, "He'll be really upset if he has to stay with strangers. I guess I'll just have to deal with it. I don't know why anything should change! It's been like this all my life! My sister already thinks I'm a terrible mother." Carol said, "Well, I think it takes guts to face the truth, and to make a plan that meets your son's needs, even if it is embarrassing and uncomfortable for you. In my mind, that's being a good parent, and I think you've just shown me that you can make good choices for Jon." Carol sat quietly while Ms. Forrester digested this last information. Finally, Carol got up from the chair and said, "Shall we go check Jon into the hospital, and then call your sister?"

Carol's final strategy was to involve Ms. Forrester in developing an immediate safety plan for Jon, thereby reinforcing Ms. Forrester's responsibility as a parent to plan for her child, and commending her when she did it well. Carol also shared her first suspicions about the dynamics of the abuse, acknowledging that personal factors, including uncontrollable anger, may have precipitated it. Yet, she said this in a factual, nonjudgmental manner. Finally, Carol helped Ms. Forrester see both her admission of the truth, and her willingness to confront the truth with her family, as significant strengths. Carol has reinterpreted as strengths what would have been construed by Ms. Forrester as personal failures. Carol has communicated that she expects Ms. Forrester to retain a measure of control in a threatening situation; that she believes Ms. Forrester can be an effective parent; and that Carol appreciates her honesty and willingness to make good decisions for her son.

Summary

Through this intervention, Carol's behaviors and responses were calculated to begin development of the casework relationship, which then provided a supportive environment in which Ms. Forrester could begin to confront the truth. Carol's honest but nonjudgmental responses to Ms. Forrester's admissions, and her willingness to continue to let Ms. Forrester make choices for her son also reaffirmed that the casework relationship would be honest and collaborative. While this relationship is still fragile at best, and will need considerable additional development, Carol has assured Jon's immediate safety without alienating his mother. Carol has also developed an initial agreement with Ms. Forrester that paves the way for the next steps in the casework process—determining how and why the abuse occurred (assessment), and developing a plan to prevent further maltreatment (the case plan and service interventions.)

C. CONDUCTING THE FAMILY ASSESSMENT

1. Conceptual Framework

2. Application

3. Case Example

Conceptual Framework

Randy, age two, went to his mother, lifted his leg, and in a whiny voice said, "Randy hurt." Randy's mother examined his leg and found nothing obviously wrong. However, as she watched Randy, she noticed that he was limping. She assumed he'd bumped himself, and it would probably go away. When Randy continued to limp and whine for another three days, his mother became concerned. She made an appointment with the pediatrician, who also examined Randy's leg, foot, and hip. He found nothing. He suggested they observe Randy for several more days and, if the problem didn't go away, he would make a referral to an orthopedic specialist.

While Randy's limp seemed to be better at times, it always worsened again. One day, when Randy was particularly uncomfortable, his mother called the pediatrician and requested the referral to the specialist. The specialist performed a series of X-rays and blood studies, costing many hundreds of dollars, and reported that she could find nothing significant in any of them. She suggested they recheck him in three months, if it didn't get better. Still, Randy's limp continued, and he continued to complain periodically.

Shortly thereafter, Randy's grandmother was babysitting and noticed his limp. She asked Randy what was wrong. Randy whined, "hurt," and again lifted his leg. Randy's grandmother took off Randy's shoes, and examined his leg and foot, and found nothing obviously wrong. She then examined Randy's shoe, thinking that it might be too small for him. As she put her fingers into the shoe, she felt something hard and sharp, and she pulled out one of Randy's small metal toy trucks that had become wedged tightly in the toe of the shoe. She removed the toy truck. Randy's limp disappeared.

This humorous but true story illustrates a simple, but fundamental truth of problem solving: a problem cannot be solved until it has been properly assessed and identified.

Randy's limp and pain were the visible, "presenting" symptoms of an underlying problem. Any number of problems could have created pain and a limp: a sprained ankle, a bone deformity, tight pinching shoes, or other injury. Different interventions would be called for, depending upon the nature of the underlying condition.

There are lessons to be learned from Randy's experience. First, more careful questioning of "what exactly hurts" might have identified that his foot hurt more than his leg. Careful observation would have revealed that Randy limped only when he was wearing his shoes, never when he was barefoot. Randy's mother and pediatrician quickly began looking for a medical problem. Randy's grandmother considered more obvious environmental factors in her assessment; she knew that children limped when their shoes were too tight. In our technologically sophisticated world, we often tend to overlook such fundamental factors.

Child abuse and neglect, the "presenting problems" of child welfare, are normally symptoms of personal, family, environmental, or social problems. Every family presents a unique picture of interacting problems and strengths. Unless we fully understand the interaction of factors contributing to maltreatment in a family, we cannot develop relevant safety and intervention plans. A comprehensive and accurate assessment is, therefore, the cornerstone of the casework process.

We must involve families in the assessment of their own problems and needs, since they have information we do not. We must observe carefully, and we must ask questions to assure that we are properly interpreting what we have observed. At times, we may see or understand things that families may not be aware of, or may not be able to tell us. And, we must always seek the obvious potential contributors to the problem, as well as the more obscure. In a casework model, therefore, the family assessment is always conducted jointly by the caseworker and family members. This team approach to assessment enables family members to better understand their own situation, and helps the worker understand the family's values, perceptions, needs, strengths, problems, and personal goals, from the family's perspective.

A frequent error in case planning is to brainstorm and select solutions without first fully assessing the problem. The inadequacy of this "laundry list" approach to case planning is that it generates solutions to treat only the symptoms. It is easy to see why many such solutions are likely to be irrelevant and ineffective. As an example, it can be dangerous to prescribe treatment for a chronic cough, which is a symptom, unless we know *why* someone is coughing. If the answer is "bacterial pneumonia," the best treatment is antibiotics. If the answer is "smoker's cough," antibiotics won't help; giving up smoking will. Similarly, if a parent neglects or abuses her child because she has paranoid schizophrenia, sending her to parent training classes will not resolve the problem. Treating the underlying mental disorder, or finding a more competent caregiver for the child, would be more effective interventions.

When a comprehensive family assessment is conducted to identify the underlying causes of maltreatment, the best solutions to eliminate maltreatment will follow logically and rationally from assessment data. The solutions will also be individualized to address the family's unique needs or problems, and will build upon family members' strengths, thus greatly increasing the likelihood of success.

In summary, in a properly implemented case planning process, case goals, objectives, and action steps will evolve logically from the information contained in the family assessment. Conversely, without a complete and accurate assessment, we can presume that our goals, objectives, and solutions will probably not solve the immediate problem, much less generate positive and lasting family change.

CONTENT AND PROCESS IN CASEWORK

Understanding the underlying dynamics in maltreating families is a prerequisite to an accurate family assessment. However, it is not always easy to discern these dynamics. The skilled caseworker is able to recognize, elicit, and help families properly interpret these dynamics. The first step is understanding the meaning of family members' communications and behaviors.

The terms "content" and "process" refer to aspects of communication. The "content" of communication includes the words and sentence structure in verbal communication. It is sometimes referred to as the "surface" information. "Process" refers to the underlying dynamics, such as feelings, symbolic meaning, and unrevealed intent that define the context, and thus contribute to the full meaning of a communication. In communicating with a computer, you need only deal with the content of communication. In communicating with people, both the content and the process of communication must be considered.

In casework, content usually refers to the strict, logical implication of the verbal communication between the caseworker and the family, or between family members. Content is what family members say to the caseworker, or to each other, and what the caseworker says to them. Content includes facts and descriptive information about family members, their situation, their problems, strengths, and needs. While content can give us much valuable information, the logical implication of the words themselves is only part of the picture.

Process in casework includes the observable dynamics of behaviors, interactions, and feelings (affect). It includes nonverbal behaviors, such as tone of voice, body posture, and facial expressions; emotive or affective responses; interactions between family members, or between the caseworker and family members; and family members' expressed feelings and perceptions about their situation. Process also includes the implicit meaning family members assign to their own behavior and actions.

In any communication, the content message (the logical implications of the verbal message) may not be consistent with the process message (the nonverbal, affective, or behavioral one). When a verbal and a nonverbal message are inconsistent or contradict each other, the nonverbal one is generally more accurate.

Some case examples can help clarify the distinction between content and process.

⚘ Sara

Sara told her caseworker that she had looked forward to having her son, and while she was worried that he had been born two months prematurely, it didn't really matter to her. She said she was still proud of him, even though he was so strange looking. The doctor said he'd outgrow it. She said she sometimes felt stressed that he needed so much care, and she was very tired, but she knew he would catch up eventually. She did, indeed, look tired; she had dark circles under her eyes, and she moved slowly, as if weary. As the worker observed Sara with the baby, she treated her son with gentle, if awkward, care. She responded immediately when her son cried, and she cradled and rocked him in her arms, smiling and talking quietly until he settled. And despite the difficulties she experienced in feeding him, Sara responded with patience and encouragement.

The content of Sara's communication was, "I am glad to have my son, his prematurity is a problem, but it doesn't make me feel any different about him." The process between Sara and her son was congruent with the verbal message. The worker concluded that Sara had lovingly bonded with her baby, in spite of his problems and her lack of experience.

🚶 Lucy

Lucy saw her two-months premature son for a moment in the delivery room, and then refused to look at him or hold him. She claimed she was much too tired and sore after a long and difficult labor. When encouraged to hold him the next day, she appeared afraid, claiming he was so little, and "awfully strange looking." She seemed eager to give him back to the nurses, and requested that the nurses feed him. The doctor had reassured Lucy that her baby was perfectly healthy, and would catch up within a couple years.

When her caseworker visited, Lucy talked about how cute her son was, even though he was little, and how happy she was to have him. During two follow-up home visits, the baby was in his crib in the bedroom. Lucy ignored his cries for long periods. When she did hold him, she did so awkwardly, and then quickly returned him to the crib. When the worker asked Lucy why she never held him, Lucy shrugged and said, "I hold him as much as he wants." She told the worker he ate and slept really well, and had adjusted to being home, and that she was really happy.

The worker concluded from the process-level communication that Lucy was still uncomfortable holding and handling her child, and she did not appear to have developed a strong attachment to him. Lucy's verbalized acceptance of the baby was not congruent with her apparent behavioral rejection of him. The worker believed the process message, and continued to monitor the case closely. She was correct in her assessment; she returned the small, sickly baby to the hospital two weeks after he had come home, and he was diagnosed as failure to thrive.

CONDUCTING THE ASSESSMENT

To conduct an accurate family assessment, the caseworker must elicit, observe, and interpret process-level issues and concerns. This requires expert listening, questioning, observation, and interviewing skills. (See related discussion in Section IV-F, "The Casework Interview: Implementing the Helping Process.")

Assessing a family requires tenacity. The skilled worker must continue to ask herself "Why?" until she is fully satisfied that she has an answer that is consistent with what she has observed or already learned. If she becomes aware of a discrepancy, she will continue to question and search until she can resolve it. She will work until she is comfortable that she has fully explored the issue and understands all its dimensions, and hopefully, identified its roots.

For example, if a worker observed that three young children were unusually small for their age and sickly, she would likely ask, "Why aren't they growing?"

She might learn that they're malnourished. She would again ask "Why?" and might determine it is because their mother does not feed them. She must question, "Why not?" There are multiple possible answers: the mother doesn't know how; she has no money; she is involved with her boyfriend and forgets; she's mentally retarded and doesn't understand she should; she's mentally ill and out of touch with reality; she's a member of a cult that preaches starvation as penance; she is always spaced out on crack; she is impulsive and spends her money on recreation. Once the worker has determined the answer to this last "why," she will have identified the primary origin of the children's poor development.

The effectiveness of the solution, however, is entirely dependent upon whether it correctly addresses the problem. Teaching the cult member how to properly prepare meals, and devising a feeding schedule won't result in change, unless the mother's values can also be changed. Telling a mentally ill parent she must feed her children will not eliminate the irresponsible behavior associated with her psychosis. Teaching good nutrition to a mother who has no money will not enable her to buy sufficient food for her children, regardless of good intentions.

In child welfare casework, the presenting problems of abuse or neglect are usually a manifestation of underlying conflicts, concerns, and stressors, which can only be identified by assessing the dynamics of the family's situation, i.e., the "process." (See related discussion in Section II–B, "Dynamics of Child Maltreatment.")

While most families can tell us a great deal about their situations, many are unaware of how interpersonal, social, and environmental conditions, as well as their own perceptions, needs, and feelings, contribute to the "presenting" problems of abuse or neglect. A goal of casework intervention is often to help families develop a better understanding of their own situations, and identify the factors that affect them. Helping families correctly identify the underlying problems can generate successful solutions.

Similarly, many families remain unaware of their own strengths and potentials, since these are often overshadowed by stresses and problems. Becoming aware of these valuable personal and interpersonal resources enables families to utilize them as coping and management strategies. If the family assessment is jointly conducted, it can provide families with necessary information to identify solutions to their problems, and empowers them to utilize their skills and strengths to implement them.

Application

This section reviews and discusses the relevant factors that should be routinely considered in a child welfare family assessment. The factors to be assessed are fully described, including listings of behavioral indicators. The ways in which these behaviors constitute either risk factors or strengths are also identified. Finally, relevant issues for case planning and intervention are also discussed.

DETERMINING THE COMPOSITION OF THE FAMILY

The caseworker's first task in family assessment is to determine who is included in the family. We can make serious errors if we make assumptions without asking the family members themselves.

The term "family" generally refers to persons who are related through a common genetic heritage. However, the actual composition and structure of families may differ considerably among cultures and over time, and even within a particular family, as new members are born, added, die, separate, or emancipate. Families often include grandparents, aunts, uncles, and cousins, as well as close family friends, godparents, or honorary aunts and uncles who are incorporated into the family system.

There are also significant differences in the structure of families. The stereotypical definition of an American family is a husband and wife, and their children. In reality, this isolated nuclear family is the exception, rather than the rule. Most healthy families, regardless of culture, have strong ties to grandparents, adult siblings, and in many cases, large extended family networks of cousins, aunts, uncles, and others. The relative importance of these people may vary among families and within families under different circumstances. For example, in some families, extended family members have regular, perhaps daily contact with each other, participate in each others' decisions, and serve as an important source of support. Other families manage their day-to-day living within the context of their immediate family, and communicate with extended family members less frequently. However, during times of celebration, such as a graduation, a wedding, or reunion, or during a crisis, such as the death of a family member, entire extended family networks may celebrate or grieve together. Cultural, interpersonal, and geographic factors all contribute to the degree and nature of any family's involvement with extended family members.

We must also differentiate the biological family from the psychological family. Both are important. While the biological family is determined by heredity, the psychological family is determined by attachment, and includes persons who perceive themselves to belong together as an intimate social group. This may include people unrelated by heredity, and in some cases, may exclude persons who are biologically related.

Child welfare workers must understand how each family sees itself. Who is included, and who is not? How are they important to each other? Who provides support and help to whom, and under what circumstances? Who leads or directs family activities? Whose influence is respected, and whose advice is likely to be followed? And, who can potentially interfere with a change effort, particularly if they are not engaged and involved?

The best way to determine the composition of any family and the relationships between its members is to ask its members open-ended questions, such as, "Tell me who is included in your family. Who are you closest to? Who makes the rules in your family? Whose opinion do you value? Whom do you ask for help, or advice?"

The caseworker might also ask family members to each draw their family, however they like. Using large sheets of paper and crayons or markers promotes creativity, and gives family members considerable freedom to express their views in a nonthreatening manner. They can then review each others' drawings, and discuss similarities and differences. Genograms are another means of identifying family patterns and relationships.

Finally, workers must solicit information about family members who are not currently involved with a child. This includes absent or "unnamed" fathers or mothers, and their extended families. These persons may be very important resources for children in our care. Yet, workers often fail to identify and locate these family members, or to engage them as supportive resources for children.

Several factors related to family composition, structure, and relationships should be assessed to identify problems and strengths. These are:

Strengths

- Families that include a consistent group of people who have relationships of long duration, and who have regular access to each other, in person, by telephone or letter, or through periodic visits.

- Families in which members maintain a strong identification with one another and view themselves as a family group.

Conditions That Increase Risk

- Nuclear families that are emotionally disengaged and isolated, or geographically separated from other family members.

- Families in which the pattern of membership is constantly changing, with little stability or continuity in relationships. Husbands or wives, boyfriends and girlfriends, and extended family members are continually changing.

- Family members do not agree on who constitutes their family. There is no consistent identification of members with the family unit.

- Parents who are isolated, without consistent family involvement, lack a significant source of support during times of stress. The absence of family support also increases stress, which concurrently increases risk.

FAMILY'S STRENGTHS, SKILLS, AND MOTIVATION

A thorough assessment of the family's strengths and abilities is a critical component of the family assessment process. It helps to identify areas of strength that can be directed toward resolution of current problems. A secondary benefit is the increase in self-esteem and motivation that can result when family members recognize their own positive traits and attributes, and receive validation of these strengths from the caseworker and other family members.

The caseworker considers family strengths throughout the assessment process. To fully identify a family's strengths, data collected during the assessment should be summarized, and the following factors should be assessed:

- What do the family members do well? What are they proud of? What gives them a sense of self–worth and satisfaction?

- What types of stresses and problems has the family dealt with successfully in the past? How did they do it? What resources and coping strategies did they use?

- In what ways might the family's strengths be supported and directed most effectively toward helping to resolve the current problems?

- What further education, support, or other interventions can build upon and further develop the family's existing strengths and resources?

- What are family members motivated for? What do parents want for themselves and for their children? How can they direct their energies toward the achievement of their own, self–selected goals?

- How are the family's own goals or desires consistent with the agency's expectations, and what may interfere with the family's ability to pursue these goals? What barriers can the caseworker or agency help to eliminate to enable the family to work toward achieving their own goals?

- A family's strengths must be viewed beyond the individual or nuclear family. Strengths may include a strong network of extended family and friends, identification with a larger social or cultural group, and commitment to group values and standards.

Points of Discussion

A family's strengths may not be immediately evident to the caseworker, or to the family members themselves. It is easy to lose sight of strengths and abilities when we are confronted with multiple, complicated, and challenging problems. However, a family's ability to manage under adverse circumstances should be recognized as a valuable strength. Examples are: the ability to meet basic needs on a very limited income; surviving a 24–hour day with four children under the age of five; and personal characteristics such as stubbornness, willfulness, and determination, which can be positively directed toward problem resolution.

Strengths may also be nascent. That is, precursor abilities or traits may be present, but the strength may not be fully developed. Casework intervention with a developmental focus will help the parents to identify traits, qualities, and attributes in themselves that can be considered elements of strength, and can help them learn to use and develop these abilities in productive ways. Casework strategies to promote such growth include modeling new behaviors, rehearsing, providing positive reinforcement and feedback, and rewarding the effective use of new strategies.

Families are often labeled "unmotivated" by their workers when they fail to do what the agency or caseworker believes should be done. Some of these families are actually highly motivated—to retain the status quo, to avoid change, and to avoid engaging with the caseworker. The question is not, "Are they motivated?" but rather, "What are they motivated for?" To achieve an accurate assessment of a family's motivation, the caseworker must assess the family's ability to persevere toward a goal which they have selected for themselves.

Family-centered practice supports the identification of goals and objectives that family members and the worker can agree upon. Service activities can then be formulated which the family sees as valuable. A mutual approach to case plan development, therefore, can increase the family's motivation to implement plan activities. Casework activities should also be directed toward helping the family recognize the value of agency intervention, and enlisting their involvement in the change process.

ENVIRONMENTAL STRESSORS AND RESOURCES

A family's economic stability is one of the most important factors in determining family needs and strengths. The physical environment can create stresses and challenges that make it impossible for family members to attend to anything other than daily survival. The physical environment can also offer significant resources and supports to help a family meet its needs.

Abraham Maslow's hierarchy of needs provides a framework within which to understand the profound effects of a stressful, unsupportive economic and physical environment on family functioning. Maslow's model represents human needs as a triangle, with the most basic of needs—physical survival—at the base of the hierarchy. Maslow contends that all energy will be directed toward meeting fundamental survival needs first.

Many families in the child welfare system live in economic situations that qualify as poverty. At times, the poverty is of long duration, and is not likely to change in the near future. Maslow's paradigm suggests that it is ludicrous to talk with family members about "self-actualizing" behaviors, such as attending classes or developing a hobby, when the family doesn't know how it will feed itself next week.

When families are subjected to stress from environmental and economic deprivation, they may be less able to provide for the basic needs of their children. This can result in marginal care or neglect, and can also be a precipitating stressor for abuse. One objective of child welfare services is to identify and eliminate economic stressors that contribute to risk of maltreatment in families.

The family assessment should evaluate the family's immediate economic and environmental situation, including: level and stability of income; ability to budget and manage money; availability of food, proper clothing, and home furnishings; safety and appropriateness of housing; availability of utilities and services; and the accessibility of transportation.

The availability of support systems and resources, and the family's ability to access such services, should also be assessed. This should include:

- The family's values regarding the use of formal agencies and other community support services.

- The family's knowledge of the services available to them.

- The family's current use of community support agencies, resources, and services to meet basic survival needs. Are they utilizing all supports and resources that are available to them?

- The family's current use of community and neighborhood resources for interpersonal support, including churches, neighborhood networks, parent groups, and community service agencies.

- The family's ability to access services, and potential barriers to access, including lack of transportation, lack of confidence, lack of understanding of the system, and previously unpleasant experiences with service providers.

Strengths

- The family can meet their basic needs for food, shelter, clothing, safety, and health care.

- The family is able to manage on a limited income, and can maximize the use of their resources.

Conditions That Increase Risk

- The family cannot meet immediate, daily survival needs. The family is without regular food, shelter, and other essentials for basic survival. The family is homeless.

- The family is without a dependable source of income, and cannot assure even short-term security. The ability to meet basic needs is cyclical.

- The family cannot manage on a limited income; money is not budgeted nor expended in the most efficient manner.

Services

When there are no psychodynamic factors contributing to maltreatment, the provision of support services to meet basic needs can greatly improve the quality of care given to the children. In families where there are multiple contributors, meeting their basic needs can eliminate a source of stress, and allow the family to direct energy toward resolving other problems.

The caseworker should serve as a case manager to identify and access economic and supportive services for the family. Such environmental problems should be addressed immediately.

Points of Discussion

A family that lacks the resources to meet their children's basic needs is not necessarily a neglectful family. Neglect implies a failure to provide for the children by a parent who has the capability to do so. In neglectful families, choices are made that are not in the children's best interests, even though other more appropriate choices could have been made. Poverty seriously limits choices, and day-to-day survival is a continual challenge. A family living in poverty, but doing the best they can with what they have, may need supportive services, but they should not automatically be labeled neglectful unless there is evidence to justify this.

The child welfare field has a responsibility to prevent child maltreatment whenever possible by helping families meet their children's basic needs. However, income-related social services cannot be the primary responsibility of the child welfare system. Many services needed by families living in poverty should be provided by other community service agencies, including county departments of human service or public welfare, community centers, housing agencies, and food pantries. Community-based, interagency service agreements are the most effective safety net for families experiencing economic stress. By accessing such community services, we can secure resources to eliminate significant family stress. However, the child welfare agency should allocate its own limited resources to assuring services for families in which children are at high risk of abuse or neglect.

PARENTAL CONDITIONS THAT AFFECT PARENTING ABILITY

There are several conditions that can affect an individual's ability to parent, including mental illness, mental retardation, and other psychological conditions.

Mental Illness and Other Mental Health Problems

Mental illness and other mental health problems include psychotic conditions such as schizophrenia and paranoia; bipolar (manic–depressive) disorder; personality disorders; depression; suicidal thoughts or behavior; anxiety disorders; and severe behavioral or emotional disturbance.

Psychotic individuals display pervasive thought disorders, emotional withdrawal, may have hallucinations or delusions, and may display erratic and unusual behaviors. Untreated mental disorders can render a parent incapable of providing proper care to the children. The mentally ill parent's inability to assess reality, and his or her often illogical thought patterns, can create very dangerous situations for children. Only a small percentage of parents who abuse, neglect, or sexually abuse their children are psychotic. Of those that do, many have been previously diagnosed and treated, but have failed to maintain their treatment or medication. Parents with mental disorders may be able to parent, if they are properly diagnosed, treated, and maintained on an appropriate therapeutic regimen.

INDICATORS OF PSYCHOSIS

The principal diagnostic indicators of psychosis listed below have been adapted from the Diagnostic and Statistical Manual of Mental Disorders, Fourth Edition (DSM–IV). Clients who display these behaviors should be referred for psychiatric evaluation:

- *Delusions*. Delusions are erroneous and irrational beliefs that cannot be altered by rational argument or fact. Psychotic persons may have delusions of being persecuted or controlled by others; believe themselves to be very powerful; or believe themselves to be someone else. They may also believe that gestures, song lyrics, or other environmental cues are specifically directed at them. Some delusions are quite bizarre; for example, a psychotic person may believe that a stranger has removed his internal organs and replaced them with someone else's, without leaving any scars. One psychotic mother of a neglected child insisted that the pastor of the local church had been to her house during the night, and had searched her cupboards to locate and remove all the cooking oil.

- *Hallucinations*. Hallucinations are sensory experiences not consistent with real world stimuli. They may occur in any sensory modality (auditory, visual, smell, taste, or touch), but auditory hallucinations are the most common, such as hearing voices, often threatening, that are perceived as separate from the person's own thoughts. These must be differentiated from dreams and illusions. Hallucinations may also be drug–induced, and at times are an accepted part of religious experience in certain cultures.

- *Severely disorganized thought and speech*. Thoughts may emerge with little serial connection and with loose, if any, association. Answers to inquiries may be only obliquely related or unrelated to the question. Speech may be so disorganized as to be incoherent. This is sometimes called a "word salad." The words may be clear and understandable, and the sentences may be well–constructed, but the meaning cannot be understood. For example: "My mother thinks John should go to school and visit the people in town, but when he does, he gets really upset, and in spite of this, in spite of this very fact, we just can't upset her. It's not right."

- *Grossly disorganized behavior*. May range from childlike silliness to unpredictable agitation. Activities of daily living may not be performed, resulting in unusual dressing patterns, inappropriate dressing for weather, and a markedly disheveled appearance. Grossly inappropriate social or sexual behavior may also be seen.

- *Catatonia*. Refers to a marked decrease in reactivity to the environment, sometimes reaching a degree of apparent complete unawareness. May include physical maintenance of rigid posture with resistance to attempts to be moved; maintaining bizarre postures; or displaying purposeless and excessive motor activity.

- *Flat affect and related behaviors.* Includes poor eye contact; a face that appears immobile and unresponsive (as opposed to expressive and animated); the range of emotional expressiveness in tone of voice and affect is clearly diminished most of the time. Person may sit for long periods of time and show little interest in the surrounding environment.

- *Paranoia.* Refers to the presence of prominent delusions or auditory hallucinations which are typically persecutory, grandiose, or both. The individual may have a superior and patronizing manner, and either a stilted, formal quality, or extreme intensity in interpersonal interactions. Associated features include anxiety, anger, aloofness, and argumentativeness.

MOOD DISORDERS

Mood disorders include depression and bipolar disorders, which combine manic and depressive behaviors.

A depressed parent may not have the emotional energy to attend to the children's needs. Depressed feelings and behaviors may be situational, of relatively recent origin, and may be in response to a traumatic loss. Clinical depression is more chronic, normally long standing, less related to situational causes, and often has a physiological basis. Depression can also result from taking certain medications, including those for treatment of high blood pressure.

- *Diagnostic indicators of a major depression* include the following symptoms, reported most of the day, nearly every day, for at least a two-week period: depressed mood, including feeling sad, empty, tearful, either by self-report or observation by others; markedly diminished interest or pleasure in all, or almost all, activities; significant weight loss when not dieting; weight gain; or, change in appetite; regular insomnia (inability to sleep) or hypersomnia (sleeps all the time); agitation and restlessness, or slow, lethargic motor activity; fatigue or loss of energy; feelings of worthlessness, or excessive or inappropriate guilt; diminished ability to think or concentrate; indecisiveness; or recurrent thoughts of death, recurrent suicidal thoughts without a specific plan, a suicide attempt, or a plan to commit suicide.

- *Bipolar disorders* combine manic and depressive behaviors. Indicators of manic episode include: a distinct period of abnormally and persistently elevated, expansive, or irritable mood. This may include: inflated self-esteem; grandiosity; decreased need for sleep; more talkative than usual; the subjective experience that the individual's thoughts are racing; distractibility; significant increase in goal-directed activity; and excessive involvement in pleasurable activities that have a high potential for painful consequences.

PERSONALITY DISORDERS

Parents who have personality disorders may display dysfunctional patterns of behavior in all aspects of their lives. There are several types of personality disorders with different symptomatology. The personality disorders that most often contribute to child maltreatment are borderline; antisocial; paranoid; and dependent. The following reviews some of the more prominent symptoms of personality disorders that might contribute to abusive or neglectful parenting:

- Disturbances in interpersonal relationships, such as: the absence of healthy emotional attachments; frequently changing and "shallow" interpersonal relationships; a pattern of unstable and intense relationships characterized by alternating extremes of idealization and devaluation (borderline); acute discomfort with and reduced capacity for close relationships (schizoid); preoccupation with unjustified doubts about the loyalty or trustworthiness of others (paranoid); avoidance of interpersonal contact because of fears of criticism, disapproval, or rejection (avoidant);

- An absence of empathy and concern for others;

- Chronic impulsivity in ways that are potentially self-damaging (borderline); frequent disruption and changes in life circumstances; abandonment of children; erratic parenting;

- Antisocial or criminal activity, and failure to conform to social norms with respect to lawful behaviors; deceitful, repeated lying, use of aliases, or conning others for personal profit or pleasure; reckless disregard for safety of self or others; consistent irresponsibility (antisocial);

- Identity disturbance; markedly and persistently unstable self-image or sense of self (borderline);

- Excessive dependency; cannot make even small decisions without advice and reassurance from others; lacks autonomy and initiative; needs others to assume responsibility for most major areas of life (dependent); and

- Exaggerated self-esteem and self-importance; grandiose, unrealistic self-estimation of his or her capability and talents; unreasonable expectations of favorable treatment; takes advantage of others to achieve his or her own ends; arrogant, haughty, feels entitled (narcissism).

Strengths

- Parents who have sought medical or psychiatric help to control and manage potentially problematic physical or mental conditions.

- Parents who exhibit a willingness to accept help, both from professionals and other family members.

- Parents who recognize their limitations, and allow other family members to assume a more active parenting role with their children.

- Parents who have a history of good problem-solving and management skills, and who have survived stressful and problematic situations in the past.

Conditions That Increase Risk

- When a parent's mental condition or emotional problems result in grossly inappropriate or harmful parenting behaviors.

- When parents have a diagnosed mental illness or emotional disorder, but refuse to maintain themselves in a treatment program, including refusing to take antidepressant or antipsychotic medications.

- When parental behaviors are irrational, and parents cannot be trusted to make sound decisions or judgments about their children's needs or welfare.

Services

Some mental illness, particularly psychotic, depressive, and anxiety conditions, can be treated with proper medication, individual and family therapy, and supportive services. The prognosis for parents with personality disorders is variable, and will depend upon the type and severity of the disorder. A thorough mental health assessment is necessary to determine the severity of the disorder, and the prognosis for adequate parental functioning.

Mental Retardation/Limitations in Cognitive and Social Skills

The intelligence and adaptive skills of parents with limited cognitive ability, or mental retardation, must be fully assessed to determine whether these parents have the capacity to retain primary responsibility for the care of their children. Competent parenting often requires significant cognitive and adaptive capabilities, including the ability to process information and make judgments; the ability to use language for accurate communication; the ability to logically assess and solve problems; the ability to retain information; and the ability to make decisions after having considered probable consequences and outcomes.

There are two measures of a person's cognitive ability: formal measured intelligence, or I.Q., and the level of adaptive or functional behavior. Both should be considered to most accurately determine parenting ability.

Standardized I.Q. assessments cannot by themselves always accurately predict cognitive ability or functional capability. Illiteracy and learning disabilities may reduce cognitive performance, particularly in an academic or test setting, and these may be misinterpreted as more general cognitive limitations.

Assessing adaptive behavior provides additional data with which to determine an individual's functional abilities. Adaptive behavior is broadly defined as the degree with which a person can meet the expectations of personal independence and social responsibility expected of his or her age and cultural group. Adaptive behavior is usually comprised of:

- Skills to meet basic physical needs. These include eating, dressing, toileting, and personal hygiene and care.

- Skills for functioning in a living environment or community. These include: domestic skills such as cooking, cleaning, laundry, and home maintenance; travel skills; budgeting and shopping skills, and the ability to appropriately use money; and the ability to care for belongings.

- Social living skills include: interpersonal relationship skills, the ability to cooperate and get along with other people; language and communication skills; the ability to initiate and carry out purposeful activities; behaving appropriately in social roles and in social situations; the ability to assume responsibility; and parenting ability.

In some situations, persons may score higher on adaptive behavior measures than might be expected from their measured I.Q. score. For example, a person with a learning disability, such as a reading or verbal processing problem, may have difficulty on some aspects of an I.Q. test, but may not be significantly hampered in daily living activities. Learning disabilities are usually specific to a particular area of cognitive functioning, most often information processing and/or reading. While persons with learning disabilities may not perform well in school, their general knowledge and intelligence in other areas is often normal, or even exceptional.

The same is true for illiteracy. Many adults cannot read or write, often because of lack of opportunity to learn, or because of learning disabilities. They may be embarrassed to acknowledge this, and as a result, may be misinterpreted as resistant when they fail to follow through with written agreements, such as the case plan.

Most parents with limited cognitive skills who are served by the child welfare system are in the borderline range of intelligence, or the mild range of mental retardation. A parent's level of intelligence and adaptive skill will determine whether the parent has the capability to retain primary responsibility for care of children. Many parents who function in the low–normal or borderline range, and in the upper range of mild mental retardation, can live independently in the community. They may be able to parent their children, when adequate supportive services are available. These supports may be provided by family members, friends, volunteers, or community agencies. (Additional information about serving persons with mental retardation can be found in Chapter VII, Child Welfare Services for Children with Developmental Disabilities.)

Strengths

- Parents who display cognitive strengths in their ability to process information, think through and solve problems, and communicate with others.

- Persons who are of low–normal intelligence or mildly mentally retarded, but who have well–developed adaptive behaviors, and can appropriately utilize supports and resources to assist them in their parenting.

Conditions That Increase Risk

- Parents who lack the cognitive ability to gather and process information needed to solve basic problems of day–to–day life and meet basic survival needs.

- Parents whose cognitive limitations result in harmful parenting practices and poor judgment in matters related to their children.

- Parents accurately diagnosed as mentally retarded, with significant limitations in both cognition and adaptive behavior, who have no family or community support, and who have sole caregiving responsibility for their children.

Services

Each parent who is thought to be cognitively limited or mentally retarded should be assessed by a psychologist who is proficient in assessing adaptive behavior as well as intelligence, and who has had considerable experience working with persons who are cognitively deficient, or mentally retarded. Linkage to specialized services is essential.

Supportive services for persons with mild mental retardation may be difficult to find in many communities. Most funding in the field of mental retardation is prioritized for individuals who have more severe disabilities. Volunteer programs, parent–aides, neighborhood networks, church groups, community centers, and other community–based services are possible resources.

When children remain with parents who are mentally retarded, out–of–home supportive and educational services can enhance the care they receive from their parents. The use of protective day care, preschool/Head Start programs, after school recreational programs, and involvement in community center activities provide children with stimulation, and with opportunities for social and emotional growth that may not be available to them within the home setting.

Points of Discussion

In situations where a parent with mental retardation cannot independently care for the child, and the child must be removed from the home to assure his safety, shared parenting between the primary parent and the child's foster or adoptive parent or caregiver can be an effective plan. The worker should consider the potential use of shared parenting as a permanent solution for children whose parents are mentally retarded and unable to independently care for their children, but who share close emotional attachments with their children.

Additional Psychological and Developmental Issues

As has been discussed above, some maltreating parents exhibit serious mental health, cognitive, and emotional problems, with subsequent problems in adaptive behavior. There are also less serious or pervasive psychological and developmental factors that, while not representing a particular clinical disorder, can negatively influence parenting capacity. The caseworker should be able to recognize symptoms of these psychological or developmental issues, and should know how to refer the family to a psychologist or other mental health professional for further assessment.

Personal and interpersonal maturity are developmental variables that describe the degree to which a person has developed adult ways of relating to other people, and of dealing with life tasks and events. These factors are often referred in the psychological literature, specifically ego psychology, as "ego strengths."

Several factors are included in the category of ego strengths. Well-developed ego strengths contribute to resilience, resourcefulness, the ability to cope with stress, and the ability to constructively manage the challenges of daily living. By contrast, failure to develop these abilities and emotional resources reduces adaptive coping ability, increases vulnerability to stress, and increases the potential for dysfunctional behavior and ineffective parenting. We can examine each of these factors individually, and delineate typical behaviors for various points on the continuum.

EMOTIONAL SELF-CONTROL

Strengths

- The parent has good emotional control, displays emotional stability and constancy, and can manage stressful situations without extreme and unwarranted expressions of emotional distress. The parent is reasonably even–tempered and goal–directed when faced with stressful and problematic situations. The parent reacts to minor stresses with patience, fortitude, and self-control. The parent holds his temper, and can express anger in an appropriate and nonharmful manner.

Conditions That Increase Risk

- The parent is emotionally labile and volatile, given to rapid mood swings, explosiveness, and strong emotional outbursts, with little apparent provocation. The parent flies into a tantrum when the child drips milk on the floor. The parent's moods vary widely from anger, to tears to euphoria on a moment–to–moment basis, depending on the immediate situation. The parent is easily provoked by very small, and seemingly insignificant, incidents.

ABILITY TO DELAY GRATIFICATION

Strengths

- The parent is able to plan ahead and can follow his own plan. The parent engages in behaviors that meet the children's needs before engaging in activities to meet his own needs. The parent can work toward a desired goal in small steps over a period of time. The parent budgets and saves money to purchase a costly item. The parent stays home when she cannot get a babysitter for her children, even when it means she cannot do what she wants. The parent spends money wisely to be sure she can feed the family and pay the rent, even though she sees a dress she would really like to own.

Conditions That Increase Risk

- The parent acts in ways that provide immediate gratification, regardless of whether the timing is appropriate or socially acceptable. The parent is unable to wait a long period for gratification. The parent's "plans" are transitory, and can be frequently changed depending upon the immediate context, situation, and his emotional needs. The parent does "what he pleases, when he pleases" with little attention to the effects on others, including the children. The compulsion to "do what feels good now" is overwhelming, and is often acted upon. The parent misses a school conference because a friend called and asked her to go out. The parent goes out in the evening and leaves her children alone, even though she knows she should get a babysitter and she may get in trouble if she doesn't. The parent spends her paycheck on a television, even though she knows it may mean a week without food at the end of the month.

ABILITY TO ACCEPT RESPONSIBILITY FOR OWN BEHAVIOR
Strengths

- The parent understands the relationship between his own behaviors and outcomes; and, he is able to recognize when his behavior has contributed to, or created a problem, or an undesired outcome. He can learn from his mistakes. He can assume responsibility, and will try to make adjustments to his behavior to prevent the problem from reoccurring. The parent feels shame or guilt about her behavior and its negative effects on her children. The parent understands how her anger at her own mother was inappropriately transferred when she slapped her child, and she knows she must find other ways to deal with her anger without taking it out on her children. The parent realizes that her continuing involvement in drugs is the result of her spending time with drug–using "friends."

Conditions That Increase Risk

- The parent does not assume responsibility for his own actions, and often believes himself not responsible for events and their outcomes. He inappropriately places blame on outside forces or other people for his troubles. (The key word is "inappropriately." The worker must discern whether the negative event is, indeed, the result of someone else's actions.) The parent blames the referral source for calling the agency, even when he has severely beaten his son. The parent blames his boss for firing him, even though his own behavior on the job was inadequate. The parent believes it is "fate" that resulted in his using drugs. The abusive husband claims his wife was at fault for the abuse, because she "provoked me and asked for it."

CAPACITY TO REALISTICALLY ASSESS STRENGTHS AND LIMITATIONS
Strengths

- The parent is able to participate in an introspective self-assessment, and recognizes both his strengths and weaknesses. The parent can be proud of his strengths, and can accept his faults without undue self-recrimination and chastisement. The parent recognizes his shortcomings and wants to address them. The parent can talk about what she does well and what she needs to learn to do better. The parent with limited reading ability asks for help in filling out a job application to be sure it is done well. The parent attends a parent education class because she realizes her child management techniques could be improved.

Conditions That Increase Risk

- The parent believes himself to be "faultless," and has an unrealistic perception of his own status and ability. He justifies his behaviors, regardless of their outcomes. He finds fault with people who criticize him, and believes himself undeserving of such criticism. The parent denies that he has any shortcomings. He defends his behaviors as being perfectly okay the way they are. He contends that his violence against his family is a perfectly appropriate way of keeping the family in line.

LEVEL OF SELF-ESTEEM AND CONFIDENCE
Strengths

- The parent feels confident and competent in important areas of her life. She can evaluate her own successes in positive terms. She feels good when she accomplishes something new, and she takes pleasure in her positive traits and attributes. Self-esteem and confidence support her efforts to try new things. She views new endeavors as a challenge. The parent expresses pride in her children and their accomplishments. The parent feels she did a good job in managing her tight budget to be able to buy her daughter a birthday present. The parent believes herself to be an excellent housekeeper, and wants to show the caseworker the new kitchen curtains she sewed. She shops at thrift shops to save money.

Conditions That Increase Risk

- The parent believes herself to be incompetent and incapable. She is highly self-critical, minimizes her achievements, and overestimates her faults. Her lack of self-confidence makes her afraid to try anything new, and she avoids unfamiliar and challenging situations. The parent does not follow through with case plan activities because she believes herself not capable, and is therefore defeated before she begins. The parent verbally chastises herself for all her failings, and takes more than her share of responsibility for problems. She may be depressed and immobilized. Or, she may insist defensively that she knows best what her children need, and may exaggerate the importance or effectiveness of her activities.

CAPACITY TO BE SELF-DIRECTED AND AUTONOMOUS
Strengths

• The parent can follow a planful course of action to define a problem, and to develop and carry out a proposed solution. The parent has confidence in her own ability to make decisions about day–to–day life events, can weigh the pros and cons of various courses of action, and can make the best decision based on this assessment. She can contribute information or an opinion about an issue, and is comfortable supporting her opinions or her decisions. The parent recognizes that her child is ill, and makes arrangements to take the child to the doctor. The parent learns that she is eligible for an additional subsidy and calls the agency to request application materials. The parent is able to communicate what she believes to be the best way to discipline her children, based upon their nature, and the seriousness of their behavior.

Conditions That Increase Risk

• The parent is not able to make autonomous decisions. She is dependent upon other people to tell her what to do, and how and when to do it. She defers to others to express an opinion. She vacillates, and never commits to a course of action. She is paralyzed by indecision. When asked what she thinks, she typically says, "I don't really know. What do you think?" When given options to choose from, she is unable to make a choice. She is unable to follow through with directions, unless someone else is with her to guide her. There may be many people in her life on whom she relies to make even simple, day–to–day decisions. She rarely begins and completes a course of action on her own.

Services

In general, parents with a higher level of developmental maturity have significant strengths which can be used to improve parenting. These strengths should be identified during the family assessment process, and parents should be provided with support and guidance to develop and utilize their strengths to achieve positive change.

Parents who are developmentally immature can be helped to acquire and develop more adaptive skills through consistent, supportive counseling with a trusted, caring caseworker or therapist, or involvement in a supportive peer education group. Treatment should be directed toward helping the parent meet her own emotional needs, increasing her self–esteem, and learning that planned, autonomous, and responsible behavior can be emotionally rewarding.

Points of Discussion

Some parents who display behaviors which reflect very deficient ego strengths may have borderline, dependent, or other personality disorders. An accurate diagnosis is essential in order to develop the proper service intervention. A good psychological assessment can help the caseworker differentiate between clients with personality disorders, and clients who are developmentally immature.

NATURE AND QUALITY OF THE PARENTS' INTERPERSONAL RELATIONSHIPS

Adults who are psychologically healthy are able to participate in mutually satisfying relationships with other people. Abusive or neglectful parents often have a history of painful, unsatisfying, or traumatic relationships. A parent's generalized distrust and avoidance of relationships may result in social withdrawal, sometimes referred to as "self–imposed isolation," and in chronic interpersonal conflict, both of which can be contributing factors to child abuse and neglect.

Strengths

- The parents can trust selected others, and believe that others can care about them and can be depended upon. They look to others for support, and expect to receive it. (The strength is in the intact *ability* to trust others, as exhibited by trust in close relationships. This does not necessarily mean that the parents will or should trust or accept help from anyone.)

- The parents display positive attachments to their children and to other family members. They reach out or respond to others; express affection and caring verbally and in culturally appropriate physical gestures; they appear to enjoy having their children around them, and they talk in positive or warm terms about other family members and their attributes.

- The parents can tolerate conflict in their relationships with others without feeling seriously threatened or uncomfortable. They are able to "work it out." (How this is done may vary among cultures; however, a mutually satisfactory or compromise solution is achieved.)

- The parents seek out help from others, and look to their relationships with friends and family members for support, nurturance, and guidance.

- The parents are selective with whom they choose to be intimate (emotionally, as well as physically); they show a normal degree of ambivalence or resistance in new or threatening relationships; they know when to be open and trusting, and when to be more reserved; and they are able to build intimacy with selected others over time.

Conditions That Increase Risk

- The parents are generally suspicious and untrusting of other people. They verbalize their belief that other people will harm them, or will let them down. (This may or may not be an accurate assessment of the quality of their relationships; however, the important variable is whether they have the ability to be trusting, provided the person they are with is trustworthy. Some people will not trust anyone.)

- The parents' relationships with their children appear to be distant, detached, or insecure. Parents may be withdrawn or indifferent to their children. They seem remote and unconcerned with their children's needs. They do not respond emotionally to their children's cries or discomfort. They may be negatively involved, constantly hostile, combative, or punitive toward their children.

- The parents cannot tolerate interpersonal conflict. They withdraw, take offense, become remote, and sullen. Or, they deny the presence of conflict and try to avoid confrontation.

- The parents do not seek help, support, nurturance, and guidance from anyone. They do not have a reliable support system, either within or outside their families, and this appears to be by choice, not from lack of opportunity. The parents appear to promote a "self-imposed isolation," in which their issues, concerns, and needs are not shared with anyone. This limits their access to help and support during times of stress.

- The parents are indiscriminate in relationships, and will be equally intimate or distant in all relationships. They never allow themselves to get close to anyone; or, they are immediately open, sharing, and effusively communicative with strangers. They may express being "very close" to people they have only just met.

- The parents have continually shifting loyalties and involvements; persons who were best friends yesterday are enemies today, and vice versa. Other people may be overidealized or devalued on the basis of insignificant behaviors or unimportant personal qualities.

Services

Casework counseling and family therapy can help parents improve their interpersonal relationship skills, and can increase their satisfaction in relationships with spouses, extended family members, and with their children. Success in the counseling relationship can also increase a parent's willingness to turn to other people for help and support. Other service interventions may include support groups and treatment programs such as Parents' Anonymous, or Alcoholics Anonymous, in which group participation and support are central features. While a parent who is ambivalent about relationships may initially resist participation in such groups, with outreach and support from group members, they may eventually become integrated into the group and benefit from it.

Points of Discussion

Information about the quality of parents' interpersonal relationships may help the caseworker assess whether they can be engaged into a casework relationship. Parents with seriously damaged relationship ability will often not be able to form a trusting relationship with the caseworker. Parents who have the ability to relate to others in a trusting manner may still not engage with the caseworker, if the caseworker is perceived as a threat. However, these family members can often be engaged through persistent attempts by the caseworker to gently address and defuse their anger, hostility, resistance, and suspiciousness. (See Section IV–B, "The Casework Relationship: The Foundation of Family–Centered Child Welfare.")

The casework relationship may be used as a therapeutic tool. Through a consistent, trusting, and satisfying relationship with a caseworker, at times family members can learn to trust others and can develop interpersonal skills, which can then be transferred to other relationships. The caseworker should not underestimate the potential benefits of casework for a family.

COPING STRATEGIES AND RESPONSES TO STRESS

Crisis has been described as a predictable emotional state which results when people are subjected to overwhelming and unmanageable stress. Crisis theory suggests that much human behavior is directed toward maintaining physical and emotional equilibrium (homeostasis). When problems or events (stressors) occur which lead to an upset in this steady emotional state, people engage in a series of behaviors (coping), to resolve the problem, and to reestablish equilibrium. Crisis may result when normal coping activities are not adequate to resolve the stress, and equilibrium cannot be restored.

Crisis theory also suggests that problematic events are not equally stressful for all people. The meaning of the event to the individual (perception) influences the degree to which the event is experienced as stressful.

Stress

Stress usually involves some type of change in life circumstances. Changes in the environment, in interpersonal relationships, or in a person's individual development can be stressful. Some events are universally highly stressful, such as the death of close family or friends, marital separation, serious illness and personal injury, and environmental disasters. Normally, the magnitude of a change affects the degree to which the event is stressful. (A tornado that uproots trees in the yard is considerably less stressful than one which destroys the house.)

Coping

Most effective human coping responses can be described as constructive problem-solving responses. These include assessing the problem, using appropriate resources and support systems, and developing plans and strategies to directly address and overcome the problem. When such strategies are effective in managing a stressful situation, equilibrium is generally reestablished and crisis is avoided.

When an individual's repertoire of coping responses is inadequate to master and overcome the stressful situation, crisis often results.

Perception of the Event

The same or similar events may be experienced quite differently by different individuals. The individual's perception of the event affects the degree to which the event is experienced as stressful.

Crisis intervention theory has described three ways events may be interpreted, and has identified predictable emotional responses to each of these.

1) If the event is perceived as a loss or a potential loss, the predictable emotional response is depression. The greater the loss, the greater the degree of depression and the more severe the stress.

2) If the event is perceived by the individual as a threat or a potential threat, the predictable emotional response is anxiety. The more significant the threat to the individual, the greater the degree of anxiety experienced, and the more severe the stress. Many events may be perceived as both a loss and a threat, thus causing both depression and anxiety.

3) If the event is perceived or interpreted by the individual as a challenge, and the individual believes himself or herself capable of avoiding a situation of significant loss or threat, the predictable emotional response is a mobilization of energy and activity directed toward resolving the situation.

Whether a crisis results from a stressful situation depends upon the interrelationship of stress, coping, and perception. Generally, low stress, effective coping ability, and a realistic and accurate perception of the event tend to prevent the development of crisis. Conversely, high stress, poor or limited coping ability, and a distorted or inaccurate perception of the event increase the likelihood of crisis.

Persons in a state of clinical crisis may display excessively high levels of anxiety and depression, and are generally unable to engage in purposeful, goal-directed behavior. Clinical crisis in a family is identified by assessing their recent history. If a recent event has created a threat or loss for family members, resulting in excessively high stress for them, and their psychological symptoms were precipitated or exacerbated by this event, then family members may be in crisis. The referral complaint of maltreatment, and the subsequent involvement of the child welfare agency are, at times, sufficiently traumatic to create a situation of crisis for a family, particularly if the children are removed.

The ways in which parents typically respond to problems can provide insight into their coping abilities. At times, the absence of effective coping abilities in otherwise healthy and well-intentioned parents can contribute to child maltreatment. Families who have limited coping ability and resources are at higher risk of crisis in the face of normal life stresses.

Strengths

The presence of effective coping strategies is a significant strength in families. It is evident that many coping strategies require the ego strengths that were discussed earlier in this section. These include: the ability to plan ahead; the ability to use structured, problem–solving activities to eliminate a stress or resolve a problem; the ability to take constructive action; the ability to identify and properly use community services, supports, and resources; and the use of interpersonal relationships for emotional support.

Conditions That Increase Risk

Ineffective coping strategies that tend to exacerbate, rather than resolve stress include: "flight" responses, such as denying that problems exist, avoiding problem situations, or physically leaving the environment; and "fight" responses, which include blaming others for the problem, or becoming angry, belligerent, and demanding.

Services

Families in clinical crisis can be helped significantly by providing immediate, intensive, and supportive services. The family members' inability to act in productive, goal–directed ways is a normal symptom of the emotional disequilibrium of the crisis state. Crisis theory suggests that most clinical crisis resolves within about six weeks. The outcome for the family can be either positive or negative. If the caseworker can establish a supportive relationship with the family during the crisis period, and, if the caseworker can provide services that reduce or eliminate the source of stress, the family can survive the crisis period with few long–term negative effects. In many instances, the positive actions of the caseworker during the crisis period can help the family function at an improved level after the crisis has been resolved. Families in crisis feel the need for help, and are, therefore, often more willing to accept guidance or intervention. A skilled caseworker can use the crisis period to help a normally resistive family engage in productive change.

This dynamic may help to explain the positive results obtained by intensive family preservation programs, when families are referred during a time of crisis. The crisis may be precipitated by the possibility of placement of the children if the situation does not improve. Not only are families more amenable to help and change when faced with crisis, but the structured interventions of the home-based service program provide immediate, concrete, and intensive assistance, with opportunities for families to learn new coping skills at a time when they are open to learning them.

Families who receive no supportive services when in crisis may become even more susceptible to stress, prone to further crisis, and may function at a less effective level than they did prior to the crisis. Caseworkers should be ready to identify situations in which the precipitant for crisis is the involvement of the child welfare agency, and should assure that the family receives adequate supportive services as quickly as possible.

Many parents can learn to use more effective planning and problem–solving strategies through education and counseling. Family counseling sessions may be used to demonstrate planning and problem–solving skills, and to give family members the opportunity to practice these skills by addressing their own problems. In addition, by providing links to "naturally occurring" supports within the family's environment, the caseworker can reduce the family's vulnerability to stress, and can increase their capacity to solve problems.

The worker should note that parents who have mental health problems, are mentally retarded, or developmentally immature will often perceive stressors as more threatening, or have less coping capability, or both.

Points of Discussion

The strengthening of a family's coping abilities is a central strategy of crisis intervention counseling. A family in crisis is likely to be very receptive to trying new strategies, particularly if they hold promise of resolving the crisis situation. Caseworkers should be able to teach, demonstrate, and support the development of productive coping strategies by families they serve, and should routinely include these activities in their case plans.

Workers should also assess their agency's capability to provide immediate crisis intervention and intensive in-home services to families. This necessitates rapid case transfer from intake to ongoing or in-home services, and the initiation of in-home services by a skilled caseworker within a matter of hours after receiving the case. Workers should understand that rapid provision of services to families in crisis can, at times, create a period of positive change which might not otherwise be possible. This may significantly shorten the period of time the case needs to remain open.

PARENTING SKILLS

A thorough assessment should be made of the parent's usual parenting strategies and methods. The assessment of parenting skills must be made within the context of the family's social and cultural environment. The worker must understand the accepted parenting practices of the family's cultural and social group, including the meaning and intent of parenting interventions. It is possible to misinterpret the parent's behavior as inappropriate, if it is assessed from an inappropriate cultural perspective.

The parenting practices and capability of parents should be thoroughly assessed. Most parents have some parenting skills and strengths. They may have less knowledge or skill in some areas, or emotional factors may interfere with their parenting ability. These barriers may include debilitating poverty, mental illness, or lack of opportunity to learn. By helping families to meet their basic economic needs, by alleviating depression, and by providing parents with constructive and supportive feedback, we can often strengthen parenting capability.

Parenting abilities should be assessed independently in each of the following areas:
1. Basic child care skills;
2. Nurturing strategies to promote attachment;
3. Discipline strategies;
4. Adequacy of supervision;

5. Parent's ability to encourage child's development; and
6. The degree to which the parent maintains stringent or unrealistic standards and expectations for the child's behavior.

1. *Basic child care skills: feeding and nutrition, bathing, dressing, maintaining a schedule; meeting health care needs; and health-related hygiene.*

Strengths

- Parent provides child with regular feedings that meet child's nutritional needs. Parent provides a hygienic environment for the child. Parent dresses the child in clothes that are appropriate for the weather and that protect the child from illness. Child receives basic preventive health care (immunizations, dental care), and receives medical care when ill. Parent provides basic health–related hygiene (bathing, brushing teeth).

Conditions That Increase Risk

- Parent fails to meet child's nutritional, health, and safety needs. Feedings are intermittent, irregular, and do not meet basic nutritional needs. Children are not dressed to protect them from adverse weather conditions. Children's hygiene is not sufficient to maintain good health (serious diaper rash from leaving infants in soiled diapers; changing diapers without cleaning the diaper area; serious tooth decay from lack of hygiene). Children are not provided with necessary medical care.

2. *Nurturing strategies to promote attachment: holding, cuddling, talking or playing with the child, responsiveness to the child's cues and approaches.*

Strengths

- Parent regularly engages child in interaction through talking, playing, or cuddling. Parent responds in a timely manner when child is distressed or needs care. Parent properly interprets child's verbal and behavioral communications, and recognizes when child is hungry, tired, frightened, or in need of attention. Parent responds in an encouraging and positive manner when child approaches. Parent routinely demonstrates affection for child in a manner that is appropriate within the family's culture.

Conditions That Increase Risk

- Parent consistently ignores child, or fails to respond to child's advances. Parent does not differentiate child's cues, and does not respond to child's needs in a timely manner. Parent does not typically initiate play or interaction with child. Parent does not demonstrate affection for child. Parent handles and communicates with child in an abrupt, harsh, punitive manner.

3. *Discipline strategies: including setting and enforcing limits, strategies to manage behavior, consistency in approach, and effectiveness of discipline strategies.*

Strengths

- Parent sets limits for child's behavior that are appropriate for the child's age and development. Parent is consistent in enforcing limits, and utilizes interventions that are age-appropriate, culturally appropriate, and nonharmful to the child. The extent of discipline is appropriate for the situation. Discipline is administered in a manner that protects and educates the child simultaneously. Child understands "family rules" and the reasons for them.

Conditions That Increase Risk

- Limits set by parents are extremely rigid, or are unrealistic for the age and developmental capacity of the child. Discipline is rigidly and harshly administered. Discipline is excessive for the situation. Parent sets and enforces few, if any, consistent limits on child's behavior. Parent provides no structure or consistency for child. Child does not understand the "rules" of behavior.

4. *Adequacy of supervision and parent's ability to recognize harmful situations and protect child from them.*

Strengths

- Parent is always aware of child's location and activities, and intervenes to prevent child from harm. Parent redirects child when child appears to be in danger. Child is not permitted to engage in activities that exceed the child's developmental capacity. Parent leaves children with competent babysitters/caregivers. Parent also recognizes when she is experiencing excessive stress, which may affect the quality of child care, and can ask others to care for the child temporarily, or to provide help and support.

Conditions That Increase Risk

- Parent leaves young child unattended for long periods. Parent does not monitor child's activities, or allows child to engage in activities that exceed child's developmental capability. Parent does not redirect child from potentially hazardous situations. Child is left alone, or in the care of persons who are not competent caregivers. Parent does not seek help when under excessive stress, and child is placed at subsequent risk.

5. *Parent's ability to encourage child's development: use of play, books, toys, household objects, television, interpersonal games, and other parent interactions with the child to develop cognitive, social, and language skills.*

Strengths

- Parent engages child in activities that stimulate child's thinking, language, or motor development. Parent tries to provide child with age-appropriate toys. Parent encourages child to play with appropriate household items, and helps stimulate child's imaginative play (placing a blanket over a table to create a cave; riding a broom handle "horse"; building a city with plastic containers and cups; making up stories about pictures in magazines). Parent engages in conversations with child about child's activities. Parent seeks activities that will catch and hold child's attention. Parent engages in interactive play with child.

Conditions That Increase Risk

- Parent ignores child for long periods of time. Parent does not engage child in play or mutual activities. Parent's verbal responses to child are short, abrupt, and are limited in scope and content. Parent rarely initiates conversation with child. Parent often directs child to "go play," without further interaction or assistance. Parent prohibits imaginative play, or utilization of appropriate household items in play activities.

6. *The degree to which the parent maintains stringent or unrealistic standards and expectations for the child's behavior, considering the child's age and developmental level.*

Strengths

- Parent's expectations for child's behavior are consistent with child's age and developmental level. Parent knows typical developmental milestones, and can adjust parenting strategies to be consistent with child's capacity. (Parent does not discipline young infants for "misbehavior"; parent uses simple and clear consequences for misbehavior of toddlers; parent helps a seven year old understand what she did wrong.) Parent does not expect children to behave in adult-like ways. Parent can be flexible and alter expectations for a child in different situations (understanding that children cry more often when they are very tired or sick). Parent can individualize parenting interventions to best address a child's unique personality and needs.

Conditions That Increase Risk

- Parent's expectations for child's behavior are not appropriate for child's age and developmental level. Parent expects child to think, act, and interact in ways that are more typical of an older child or an adult. Parent is rigid in expectations, and cannot be flexible to accommodate different situations. Parent does not change parenting interventions to meet child's developmental capacity, situation, or personality.

Services

Parent training is an appropriate intervention when neglect or abuse are the result of the parent's limited parenting knowledge and skill. These services can be provided through referral to parenting classes, or training in the home by a caseworker, a parent aide, a homemaker, or a trained foster caregiver.

Points of Discussion

Referral of parents to formal parenting classes is a common casework intervention, but it is not always appropriate. Many parenting classes were developed for parents with adequate parenting skills who seek techniques to improve communication, and promote the development of self–reliance and responsibility in their children. Participation in these parenting classes requires a high level of comfort in social and group situations. Additionally, unless parenting classes are offered from a culturally relevant frame of reference, many parents will refuse to attend, or will not complete the classes.

Formal programs to train parenting skills should be developed specifically to meet the needs of families in the child welfare system. Many parents need training in very basic child care practices. If such training is conducted in a group setting, the group leader must be skilled in developing group process with parents who may have limited social confidence or competence. A group setting may be very helpful for many families, if they can be made to feel comfortable and supported in the group.

For many families, one–to–one, in–home training and coaching is the preferred means of teaching parenting. Parents are often more comfortable with, and learn more, if coached individually in the familiar environment of their own homes. Regular casework visits, visits in foster or relative homes, and other casework contacts can also be used as opportunities to help parents learn more effective parenting strategies.

Parenting strategies should also be consistent with the family's values and cultural perspective. Training in parenting techniques that are unacceptable within the family's culture will generally be unproductive.

In situations where improper parenting is not the result of lack of knowledge, but rather because of the parent's personal deficiencies or emotional problems, formal parenting classes are not an appropriate intervention. The caseworker must be able to differentiate the contributing factors to poor parenting before trying to determine the best service interventions.

SUBSTANCE ABUSE

The abuse of drugs and alcohol by parents has become an increasingly frequent contributor to child maltreatment. The risks to children can be quite high. Children of alcoholic mothers may be born with fetal alcohol syndrome, which is characterized by growth deficiency, learning disabilities, behavior problems, and various degrees of mental retardation. Infants whose mothers used crack cocaine during pregnancy are likely to have neurological, behavioral, and other developmental problems. (Refer to Section VII-C, "The Primary Developmental Disabilities: Identification and Early Intervention," for more information on developmental conditions resulting from substance abuse.)

Children with substance–abusing parents are also at higher risk of physical abuse, neglect, and sexual abuse. As an example, it has been estimated that up to 75% of all incest incidents involve use of alcohol on the part of the perpetrator [Thompson 1990].

Drug abuse can be defined as the use of a drug for other than medicinal purposes, which results in the impaired physical, mental, emotional, or social well-being of the user, or others who are dependent upon the user. Commonly abused drugs are alcohol, prescription drugs, sedatives, stimulants, marijuana, narcotics, inhalants, hallucinogens, phencyclidine, cocaine, and crack. These drugs affect the user's feelings, perceptions, and behavior by altering the body chemistry. Users often experience these physiological changes as mildly to intensely pleasurable–altering mood, reducing anxiety and depression, and creating feelings of euphoria sometimes referred to as a "high."

With some drugs, continued use sufficiently changes the body chemistry to increase tolerance. The user then requires increasing amounts of the drug to produce the same effect. The user may also become physically and/or emotionally dependent on the drug to function. This dependence, also referred to as addiction, makes it extremely difficult to control or stop use of the drug. Withdrawal can cause a wide range of unpleasant, painful, and potentially dangerous physical and psychological symptoms.

Clearly, not all persons who use drugs or alcohol are drug dependent. The scope, frequency, and circumstances of parents' drug or alcohol use will determine the ultimate risk to their children. Drug use can be limited in scope and frequency, more or less controlled, and it may not significantly affect the user's functioning or parenting ability. However, for many people, recreational use of drugs and alcohol can be a "slippery slope," quickly becoming more chronic and serious, leading to abuse or addiction. This is particularly true of crack cocaine, a highly addictive substance. Zuckerman [1994] states that while becoming addicted to alcohol, heroin, or intranasal cocaine may take years, with crack cocaine this progression from recreational use to addiction can occur within weeks or months of first use.

Once addicted, the user has a "chronic, progressive disease in which there is a loss of control over the use of, and a compulsive preoccupation with, a substance, despite the consequences" [Zuckerman 1994]. The addict's primary goal is to maintain use of the drug. Pervasive disruption in all aspects of the addict's life –physical, psychological, economic, familial, interpersonal, and social–is a common result. The effects of substance abuse on parenting can be pervasive. Since addicts consider their own needs first, their children's needs for basic physical care, nurturance, and supervision are often not met, placing them at high risk of harm. According to Zuckerman [1994] the "primary relationship" of mothers addicted to crack "is with their drug of choice, not with their child." Howard [1994] reports that mothers who are dependent on crack were found to be significantly less sensitive, responsive, or accessible to their children, and without exception, their children exhibited insecure attachments. Secure attachments were seen only in children whose mothers had been sober for at least six months prior to the testing procedure.

It is important to stress that in spite of the potentially serious outcomes of parental drug use for children, most drug addicts do not intend to harm their children, nor are they deliberately indifferent to their needs. They frequently exhibit extreme shame and guilt about the problems their drug use causes their children [Schottenfeld, Viscarello, Grossman, Klerman, Nagler, & Adnopoz 1994]; and they often devise complicated strategies to protect their children from the effects of their drug use [Kearney, Murphy & Rosenbaum 1994].

The deleterious effects of drug use on parenting are pervasive. Heavy use of drugs and alcohol typically interferes with thought processes, judgment, organization, and self-control. Substance abusing parents are often disorganized in their thinking and actions, they lack follow-through in all their activities, and their parenting responses are unpredictable and inconsistent [Howard 1994]. In addition, blackouts, binges, and drug or alcohol-induced stupors, which are common with heavy substance abuse, can create very dangerous situations in which children are left totally unsupervised, placing them at high risk of harm. In fact, Zuckerman [1994] contends that, "If the mother is addicted, the child's safety can be assured only if an adult who does not use drugs is in the household and is willing to take care of the child, or if the mother is actively involved in treatment that regularly monitors the child."

In spite of high correlations between substance abuse and child maltreatment, substance abuse in maltreating families is not always identified. Many caseworkers are not aware of the signs and symptoms of substance abuse or addiction, and they may be uncomfortable asking the pointed questions necessary to determine the scope of drug or alcohol involvement. Denial is also a typical symptom of addiction. Substance abusers often deny that they use drugs or alcohol, or they may contend that their drug use causes no problems for themselves or their children.

In addition, research by Kearney, et al. [1994] suggested that mothers on crack devised many strategies to hide their drug involvement, to shield their children from drugs and the drug life, and to make up for crack's negative effects on mothering. These strategies included keeping children physically apart from cocaine by never using the drug in front of the children; hiring babysitters or leaving children with relatives prior to using the drug; or waiting until the children were asleep or safely situated. Mothers also made certain their appearance did not reveal their drug-using status when they visited schools or other child-related settings, and they lied to agency officials or family members about their drug use. Most women described how they separated family money from drug money to assure that their children's needs were met. As their crack use became more frequent, they reported paying all their bills as soon as their paychecks or welfare checks arrived, because any unspent money was vulnerable. As a result, many of the mothers were able to hide the fact of their drug use from family, friends, and the community.

However, these compensatory strategies eventually broke down for almost 70% of the mothers in the study. Many were unable to reduce or stop drug use, and they eventually exhausted their emotional and financial resources. Many of the mothers then voluntarily entrusted the care of their children to family members, or their children were removed by protective service agencies. The mothers appeared to be more readily accepting of placement of their children if they themselves made the placement arrangements, than if the child protection agency removed their children without their consent. Drug use often escalated after placement of the children, reportedly as they now had no mothering responsibilities, and as an attempt to deal with the pain and sadness of losing their children.

Recognizing Signs and Symptoms of Substance Abuse

Because there are a wide variety of substances used, and an equally wide variety of indicators and symptoms, it is usually not possible for caseworkers to accurately diagnose which drug is being used or to what degree. Users may also concurrently use more than one substance. Anyone suspected of drug abuse or addiction should be evaluated by a professional in the field of substance abuse.

The most common general indicators of substance abuse are: altered mood states (euphoria, anxiety, irritability, excitability, sluggishness, or depression); changes in appetite and sleep patterns; temperamental or erratic behavior; poor memory and judgment; confusion and inability to concentrate; moodiness and restlessness; lack of concern about personal appearance; lack of attention to the environment; and clumsiness and coordination problems.

The following descriptions of the most commonly abused substances are designed to help caseworkers recognize when substance abuse is a contributor to maltreatment. (The information that follows has been adapted from pamphlets distributed by the Michigan Substance Abuse & Traffic Safety Information Center, and the United States Department of Education.)

ALCOHOL ABUSE

Alcohol is a sedative and a central nervous system depressant. In even small amounts it has a tranquilizing effect on most people, and it depresses the brain centers for self-control and inhibition. Lowered self-control often leads to loud or aggressive behavior, and makes alcohol appear to be a stimulant. Alcohol dulls sensation, impairs memory, decreases muscular coordination, impairs vision and other senses, and impairs judgment. The greater the amount of alcohol consumed in a particular time period, the more pervasive the effect. However, individuals often react very differently to comparable levels of alcohol.

When ingested in large quantities, alcohol can cause unconsciousness, coma, respiratory failure, and death. It can also damage many body organs including the liver, heart, and brain. Use of alcohol by pregnant women can cause fetal alcohol syndrome or fetal alcohol effects in their infants. (See Section VII-C, "The Primary Developmental Disabilities: Identification and Early Intervention," for discussion of fetal alcohol syndrome and fetal alcohol effects.)

Alcohol can be both physically and psychologically addicting. Dependence on alcohol is called alcoholism. The user loses control and continues to drink, despite major and continuing negative consequences. Signs and symptoms of alcohol intoxication include slurred speech, unsteady walk, poor muscle tone, relaxed inhibitions, impaired fine and gross motor coordination, stupor, and slowed reflexes.

Indicators include the odor of alcohol on clothes or breath, and the presence of empty beer, wine, or liquor cans or bottles in the user's environment. Denial may be present. Users sometimes hide alcohol, or may greatly minimize how many drinks they have had. Many alcoholics describe themselves as "social drinkers," and insist they only drink because it's enjoyable and they can stop any time they choose. However, to them it is always enjoyable, and they never want to stop.

INHALANTS

Inhalant abuse is the deliberate inhalation of a volatile substance for the purpose of getting "high." Commonly inhaled substances include: glue and other adhesives; paints and lacquers; household cleaners and solvents; fuels and fuel exhaust; hair spray and other chemicals in cans with propellants; nail polish and remover; typing correction fluid; marking pens; and other similar products. Many of these chemicals are extremely toxic.

The inhaled substances are often quickly absorbed into the blood stream and carried directly to the brain. They can depress the central nervous system, and can cause fatal cardiac arrhythmias (irregular heart beat), asphyxiation, accidents, and suicide. Use during pregnancy can damage the fetus. Because inhalant substances are easy to obtain and are low in cost, they are often abused by youths and other persons who can't afford more costly substances.

Indicators of inhalant abuse vary among individuals and with the substance abused, but often include sores or a rash around the mouth or nose, hand tremors, a chronic cough, red or runny nose, nosebleeds, a chemical smell on the user's breath or clothing, and other signs of acute intoxication (drowsiness, unconsciousness, slurred speech, loss of muscle coordination, slowed reflexes, and a dazed or dizzy look). Users may become abusive or violent toward others. Environmental clues include the prevalence of spray cans or soda cans that smell of chemicals around the house, car, or bedroom. Abuse paraphernalia may include plastic bags, and old rags or socks with peculiar chemical odors.

Street names for inhalants include: laughing gas, whippets, poppers, snappers, rush, bolt, locker room, bullet, and climax.

COCAINE AND CRACK

Cocaine in its pure form is a white crystalline powder extracted from the leaves of the South American coca plant. Cocaine is normally mixed with other substances before being sold on the street, usually to increase the profit for the seller. The purity may range from 30 to 90%, making it extremely difficult for a user to determine how much is actually being ingested. Accidental overdose is a common cause of death with cocaine abuse. The substances mixed with cocaine are themselves often dangerous.

Cocaine in powder form is usually inhaled into the nose, or "snorted." Cocaine may also be converted to be smoked ("freebase") or can be injected. Cocaine is physically risky in all forms; overdose can result in heart failure, convulsions, respiratory failure, and death. In a sensitive individual, even small amounts of cocaine can have life–threatening consequences. Smoking or injecting cocaine greatly increases the risk of overdose, because very large doses reach the brain within seconds.

"Crack" is a crystallized form of cocaine. When smoked, crack transmits cocaine in very high concentrations to the small blood vessels of the lungs, producing an effect comparable to that of an intravenous injection. Because of its rapid absorption, crack is a very dangerous drug; overdose is frequent, and many deaths have occurred. A high percentage of users quickly become addicted to the drug.

Some effects of cocaine include dilated pupils and increases in blood pressure, heart rate, breathing rate, and body temperature. Initially, the user usually feels exhilaration and a sense of well–being, with more energy, and alertness. Cocaine is a short–acting drug; when snorted, its effects begin within several seconds to a few minutes, peak in 15 to 20 minutes, and disappear within an hour. When injected or smoked, cocaine effects occur almost immediately and diminish sooner. Once the effects of the drug wear off, users are likely to feel more depressed, less alert, and more anxious than before they took the drug ("coke blues"). Use of the drug is then increased to feel "normal." Users often get caught in "binge and crash" cycles, in which other drugs are taken to get rid of the depression that follows the short cocaine high.

Signs of regular use include weight loss, chronic runny nose with damage to the nose and sinus, lowered resistance to infections and disease, and high blood pressure. Needle marks may be visible if cocaine is injected. Behavioral signs include increased irritability, short temper, paranoia, difficulty with concentration or memory, loss of interest in sex, and panic attacks. After weeks or months of binges, depression can become chronic, and hallucinations and other signs of psychosis may appear. Signs of withdrawal include exhaustion, irritability, sleepiness, loss of energy, depression, and an intense craving for more cocaine. Environmental clues include the presence of white crystalline powder (cocaine); light brown or beige pellets, or crystalline rocks (crack); glass vials; glass pipes; razor blades; and syringes.

Street names for cocaine include: coke, snow, flake, white, blow, nose candy, Big C, snowbirds, and lady. Other names for crack are rock and freebase rocks.

STIMULANTS

Stimulants are a class of drugs that stimulate the central nervous system, and produce an increase in alertness and activity. They include amphetamines (dexadrine, benzedrine), methamphetamine, ephedrine and phenylpropanolamine (decongestants that are used in a variety of nasal inhalers and cold medicines); caffeine, nicotine, and some prescription drugs (methylphenidate, used to treat Attention Deficit Hyperactive Disorder). Cocaine also has stimulant effects.

People take amphetamines to feel alert, energetic, or to get high. They often report a euphoric sense of well-being. Regular use of amphetamines at high doses can cause drug dependence. Dependent users often feel that they need the drug to get by, and they increase its use and dosage to avoid the "down" mood they experience when the "high" wears off.

Heavy and frequent doses of amphetamines can produce brain damage, resulting in speech disturbances and difficulty expressing thoughts. While limited amphetamine use generally does not compromise parenting, toxicity can produce a condition known as amphetamine psychosis; the user becomes extremely suspicious and paranoid, hallucinates, may become delusional, and frequently exhibits bizarre and sometimes violent behavior. Death can result from amphetamine overdose through injection.

Signs and symptoms of heavy amphetamine use can include restlessness; anxiety; mood swings; panic; paranoid thoughts; and hallucinations. Physical effects may include sweating, headache, blurred vision, and sleeplessness. Physical symptoms of long-term use includes acne resembling a measles rash; trouble with teeth, gums, and nails; and dry, lifeless hair.

"Ice" is a smokable crystal form of methamphetamine. Known also as speed or crystal meth, it is a powerful synthetic stimulant. The smoke is odorless and the residue that stays in the pipe can be resmoked. Methamphetamine is often smoked in "runs," periods of continuous use that last an average of five days, with an average of four days between smoking periods. The days of abstinence are generally spent sleeping. Marijuana and alcohol are often used to "come down" from a methamphetamine high.

Users of methamphetamine report increased physical activity, restlessness, and anxiety. They repeat simple acts, become very talkative, and can be difficult to understand because of abrupt shifts in thought and speech. Impaired judgment, impulsiveness, and insomnia are also present. Methamphetamine is highly and rapidly addictive, and drug tolerance develops quickly. Drug-induced psychosis is also common with high doses of methamphetamine.

Withdrawal symptoms during abstinence from methamphetamine include severe depression, decreased energy, agitation, anxiety, and limited ability to experience pleasure. A "crash" often immediately follows a binge, characterized by extreme exhaustion and an overwhelmingly powerful need for more of the drug.

Street names for amphetamines include: speed, uppers, ups, black beauties, pep pills, copilots, bumblebees, hearts, footballs, crank, crystal methedrine, or crystal meth. Most stimulants are taken in the form of capsules, pills, or tablets. Methamphetamine crystal (ice, or crystal meth) is a large clear crystal that resembles a block of paraffin.

DEPRESSANTS

Depressant or sedative drugs depress the central nervous system, causing relaxation, sedation, and producing sleep. Tranquilizers and sleeping pills are commonly used sedatives.

Barbiturates, the most commonly abused sedatives, include pentobarbitol (Nembutal), secobarbital (Seconal), and amobarbital (Amytal), all of which are legal prescription sleeping aids. Other nonbarbiturate sedatives include glutethimide (Doriden), meprobamate (Miltown), methyprylon (Noludar), and ethchlorvynol (Placidyl). Another category of depressants, the benzodiazapines, include Valium, Serax, and related drugs. Methaqualone (Quaalude, Sopor) was once commonly abused, but is no longer legally available in the United States.

The effects of depressants are in many ways similar to the effects of alcohol. Small amounts can promote calmness and relaxation, but larger doses lead to slurred speech, staggering gait, and altered perception. Very large doses can cause respiratory depression, coma, and death. Combining alcohol with depressant drugs can multiply the effects of both drugs, and increases the risks of side effects and overdose.

Depressants can be both physically and psychologically addictive, and tolerance is often developed. Infants of mothers who abuse depressants during pregnancy can be born physically addicted, and can experience withdrawal symptoms shortly after birth. When used improperly, sedatives can be very dangerous; barbiturate overdose is implicated in nearly one–third of all reported drug–induced deaths. Nonlethal overdoses can cause a coma. Moderately large doses produce an intoxicated stupor. While many people have legitimate prescriptions for these drugs, they may take more than is prescribed, or they may share prescribed drugs with other persons. Some users obtain sedatives by using faked prescriptions. Withdrawal symptoms range from restlessness, insomnia, and anxiety, to convulsions and death.

Street names for depressants include: downers, barbs, blue devils, red devils, yellow jackets, yellows, ludes, and sopors. They are orally administered tablets and capsules. The red, yellow, blue, or red and blue capsules give the barbiturates their common names.

NARCOTICS

Narcotics are drugs that relieve pain and often produce a sense of well–being and a sedative effect. They include opiates such as opium, morphine, codeine, and heroin, and certain synthetic chemicals that have a morphine–like action, such as methadone. They also include meperidine (Demerol), and other narcotic pain killers (Percocet, Percodan, Darvon, and Talwin).

Heroin is the most widely abused narcotic drug, and continued heroin use can cause addiction. Tolerance develops quickly, and dependence is likely. Addiction in pregnant women can lead to premature, stillborn, or addicted infants who experience severe withdrawal symptoms.

Heroin is normally injected intravenously, inhaled through the nose or smoked. Other narcotics can be taken orally or injected. Overdose through intravenous injection can cause death. Unsterile syringes and needles can transmit disease, including HIV (AIDS) and forms of hepatitis.

When a heroin–dependent person stops taking the drug, withdrawal begins within four to six hours after the last injection. Withdrawal symptoms can become severe in 12 to 16 hours from the last dose, and includes shaking, sweating, vomiting, runny nose and eyes, muscle aches, chills, abdominal pain, and diarrhea.

Methadone is a synthetic narcotic often used to treat heroin addiction. When given in daily measured and decreasing doses to relieve the physical craving for heroin and prevent withdrawal symptoms, methadone can allow the heroin addict to both withdraw from his heroin addiction and lead a more normal life. However, methadone itself causes physical dependence, and it is under strict regulation to prevent misuse. Some heroin addicts must also be eventually withdrawn from methadone.

Signs and symptoms of narcotic use include euphoria, drowsiness, sensitivity to pain, nausea and vomiting, watery eyes, runny nose, cold clammy skin, and constricted pupils that fail to respond to light (pinpoint pupils). Other signs include needle marks on the insides of the arms, syringes, needles, and spoons. Heroin is sold as a white to dark brown powder or tar–like substance. Prescription narcotic pain killers come in tablet, capsule, or liquid form, including injectable solutions.

Street names for heroin include: smack, horse, brown sugar, junk, mud, Big H, and black tar.

HALLUCINOGENS

Hallucinogens, also called psychedelics, affect sensation, perception, thinking, self–awareness, and emotion. Common hallucinogens are LSD (lysergic acid diethylamide); mescaline, peyote, and psilocybin.

LSD, mescaline, and psilocybin cause delusions and hallucinations, changes in time and space perception, and alterations in an individual's sense of self. The perceptions of sensation may be reported as experienced across sensory modes; that is, users report that music is seen, or color is heard. Physical reactions include dilated pupils, rise in temperature, changes in heartbeat and blood pressure, and tremors. Some illusions and hallucinations may cause panic, confusion, and loss of control, or may lead the person to dangerous delusions, such as the belief that he or she cannot be harmed. This may promote irresponsible, self-destructive behavior. Longer–term harmful reactions include anxiety, depression, or more pervasive emotional disturbance. Delayed effects, or "flashbacks," can occur long after use has ceased. There have been reports of diverse and significant brain damage from the abuse of these drugs.

PCP (phencyclidine), sometimes categorized as a hallucinogen, is a very dangerous drug. Also called "angel dust," PCP was developed as a surgical anesthetic in the late 1950s, but its use was discontinued because of its unusual and unpleasant side effects. Effects vary among individuals and according to dosage levels. Low doses often provide euphoria and a feeling of numbness. Increased doses result in excitement and confusion, muscle rigidity and incoordination, loss of concentration and memory, visual disturbances, delirium, convulsions, speech impairment, violent behavior, fear of death, and changes in the users' perceptions of their bodies. Chronic PCP users report persistent memory problems and speech difficulties.

PCP can produce violent and bizarre behavior, even in people not otherwise prone to such behavior. PCP interrupts the functions of the neocortex, the higher cognitive centers which keep aggressive behavior in check. Violent behavior may be self-directed, or directed at others, and often results in serious injuries or death. More people die from the erratic and unpredictable behavior produced by the drug than from the drug's direct effects on the body. The drug also blocks pain receptors, and violent PCP episodes may result in self-inflicted injuries. In addition, a temporary, schizophrenic-like paranoid psychosis may occur which lasts from days to weeks. Users may be excited, incoherent and aggressive, or they may be uncommunicative, depressed, and withdrawn.

The hallucinogens can all be taken orally (chewed, swallowed, licked off paper). PCP can also be injected or smoked. LSD in liquid form can be put in the eyes. Mescaline and peyote can also be smoked.

Street names for PCP include: angel dust, loveboat, lovely, hog, and killer weed. Names for LSD include acid, green or red dragon, white lightning, blue heaven, sugar cubes, and microdot. Names for mescaline and peyote are mesc, buttons, and cactus. Psilocybin is known as magic mushrooms or 'shrooms.

Prognosis for Treatment

Currently, the prognosis for the treatment of substance abuse is quite equivocal. Different treatment programs report widely differing degrees of success with addiction to different drugs. Further, the need for drug abuse treatment far exceeds the availability of treatment resources. For example, in 1990 it was estimated that of the 105,000 pregnant women who needed drug treatment annually, only 30,000 received it [Nunes–Dinis & Barth 1993].

The prognosis for treatment of crack cocaine addiction is, at present, limited. Howard [1994] reports that most of the mothers in their study continued to use drugs, despite efforts by program staff to help their clients identify, enter, and stick with drug treatment. Only 15% of the mothers in the study remained abstinent for one year. Besharov [1994] concurs, suggesting that with crack cocaine addiction, "relapse is the rule, not the exception," and treatment success is defined as successfully increasing periods of remission, and controlling the damage done during relapses, rather than achieving permanent abstinence.

Wald [1994], however, cites a growing body of evidence to support the claim that the lack of success in treating crack cocaine addiction is at least partially related to the inadequacy of available treatment programs.

Substance abuse is difficult to treat because of the complexity of conditions and factors related to drug use. Several studies have noted the high percentage of drug-abusing mothers whose personal histories included physical and/or sexual abuse, neglect, drug use, violence, multiple separations, discontinuous relationships, and other physical and emotional hardships [Howard 1994; Kearney et al. 1994; Chavkin, Paone, Friedmann, & Wilets 1993]. It is posited that the euphoric mood and feelings of well-being that are typical effects of many drugs may be used as an antidote to anxiety, depression, hopelessness, and shame. However, the etiology of drug addiction is not that simple, and the effects of individual personality, physiological make-up, environmental factors, and social factors must be considered concurrently with the user's history.

The prognosis for individual drug users varies considerably, depending upon several factors: the type of drug used; the scope and frequency of drug use; the longevity of the user's habit; the degree of tolerance or dependence; the individual's personal, and interpersonal strengths and resources; and the supportiveness of the user's family and social environment. The following "strength" conditions would, in general, increase the likelihood of successful treatment. The "risk" conditions, in general, are likely to make treatment more difficult.

Strengths

- Parents acknowledge their substance abuse, and fully understand the negative impact it has on their children.

- Parents are willing to engage in some form of substance abuse treatment, and attempt to remain involved in a treatment program. This may include self-help and peer-help organizations such as Alcoholics Anonymous and Narcotics Anonymous.

- Parents make alternative caregiving arrangements for their children when they recognize themselves to be incapable of providing proper care.

- Parents are willing and able to separate themselves from friends, family-members, spouses, or others who continue to use drugs and support their continued use by the parent(s).

- Parents have a strong support network of family and friends who do not use drugs, and who support their attempts to discontinue drug use.

- Parents have a history of adequate social, occupational, and personal functioning prior to the onset of drug use.

- Parents are able to recognize when a relapse is likely, and make plans for their children, call in friends or family members to provide care for the children, or seek help.

- Parents exhibit shame and distress about the effects of drug use on their parenting.

- Parents have a history of successful parenting prior to the onset of drug use, and have a strong identity as a parent.

Conditions That Increase Risk

- Parents whose drug abuse seriously impairs their judgment, reliability, and ability to meet their children's needs.

- Parents whose involvement in a drug culture lifestyle places their children at continuous and serious risk of harm.

- Drug abusing parents who deny the existence of the problem, and refuse to consider treatment, or who verbalize a desire for help but never follow through.

- Parents with no history of adequate social, occupational, and personal functioning prior to the onset of drug use.

- Parents whose primary social contacts and support networks are also habitual drug users; parents with no social support network of nonusing family or friends.

- Parents with little or no history of successful parenting prior to onset of drug use, and limited identity as a parent.

Services

Highly specialized treatment must be provided to address the problems related to substance abuse. When substance abuse is a primary contributing factor to child maltreatment, little change in the home situation can be expected until the substance abuse problem has been dealt with and resolved.

Self–help and step programs such as Alcoholics Anonymous have reported considerable success in helping persons with alcoholism remain sober. A similar program, Narcotics Anonymous, utilizes the same strategies to help drug users remain drug free. Pharmacological interventions are helpful in treating some addictions. Methadone is often used to treat opiate addiction, particularly heroin. Disulfiram deters alcohol abuse because drinking while on the drug causes severe headaches and protracted vomiting. Antidepressants may be used to combat the depression that often precedes, and may be exacerbated by, the use and abuse of some drugs.

Most theorists contend that successful treatment for drug addiction must be multifaceted and ongoing. Nunes–Dinis and Barth [1993] suggest that outpatient drug treatment programs should include multiple weekly contacts with peer–support groups; family or couples therapy; treatment contracts for activities related to abstinence; urine monitoring; education sessions; and individual counseling. They also suggest treatment programs must help users learn to prevent relapse. Strategies might include "predicting situations in which relapse risk is high; rehearsing avoidance strategies; changing lifestyle; developing a drug–free network of social contacts; and developing memories of the negative consequences of abuse to counteract memories of drug euphoria." The authors contend, however, that while these strategies are known to be effective for the treatment of other drugs, their ultimate effectiveness with crack cocaine remains unknown.

Drug treatment must also directly address parenting, if recovering users are to retain custody of their children [Schottenfeld et al. 1994]. Chavkin et al. [1993] reported that for many drug–using mothers, their concern for their children's well–being motivated them to enter drug treatment, and their preferred treatment modality was family therapy aimed at strengthening their relationships with their children. Since many drug programs have focused on treating male addicts, and have not incorporated improved parenting as goals of treatment, they have not always been appropriate treatment for addicted mothers [Nunes-Dinis & Barth 1993; Zuckerman 1994]. Mothers often feel stigmatized by attending drug treatment programs, and they avoid residential treatment because they do not wish to put their children in foster care, or are fearful of losing custody [Zuckerman 1994].

Zuckerman [1994] describes a community-based outpatient program with a parent–child focus. A pediatric primary care clinic was chosen as the setting, as it was nonstigmatizing, and supported the mothers' interest in their children. The services provided were pediatric child care, child development services, and drug treatment, including a weekly clinic session, a relapse prevention group, and a mother–child group. Schottenfeld et al. [1994] describe a community-based day treatment program, with interventions occurring both on–site at the center and in the families' homes. The program offers six hours of structured daily activities including group, family, and individual therapy; relapse prevention training; leisure and exercise activities; and education about pregnancy, parenting, and the effects of drug use. Contingency contracting is used. Abstinence, documented by twice-weekly urine screening and self-reports, is strongly rewarded. On–site child day care permits recovering women to observe trained teachers interact with the children, and learn parenting skills in a nonthreatening setting. The on–site day care also removes a significant barrier to accessing treatment for many mothers. The recovering mother is also paired with a trained family support worker. These women are recruited from the community. This "buddy system" provides the women in treatment with a consistent and ongoing relationship with a caring and concerned advocate, who helps the recovering women with all aspects of life and child management. This also helps recovering women develop a drug-free social network.

Barth [1994] recommends multi-faceted approaches to treatment that include the following service components:

- Prevention of subsequent unwanted pregnancies through education and family planning;

- Intensive family preservation services as an initial response for drug-involved families. Many families will also need a much longer-term program than is usually provided through an intensive services model;

- Ongoing case management to assure aftercare. In cases where risk to the children has been sufficiently reduced to warrant closing of the case, the child welfare agency should not be responsible for the long-term provision of services. Families should be referred and maintained in other community-based and developmentally focused services. The child welfare agency should be informed if these service providers continue to have concerns about the protection of the user's children;

- Developmental and protective day care services to afford immediate protection to the children, while making it possible for mothers to attend treatment programming; and

- If children cannot be sufficiently protected at home, the mother and her children should be placed in a residential treatment group home to provide intensive family treatment without separating children from their families.

Multi-faceted treatment approaches, such as those found to have had some treatment success for drug-abusing mothers, are complicated and costly. Unfortunately, in times of diminishing resources, it is difficult to see how social service systems in general, and child welfare programs in particular, will be able to find the resources to address this growing need.

Placement Issues

Whether, and when, children of substance-abusing parents should be placed into substitute care should depend upon a comprehensive assessment of the risks to the child of remaining in the care of the drug-involved parent. As with all child welfare cases, agencies should first consider services that strengthen the family and protect the child in the home. Only when the child cannot be sufficiently protected at home with intensive family support services should placement be considered.

However, the complexity of cases involving substance abuse, and the unavailability of community-based and outpatient drug treatment programs, can limit an agency's success in preserving families, and placement of the child outside the home may become necessary. But, the manner in which the agency approaches this can have significant effects on the outcomes of the case. Kearney et al. [1994] report:

> Custody loss and its properties—voluntary vs. involuntary, and short term vs. long term—in turn affected a woman's identity as a mother. Those who voluntarily found a better place for their children were sorrowful, but retained relatively intact self-images as mothers. When children were forcibly removed, women harbored anger, fatalism, guilt, and images of failure as mothers. Women who believed in their ability and integrity as mothers were more likely to attempt to pull away from drugs in order to regain custody, whereas those who saw this central social role as shattered beyond repair were less likely to make this effort...In the most negative scenario, a woman who had lost custody, felt herself to be a failed mother, and believed her children were happier and healthier with an alternate caregiver, was very unlikely to fight for reunification. In a more positive interaction, a mother who had voluntarily relinquished custody, had successfully cared for her children for a number of years and had confidence in herself as a mother, and whose children were unhappy or improperly cared for in a substitute care situation, would be likely to take steps to maintain her mothering influence and regain custody.

This would suggest that if drug use seriously compromises a parent's ability to care for her children, the parent should be encouraged and empowered to develop a safety plan for the children. This might include protective day care, and/or kinship or family-based care. Where parent-child group home placement is available, it should be strongly considered. If foster care is necessary, the parent should be engaged to participate in all aspects of placement planning (See Section IX–B, "Empowering Families to Participate in Placement Activities.") Workers should also stress the importance of the parents' continued involvement with their children while in placement, and support this through regular visits. By supporting continued parental involvement, combined with a family–focused treatment intervention, reunification may be more likely.

It appears that the converse is also likely; if the child welfare agency adopts a punitive approach, and removes the children without first trying to engage the parent, the most powerful motivator for drug–abusing mothers to seek and stay in treatment is removed. It can then be assured that reunification will be more difficult. Wald [1994] also claims that when social workers take a punitive view toward drug-involved parents, expecting them to "do everything on their own," and courts and agencies make unreasonable demands with regard to treatment "success," this greatly reduces the success of interventions.

Finally, our overriding concern for children with drug–abusing parents is permanence in a safe environment. In spite of our best efforts, some drug users will not be able to provide their children with safe and nurturing environments. We must then strongly consider permanent alternative placements through kinship care or adoption.

(Refer to related discussion related to placement of cocaine–exposed infants in Section VII–C, "The Primary Developmental Disabilities: Identification and Early Intervention.")

Safety Issues for Child Welfare Caseworkers

Because of the unpredictability of behavior when people are using certain drugs, workers should take steps to assure their own safety when interviewing persons suspected to be under the influence of dangerous drugs. Some strategies for self-protection are:

- Do not conduct interviews in the kitchen, where knives, pots, pans, and other utensils that could be used as weapons are in easy reach.

- Do not accept an offer for a hot cup of coffee or tea that could burn you if spilled or thrown.

- Do not be accusatory or demanding. Moods of drug and alcohol users can be volatile and quickly become dangerously aggressive.

- Do sit around a barrier, such as a dining room table or a coffee table in the living room, so that a boundary is established between you and the client.

- Do maintain a position close to an exit, and make sure there are no barriers to quick exit.

- Do anticipate problems, and "expect the unexpected." Determine early who else is in the house and where they are.

- Do carefully observe the client's physical appearance and behavior. Look around for evidence of drug use…empty vials, bottles, or cans and drug paraphernalia.

- If you believe that drug dealers live in the home, or that the level of drug use makes the neighborhood dangerous, request accompaniment by law enforcement.

Case Example

⚐ The Forrester Family

The following example describes the family assessment process conducted by Carol Johnson, caseworker, with the Forrester Family. (See previous case examples in Section IV–A, "Integrating Casework and Protective Authority," and Section IV–B, "The Casework Relationship: The Foundation of Family–Centered Child Welfare.")

For purposes of illustration, this assessment was condensed into two interviews. While this may be an unrealistic time frame for some families, an initial assessment can be made in a few interviews, when the caseworker is skilled, and the client family is easily engaged into the casework process.

The format utilized in this assessment dictation includes the dialogue between Carol and Ms. Forrester (in regular type), and Carol's thoughts about what was occurring (in italic type, indented.) Carol's thoughts are included to illustrate the conclusions she drew from their interaction, how she decided to choose the direction of the interview, and her rationale for her interviewing and intervention strategies.

The case plan interview, which followed the assessment interviews, and the case plan document developed by Carol and Ms. Forrester in response to this assessment can be found at the end of Section IV–D, "Developing the Case Plan.")

Family:	Forrester, Susan, age 29
	Forrester, Jon, age nine
	Forrester, Wendy, age four
Worker:	Carol Johnson

SUMMARY TO DATE:

Jon remained in the hospital overnight and was released to Carol and Ms. Forrester. Carol had determined that Ms. Forrester's four–year–old daughter, Wendy, was at no risk of imminent harm. Carol and Ms. Forrester jointly placed Jon at Ms. Forrester's sister's house for the weekend, and Carol indicated she would meet with Ms. Forrester at her home on Monday, after Ms. Forrester returned from her job training class. Carol offered to pick her up, since the training class was located near the agency, and this would save Ms. Forrester an hour in travel time on the bus.

GOAL OF CURRENT ACTIVITIES: STRENGTHENING THE CASEWORK RELATIONSHIP

The purpose of these contacts was to strengthen the casework relationship, and to begin the family assessment. Carol had laid the groundwork for a collaborative relationship with Ms. Forrester at their previous meeting three days earlier. However, she fully expected that Ms. Forrester might still be angry and defensive, and she would probably continue to test Carol. Carol and Ms. Forrester had agreed that they would begin to explore the circumstances that led to Jon's injuries, and develop a safety plan for Jon.

ASSESSMENT INTERVIEW #1

Carol picked Ms. Forrester up at her training program as planned. Ms. Forrester rode most of the way without talking. Carol asked her more about her job training. Ms. Forrester answered in monosyllables, and volunteered very little information. This was notable, since she had talked openly with Carol about her training program while they were waiting at the hospital.

> *Carol noted Ms. Forrester's reticence to talk. Ms. Forrester would not look directly at Carol, but stared out the side window as they drove. Her body posture was stiff. She did not fidget. Carol considered the possibility that Ms. Forrester was angry, and made note to continue to explore this later, if it continued at the house.*

They drove first to the day care center to pick up Wendy. When Wendy saw her mother at the door to her classroom, she immediately left her activities and ran to her mother for a hug. Ms. Forrester related to Wendy with affection, and stroked her head while talking to the day care provider. On the ride home, Wendy chatted amiably with her mother about the zoo animals that had visited the center that day. Carol's initial impression, that Wendy was developmentally at age level, was reconfirmed by her observations.

When they arrived at the house, Ms. Forrester unlocked the door and walked straight to the back of the house with Wendy, allowing Carol to find her own way in. Carol took off her coat and waited in the living room. About five minutes later, Ms. Forrester returned to the living room, and said Wendy was playing in her room. Carol asked Ms. Forrester if she wanted to talk at the kitchen table again. Ms. Forrester said she didn't care, but walked toward the table and sat down.

Carol asked Ms. Forrester how her weekend had gone. She said fine. Carol asked if she had seen Jon. She said yes. Carol asked when she had seen him, and Ms. Forrester said Sunday afternoon. Ms. Forrester still would not make eye contact with Carol. Carol then said, "You don't seem to want to talk." Ms. Forrester looked at Carol and in a terse, hostile tone of voice said, "Just what is it you want me to say?" The question was issued as a challenge.

> *Carol recognized Ms. Forrester's tension, which confirmed her earlier suspicion that Ms. Forrester was angry beneath her controlled and distant demeanor. Carol attempted to acknowledge and understand Ms. Forrester's anger, rather than ignore it, or pretend it wasn't important.*

Carol said, "You know, you seem pretty angry to me." Ms. Forrester responded, testily, "What of it?" Carol said, "I'd like to hear what you're angry about." Ms. Forrester said, "Yeah, like you don't know." Carol responded, "Well, I'd guess, since it's me you're angry at, it must be related to what happened on Friday." Ms. Forrester was silent. Carol said, "I meant it when I said honesty was important, and that includes honesty if you're angry at me. Can you tell me what made you so angry?" Ms. Forrester was quiet for several seconds, and then said, "You suckered me." Carol waited. Ms. Forrester said nothing. Carol continued to encourage her. "Tell me what you mean." Ms. Forrester said, "You come in here and act so nice, and pretty soon I'm agreeing to let you take my son. I don't know how you did it, but I know I'll never get him back now."

Carol knew this kind of delayed anger was neither abnormal nor unexpected, and Ms. Forrester's anger likely resulted from a combination of feelings. Ms. Forrester might feel embarrassed and ashamed at having been "caught" mistreating her child. She may have had second thoughts about letting Jon go to her sister's, and she may still mistrust Carol's intentions. Other people may have told her not to trust the caseworker. Carol also wondered whether, perhaps, Ms. Forrester generally expected other people to harm her. Carol needed more information. She started by responding directly to Ms. Forrester's last statement about never getting Jon back. She did this by summarizing and reiterating her purpose and intent, and her commitment to working collaboratively with Ms. Forrester. Then she used an open-ended question to encourage Ms. Forrester to tell her why she was hesitant to believe this.

Carol said, "Well, as I told you on Friday, I want you to have Jon back. My job is to help you so Jon can live at home without risk of being hurt. And, I'll tell you again that it's very important that you and I work together on this, because the decisions will be better if you are involved in making them. I've said all this before...but, for some reason, you don't seem quite convinced. Can you tell me why?"

Ms. Forrester said, "I just don't trust you, or your damned agency. And why should I? Everyone I know says you people take kids, and their parents don't see them for months... and some never see them again. Even my neighbor said I was a fool for talking to you. She said I should have gone to court right away and fought for Jon. You're probably no different from the other social workers I know. I don't know why you would be!"

Carol summarized what she had understood Ms. Forrester to say. "I guess you don't really believe I'm going to help you keep Jon. I can assure you, again, that *is* my intent. I also understand I'll have to prove it by my actions. But I can't promise you that Jon can come home no matter what, because I can't let Jon stay at home if he's at risk of being hurt. However, if we work together...and I think we made a good start on Friday...we can help you understand what caused Jon to get hurt, and help you learn how to prevent it. As soon as you're able to do that, and he can live safely with you, he'll come home." Ms. Forrester was listening quietly, but her facial features still reflected anger.

Carol continued. "So the real issue is whether we can work together to keep Jon from being hurt again. Do you understand what I'm saying?" Ms. Forrester nodded. Carol then said, "I'd like you to tell me, in your own words, what you think I just said. I want to be sure we both understand the same thing." Ms. Forrester said, "You want to help me learn how Jon gets hurt, and learn how to stop it from happening, and if I can do that, I can keep him." Carol said, "That's basically it. Now, let's talk about the second thing I heard...that part about my being just like all social workers, and how that's a problem for you."

Carol wondered whether Ms. Forrester had begun to doubt whether her concession to work with Carol was really a good idea, particularly when Ms. Forrester's neighbor implied that she had been a fool to trust Carol. Carol was able to reengage her and restate her contract, but Carol expected that the issue was not settled, and would need to be revisited. Carol decided to explore how her position of social worker posed a barrier in Ms. Forrester's ability to trust her.

Ms. Forrester said, "When I was younger, I had to see the social worker at the court house. You all can't be trusted. I've known that all my life. So why should I trust you? But, it looks like I don't have much choice in the matter." Carol said, thoughtfully, "Well, trust is very important to me, and I work hard to be worthy of trust. You don't know me well enough yet to trust me. But, it sounds like you have a bad history with social workers." Ms. Forrester said, "You got that one right!" Carol said, "Can you tell me about it?" Ms. Forrester said, "What business is it of yours?" Carol said, "I'm not just being nosy. If we're going to work together, you need to feel confident that I'm on your side. If I understand how you feel, I'll be less likely to do something to hurt or upset you. I also want you to feel comfortable telling me when I've done something you don't like."

Carol has acknowledged that her being a social worker could pose a barrier to their collaboration if not dealt with. In encouraging Ms. Forrester to discuss this, she is communicating that she is supportive and accepting of Ms. Forrester's feelings, rather than becoming angry or defensive. Carol clarifies that trust and honesty are important to her, and she gives Ms. Forrester permission to be honest, even if that means confronting Carol. This both defines the parameters of their relationship, and potentially strengthens it. Carol also sees this discussion as an entry into assessing Ms. Forrester's feelings about relationships and people in general, both of which are important to the family assessment.

For the next 15 minutes, Ms. Forrester talked angrily about how often she'd been "suckered" by people, who "make all kinds of promises, and then never do what they say." She first talked about the "welfare people" and "court people" who worked with her family while she was growing up, and then the "counselors" at the juvenile detention center. She said they had all claimed to want to "help," but never did anything but harass her. Carol said it seemed like Ms. Forrester had some bad experiences with "helpers." She then asked Ms. Forrester about her trust of people in general. Ms. Forrester shrugged and said, "In this world, you're dumb to trust anybody. It just comes back to haunt you."

Carol saw this as an opening to discuss issues related to trust, but also saw it as a way to learn about Ms. Forrester's personal history. Carol knew that parents who could trust other people to provide guidance and support had a valuable resource in preventing future maltreatment. Conversely, a lack of ability to trust often results in self-imposed isolation, which can greatly increase the risk of future maltreatment. Carol knew an assessment of Ms. Forrester's ability to trust others would be important in determining the ongoing risk to Jon in his mother's care. However, since it was very early in their relationship, Carol decided to use open-ended questions to encourage Ms. Forrester to talk about her past, which would be less threatening than directly confronting the issue of trust.

Carol said, "Do you feel that way about everybody?" Ms. Forrester said she did, in general, and that the only people you could trust were small children. They were innocent and loving. When they grew up they got devious and hurtful. With Carol's encouragement, she gave several examples of people who had fit this description, including several boyfriends and her ex–husband. She said her husband had a good job, and promised he'd look after her. It was only after they were married that he "showed his true colors." Ms. Forrester said she kicked him out after she learned he had been seeing another woman. She said her husband drank a lot, and they always fought. "It really was better after he left…we weren't fighting all the time. The fighting really upset Jon…and Wendy would just scream and scream, and it took me hours to get her quieted down after a fight. Most times I know he was doing it just to hurt me. He'd get me so mad, and then he'd say he couldn't stand it at home any more, and he'd go out and have a good time and leave me home with screaming kids. I think he just wanted to go to the bar with his buddies all the time." Then she said, "Jon's a lot like him." Carol asked, "How so?" Ms. Forrester responded, "He can act so sweet, and the next thing you know, he's doing something behind your back, or not doing what he's supposed to do, or he's lying about something or other."

> *Carol made a mental note that Ms. Forrester saw Jon as "a lot like" his father. Carol wondered whether this might contribute to her feelings about Jon, including the strength of her anger at his behavior. Carol felt it was too early in their relationship to deal with this topic directly, and continued to examine trust issues from a broader perspective, instead.*

Carol asked if there were anyone Ms. Forrester trusted and confided in. Ms. Forrester said she had one girlfriend who always listened and was helpful. When Carol asked Ms. Forrester about her relationships with her family, Carol began to hear a pattern of ambivalence and conflict. Ms. Forrester said her mother and older sister were the only family she had, and they both continually criticized her for what she called her "failures at life." Carol asked Ms. Forrester about her father, and learned he had left the family when Ms. Forrester was four. He would visit every few years, hang around for a while, make promises to her, and then disappear again. Ms. Forrester had been a poor student, and was often suspended and in detention because of her temper. "I just couldn't put up with it. Finally I just quit. Then things got really bad." She said her mother told her she'd never make anything of herself if she didn't finish school. Ms. Forrester said, "Talking to me was like talking to the wall." She said her mother "tried everything…she even tried to beat it out of me."

After she dropped out of school, she tried working, but couldn't keep a job more than a few weeks…she kept getting mad at the boss and quitting, or flying off the handle and getting fired. She was "in trouble with the law all the time," used drugs, was arrested twice for shoplifting, and eventually stole a car with a boyfriend. She'd had a baby when she was 16. The child was adopted by her aunt in another state. The child was now 13, and didn't know Ms. Forrester was her biological mother. She said, "I couldn't even make a marriage work, and now, the welfare people are after me." At this point, her eyes began to fill and she turned away angrily, as if embarrassed. Carol said, "You seem really angry, and you also sound depressed." Ms. Forrester said nothing. Carol said, "Well, it sounds like you've had a whole lifetime of feeling like you can't do anything right. Now I understand why doing well at this job training program is so important to you, and I understand why having children's services involved is such a problem for you. It must feel like just one more thing in a whole line of problems." She was quiet for a minute. Then Ms. Forrester said angrily, "I haven't got any problems that I can't handle. Life was never meant to be easy. I'd say I do pretty good, considering what I've been handed."

> *Carol recognized considerable hurt beneath Ms. Forrester's testy facade, but Ms. Forrester also was defensive about acknowledging it to Carol. Carol felt this was to be expected at this stage of their relationship. Ms. Forrester had implied that she had little support, and that few people had ever acknowledged her abilities. Carol recognized that while her comment about "not having any problems she couldn't handle" was basically defensive, in many respects, she had done well. Carol believed it was important to communicate this.*

Carol said, "Well, I'd have to agree with you. You appear to have handled a lot and done pretty well. You seem to have strengths that we can use to help resolve the problems with Jon. I'd be interested to know what you think those strengths are." Ms. Forrester wiped her eyes, composed herself, thought for a minute and said, "I guess I've never much thought about it." She paused for several seconds. "I'm a survivor...I've been through a lot, and I'm still here. I guess that counts for something." Carol said she thought it did, too.

> *Carol noted that while Ms. Forrester staunchly defended herself and her worth, she couldn't articulate anything she saw as a personal strength, other than the fact of her survival. Carol concluded that Ms. Forrester was not aware of her strengths, or was unable to consider or communicate them. Carol summarized what she had observed and believed to be strengths.*

Carol said, "Having survived is only a small part of it. You've kept a home for your children. You live on a very limited income, yet your home is very comfortable and nicely furnished." Ms. Forrester half-smiled and said, "Salvation Army and garage sales." Carol said, "It doesn't look it. I'm impressed." Carol then said, "You already know how much I admire your going back to school. That had to take guts, after dropping out the way you did. Was it hard?" Ms. Forrester said, "Yeah, sort of. I was scared at first, but after a while, I figured I was just as smart as anyone else there, and if they could do it, so could I." Carol then said, "What do you think you do well as a parent?" Ms. Forrester said, "I don't know...my kids are always fed, they're always clean. Heaven help them if they go out of here with dirty clothes. And I teach them to respect people, to do good in school, and I try to teach them to be kind." She paused, and looked at Carol. "Why do you want to know all this?" Carol said, "Because I'm interested. Do you doubt my intentions?" Ms. Forrester said, "Well, it's like you're trying to get me to tell you things so you can decide if I'm a fit parent." Carol said, "I'm trying to get to know you, to understand your strengths, and to help you recognize areas where you may need help. We need to consider both, if we're to help you get Jon home."

Ms. Forrester appears to be trying to discern Carol's tactics. This is typical early in the development of a casework relationship, and is also common for people who are cautious and suspicious of other people. Ms. Forrester expects people to be devious. Carol responds with honesty, further strengthening her previously stated commitment to be straightforward with Ms. Forrester. She also picks up on Ms. Forrester's lead.

"Since you brought it up, can you tell me what kind of parent you think you are with Jon?" Ms. Forrester said emphatically, "A good one. He's lucky that I put up with him. I could have thrown him out with his father, but I believe the Lord puts us on this earth to do good for others, and if it's the last thing I do, I'm going to get him to mind me and make him a better person for it. Of course, he doesn't see it that way. He just whines and complains for no good reason."

This brief exchange illuminates some important dynamics in the Forrester family. First, Ms. Forrester appears to have stringent expectations for Jon's behavior, and she seems to genuinely think that she has Jon's best interests at heart. She also intimates that Jon should be grateful for the care she's given him; after all, she could have thrown him out, but she didn't, and that he should somehow appreciate her efforts. Carol recognizes these as common dynamics of many abusive parents. They may have overly demanding, sometimes rigid expectations for their children's behavior, and may believe their children's behavior is a direct reflection of their own self-worth and parenting ability. Jon's willfulness is a challenge to Ms. Forrester's self-esteem, and his lack of "appreciation" for her is perceived as inconsiderate.

Ms. Forrester also alludes to a power struggle when she talks about getting Jon to mind her "if it's the last thing I do." This battle for control is also common in abuse situations. The parent interprets the child's willfulness as a personal assault on the parent's authority, and an indication of the child's dysfunction. The more the child subverts or thwarts the parent, the stronger the parent's need and determination to regain control. This, then, escalates the struggle. Carol recognized that this dynamic might be important in assessing the roots of the abuse in this family.

Carol also knows the interview could go two directions from here. She could ask Ms. Forrester to elaborate on Jon's behavior. This would probably result in a lengthy description of all Jon's problematic misbehaviors, which would not be productive, since Carol believes that Jon's behavior is largely governed by his mother's interactions with him, and if her attitudes and behavior can be changed, Jon's will likely change, also. Information from Jon's teacher suggests that while willful, Jon can be brought around with firm, but gentle guidance. Carol notes that at some time, if Jon's behavior appears to be particularly extreme, a psychological assessment could be utilized to identify or rule out emotional disorders.

Carol believes a better approach to the assessment would be to further explore how Ms. Forrester interacts with Jon, how she responds to his behavior, and how she feels when she tries to parent him. To do this, Carol needs to keep the interview focused on Ms. Forrester's beliefs and feelings rather than Jon's behavior. However, this will take more time than remains in this interview, and Carol does not want to begin and have to end before completing the discussion. She summarizes her thoughts, contracts with Ms. Forrester for topics to discuss at their next meeting, and closes the interview.

Carol explained to Ms. Forrester that the time was up. She said, "I have to leave now, but I think I understand some things better. You've evidently had some very hard times in your life. But, I believe you've done a lot that's right. I also think you're really trying to do the right thing for Jon, and that's a good place to start next time. Perhaps you can help me understand what happens when you try to guide and discipline him. Maybe we can figure out what happens that leads to his being hurt. Would you agree?" Ms. Forrester shrugged and said, "I guess." Carol decided not to confront her ambivalence. The small concession was a step in the right direction. Carol then spent several minutes arranging for Jon to continue to stay at Ms. Forrester's sister's house until their next meeting, and agreed to meet with her several days later to continue talking. She also said that the next time they met, they would begin to think about a plan for services to help Jon and her.

ASSESSMENT INTERVIEW #2

Carol met with Ms. Forrester in her home several days later. She was sullen and withdrawn, in spite of Carol's efforts to draw her out. Finally, after considerable prodding, Ms. Forrester told Carol she was angry because she had failed a test at job training. Carol asked her why she thought she had failed; Ms. Forrester lashed out in an accusing voice, "Everything–especially you being on my case, and Jon being at my sister's; I've just been too upset to study." Carol ignored Ms. Forrester's accusatory tone, and said gently that she wasn't surprised, since she knew Ms. Forrester was under a lot of stress because of the agency's involvement. She asked what the failed test meant. Ms. Forrester said, "They'll probably kick me out." Carol said, "Why would you think that?" Ms. Forrester said she didn't know...it always worked that way. Carol said firmly that it *didn't* always work that way, and suggested it might help to talk with her advisor, explain that she had been under extreme stress due to family problems, and ask to take a make-up test. Ms. Forrester said she really doubted it would work. Carol said she would help Ms. Forrester talk to her advisor, if Ms. Forrester wanted her to. Ms. Forrester said, brusquely, that she could do it herself, that she wasn't incompetent. Carol agreed with her, and asked if she wanted to take a few minutes and phone the school before they started talking. Ms. Forrester shrugged, said, "I guess," and went into the kitchen. A few minutes later, she returned and said, "They said okay, but just this once." Carol said "Good. Do you have enough time to study?" She said she did, but she still didn't feel like studying. Carol said, "I can under-stand that. I know this whole thing is weighing heavily on you. So, I'd suggest that we keep moving and try to get it resolved. What do you think?"

> *Carol intervened in a constructive way to help eliminate a source of stress. This communicated several things to Ms. Forrester: Carol really was there to help; her suggestions were useful; and, she empathized with Ms. Forrester's problem without being critical. She then reaffirmed her contract with Ms. Forrester, and helped her understand how resolving the issue with Jon would alleviate considerable stress. To do this, they must fully assess the scope of the problem and its causal factors, then identify strategies to address them. Carol shares her thoughts with Ms. Forrester, summarizes their agreement from the previous interview, and describes the next steps.*

"First we have to understand how Jon gets hurt, and why it happens. Every family is different, and until we both understand exactly what happens in your family, we won't be able to choose the best solutions. Will you tell me how it happened this last time?" Ms. Forrester was silent, but began to fidget nervously with a button on her sweater. Carol noted her nervousness, and commented on it. "You seem really nervous and tense. Are you worried about talking about this?" Ms. Forrester said angrily, "Of course not. I didn't do anything wrong. I was just keeping him out of trouble." Carol did not respond to her outburst and continued. "That's what I'd like to hear about. How you do that, and what happens. And in spite of what you say, most people *are* very nervous talking about this. I know it's not easy. Why don't you tell me in your own way. I won't question you to death, and I won't force you to tell me anything you're not ready to tell me, okay?" Mrs. Forrester nodded.

> *Carol has made the purpose of the interview clear to Ms. Forrester. She has also noted Ms. Forrester's nervousness and anxiety about disclosing this personal information, and Carol has reassured her. Carol understands that if she pushes too hard, Ms. Forrester will resist and withdraw. By letting her tell her own story in her own way, Carol gives Ms. Forrester more control of the interview. Carol expects Ms. Forrester will probably initially skirt the issues, or she may test Carol by disclosing less significant information first. Carol will use clarifying and supportive interviewing methods to help get to the underlying issues.*

Ms. Forrester began by telling Carol that she was feeling a lot of stress. Carol asked her why. Ms. Forrester rattled off the list of stresses in her life–the divorce, trying to raise two children by herself, the constant interference from her mother, trying to pass the job training, worry that she wouldn't be employable, even with the training. She was always running behind, never getting on top of things. Just surviving the day was hard. Carol agreed that it truly could be stressful, just getting by. She asked, "Do you sometimes feel more stressed than other times?" Ms. Forrester said she did. "What makes the difference?" Carol asked. Ms. Forrester thought for a minute, and then said, "I guess on some days, it all just builds up at once." Carol asked her how she reacted when she was feeling really stressed. She said, "I get mad." Carol said she remembered Ms. Forrester had told her about her temper, and how easily it flared. Carol asked what happened when she got mad. Ms. Forrester said, "It depends." Carol asked, "What's the worst?" Ms. Forrester said, "I lose it. I know I shouldn't, but I just can't help it." Carol asked gently, "What do you mean, 'lose it'? Can you describe it?" Ms. Forrester was quiet, and then said, "I yell and scream, or swear. Sometimes I throw things. If people get up in my face, I might shove them away, and every so often I've been known to take a swing at them."

> *Ms. Forrester chose to begin talking about stress. Carol didn't say, "Let's not talk about stress. Let's talk about your relationship with Jon." Instead, using open-ended and clarifying questions, Carol helped Ms. Forrester consider how she felt and acted when under stress, and related these feelings to her temper outbursts. Carol knows if Ms. Forrester can understand this connection, she has the capacity for insight. This is a critical piece*

of information. If Ms. Forrester is able, even on a rudimentary level, to eventually see a connection between her feelings and her behavior toward Jon, she will have a valuable tool toward controlling the abuse.

Carol asked, "What kinds of things make you so mad that you lose it?" Ms. Forrester thought for a long time, and said, "I don't know, just everything." Carol said, "Everything?" She nodded. Carol then said, "Does it make you mad when Wendy comes home with a happy face on her school paper?" Ms. Forrester rolled her eyes and said, "Of course not." Carol then said, "What do you feel then?" Ms. Forrester said, "Pride. I'm really proud of Wendy. She's a good girl." Carol said, "She is awfully cute. Seems smart to me, too." Ms. Forrester smiled. Then Carol asked, "So, what kinds of things make you *really* mad?" Ms. Forrester paused and thought, then said, "When people treat you badly. Act like they don't care about you. People who take advantage of you. They walk on you when you're down. They do what they want, and don't care who they hurt. They turn on you, after you've given them everything. When you try so hard and they're never satisfied." Carol asked, "Who do you think isn't satisfied with you?" Ms. Forrester said, "Nobody ever is. My mother, for example. No matter what I do, she's never been satisfied. I don't even talk to her about my job training any more; she just says, "Well, it's about time. You're only about ten years late!"

Carol then said, "And what do you feel when people are like that?" She said, "I don't know, like I said, mad." Carol said, "Anything else?" Ms. Forrester said, "Well…I don't feel too good. I feel," she paused, thinking, "like it's hopeless. Like nobody really gives a damn about you. Like you have to look out for yourself." Carol prompted, "There's that issue again…of not being able to depend on other people. That must feel pretty lonely, to think you're completely on your own." Ms. Forrester thought about that for a moment.

Ms. Forrester has told Carol that disappointment in interpersonal relationships precipitates her anger. Carol wonders if Ms. Forrester feels disappointment in Jon, and whether this is a factor in precipitating her anger at him. Ms. Forrester has also demonstrated that she can identify feelings, and can talk about what prompts them. This is a significant strength. Carol decides it is important to give her this feedback. In doing so, she is pointing out process-level issues, and helping Ms. Forrester learn to pay attention to these. She summarizes what she has heard Ms. Forrester say.

"I want to point out something important. It may not seem to be important to you, but it is. I asked you how you felt, and you were able to tell me. You were also able to tell me what makes you feel that way. Not everybody can do that. I think it's a valuable ability in helping to solve problems." Then she said, "I also want to see if I understood you. It sounds like a lot of your anger comes from feeling disappointment, or hurt by other people. Is that right…somebody does something that really hurts you, and you get angry?"

Carol is using summarization and clarification to help Ms. Forrester establish the connection between hurt and her anger. This connection is more subtle. Ms. Forrester already understands the connection between people's behavior and her anger, but her feeling of being hurt is actually the intervening variable that sparks her anger.

Ms. Forrester said, "No, they can't hurt me any more. I learned a long time ago not to let people hurt you. You wouldn't survive."

Carol realizes Ms. Forrester is not ready to fully acknowledge her hurt. It is too soon to confront her with this directly, but Carol will let her know she believes Ms. Forrester is hurting, and that she will continue to support her.

Not surprised by Ms. Forrester's denial, Carol said, "Sounds like you're saying it hurts too much to hurt, and you've gotten tough to protect yourself. It may make you stronger, but it doesn't always make the pain go away." Ms. Forrester said quietly, "No, it doesn't." Carol was pleased that Ms. Forrester had gotten the point, even if she didn't directly acknowledge it. Carol returned control of the interview to her. "Okay, what else can you tell me that might help us understand what happens with Jon?"

Ms. Forrester thought for a minute and said, "I guess I get mad at Jon more than I should. But, he really asks for it sometimes! And sometimes he deserves what he gets!" Carol said, "Tell me more about that. What do you mean?" "Well, it's like he does things on purpose, just to get me mad. It's like he's not satisfied unless I'm yelling at him. I talk to him, and he just stands there and looks through me, like I'm the wall or something. I tell him red, and he says blue. I tell him run, and he sits down. I don't know how he got to be that way. I never taught him to be like that. Must be in the blood." She paused. "He is a lot like his father. I really want Jon to be a good boy...nice, respectful...I thought maybe with his father gone, he'd listen to me better. You know, they say how you treat a child is important...helps them grow up better. But I'm not sure it matters...seems like it's born in them. You can't fight it." Then she laughed and said, "Wouldn't you know, I sound just like my mother talking about me! She always said I was too much like my own father for my own good."

Carol noted the similarity between Ms. Forrester's own experience as a child and her perceptions of Jon. But Carol felt exploring this issue would divert discussion away from Ms. Forrester's feelings about Jon, and so she continued to gently push Ms. Forrester to explore them.

Carol then said, "Can you tell me what it's like for you when Jon acts that way toward you?" Ms. Forrester was quiet, and then shrugged. Carol helped prompt, "Let me tell you what some parents feel. Like you're not really worth listening to. Like he doesn't respect you...like he doesn't much care about what you think. Help me out...I'm guessing." Ms. Forrester said, "All of that." Carol nodded.

Carol understands that Ms. Forrester perceives Jon's behavior as deliberate, and intended to thwart her. She also believes his oppositional behavior is inborn, and therefore, not affected by his environment. In both beliefs, Ms. Forrester is communicating that she feels powerless to control Jon, or to guide him to become the kind of person she herself values. This helps to support Carol's earlier suspicion that Jon does not live up to Ms. Forrester's expectations, and she views him as a problem child. Carol also knows she can't logically argue away Ms. Forrester's misperception by explaining that all chil-

dren behave in a belligerent manner at times, and that good parenting can make a difference. Some of Ms. Forrester beliefs are defensive—if she perceives Jon to be at fault, she can avoid blaming herself. Carol's other suspicion, that Jon and his mother are locked in a battle of wills, may also be correct. She tries to explore this further.

"Well, it sounds as if Jon is a difficult child for you to handle, and you get really frustrated. Actually, it sounds like you may feel pretty helpless to deal with him—like whatever you do, nothing seems to work." She said, "Yeah, that's about it." Carol then said, "Tell me what you can about how he gets hurt."

Carol knows they are at a watershed point. She has tried to demonstrate her empathy and support. She has talked around the abuse up until this point. She has led Ms. Forrester to acknowledging her anger at Jon, and her difficulty in managing him. The logical next step is to talk about how she behaves in response to her feelings. If she is able to acknowledge the maltreatment, Carol knows this is a strong indicator that she can be helped. If she continues to be defensive and deny her role in the maltreatment, Carol will have to reconsider her strategies.

Ms. Forrester was silent for a long time. Carol said, "Let me say something first. If we understand what leads up to Jon's being hurt, it gives us better control; we can then figure out how to stop it. And that's my goal…stopping Jon from being hurt…not taking him away from you."

"Second, I want to tell you, again, my job is not to punish, but to help. And I guarantee you that's what I'll try my best to do. But, I can't do it alone. You'll have to help me. But, you're a strong lady. You've survived a lot. You understand how you feel about things, and you are willing to talk about it. However you feel about what's happened, however bad you may feel about what you may have done, you need to know that I believe you have the ability to make it different." Ms. Forrester said, "How can you know that?" Carol said, "Just from what I've learned about you as we've talked. Of course, I can't say for sure, but I'd bet in your favor. So, why don't you tell me what happens." Ms. Forrester was quiet for a long time, and then quietly said, "I give him too many whippings, and I guess I hit him too hard."

Carol breathes a sigh of relief at this point. She has apparently earned Ms. Forrester's confidence sufficiently to warrant this initial acknowledgment that she hurt her son. Carol knows they have work to do, but she has helped her take the first step toward taking responsibility for a safety plan.

Carol said, "That makes sense. It explains the bruises. And what about Jon's head injury?" Ms. Forrester said, "Oh, that…that wasn't my fault. He fell off his bike." Carol looked directly at Ms. Forrester and said gently, "It's really important that you tell me the truth about that, too. It's difficult for us to work together on this until you tell me." Ms. Forrester started to protest, then stopped, and said, "No mother worth anything would hurt a child like that!" Carol said, "You're wrong. Do you think you're the only parent who has ever harmed a child? I feel lucky with Jon. We caught it early. There are families where we don't get to it soon enough, and children die. We're very lucky. Jon's okay, and we can still do something about it. So, please tell me how it happened."

Ms. Forrester started to cry, and said, "He'd been on my nerves all day. All day. I'd had a terrible day. My mother had been yelling at me. Wendy had been sick. I didn't feel great myself, and I didn't feel like cooking. So I made those frozen fish sticks. Wendy likes them, and they're easy. Well, first off, Jon didn't come home from his friend's on time, and everything was getting cold. When he finally came in, dinner had been sitting for an hour. I told myself I wouldn't get mad. I got him a plate, and he began to whine that he wasn't hungry. I told him he had to eat something. I was standing at the stove, ready to take the fry pan to the table when he yelled, 'You never cook anything that's any good. I HATE FISH STICKS!!! Why don't you ever cook real food?' That did it. I lost it. I threw the whole frying pan at him, fish sticks and all." Ms. Forrester began to sob. "I didn't mean to hit him in the head with it, I really didn't. Like I said, I just lost it."

Carol said, "So that's what happens. Jon says and does things that set off your anger, and you can't control it." Ms. Forrester nodded and said, "That's why I think you're wrong about me changing. I've been like that all my life, and it's never changed." Carol said, "Well, it's very hard to change something like that by yourself. But, you're not the only person in the world with a violent temper, and there are ways to help." Ms. Forrester continued to cry quietly. Carol said, "You know, I'd guess that your feelings about Jon are pretty mixed up." She nodded. "I get so mad at him, I really think I hate him. How can you hate your own child? What's so funny is how much I wanted him. And when he was little, he was so sweet. I do love him. I can't believe it's come to this."

> *Carol feels Ms. Forrester has been through enough for one interview. She has the information she needs to help Ms. Forrester begin to develop a safety plan for Jon, and a case plan for continuing services. She knows Ms. Forrester needs considerable support, and will probably worry after Carol leaves about repercussions from her admission. Carol needs to reaffirm her confidence in Ms. Forrester and outline her next steps, including stating clearly what she will not do. Carol also wants Ms. Forrester to call her, if she has any second thoughts. She does not want Ms. Forrester to worry and change her mind without talking to Carol first.*

Carol said, gently, "As rough as that was for you, I know it took courage to do it. Admitting it happened is the hardest part. I think, since this all began, you've acted like a very strong and responsible parent. You didn't run away. You didn't make a million excuses." She paused, and smiled. "And you've put up with me." Ms. Forrester smiled. Carol continued. "The next time I come, we'll start talking about what we can do to help, and we'll work on a plan for services. I'd like you to think about what might help you be a better parent to Jon. Will you?" Ms. Forrester nodded. She then said, "Can Jon stay with your sister for a while longer?" Ms. Forrester said she thought so. Carol asked Ms. Forrester for permission to talk directly with her sister, and invited Ms. Forrester to be present, if she wanted. She also asked Ms. Forrester's permission to talk further with Jon's teacher. She thought the teacher might help them both understand some effective ways to handle Jon's behavior. Ms. Forrester agreed to sign a release of information so Carol could talk with the teacher.

Then Carol said, "Once before, when we'd agreed to a plan, in the space of the weekend, you had second thoughts. When I got back here, you were angry at me, and felt you'd been suckered. I'm worried that you might feel that way after I leave. After all, now you've told me a whole lot more. I want to know if you trust that I'm here to help you, and whether you'll be all right until I get back here?" Ms. Forrester said she thought she would. Carol gave her a card with her phone number, and said, "I'm serious about this. If you start worrying, call me. I'd rather you call than find you worried and angry with me the next time we meet." Ms. Forrester nodded her agreement. Carol scheduled an appointment for early the following week.

SUMMARY OF ADDITIONAL CONTACTS

Carol talked with Jon's teacher, Ms. Forrester's sister, and Ms. Forrester's advisor at her job training program, all with Ms. Forrester's written permission.

Jon's teacher reiterated that Jon was generally a good child. He occasionally became obstinate and willful, but it was not difficult to talk with him and engage him to be more cooperative. He often seemed distracted, and at times, uninterested in school activities. He fought with peers on the playground, and had been seen bullying younger children. The teacher thought that he was developmentally on the lower side of normal, but couldn't tell if this was because of lack of interest, distraction, or emotional problems. She said Jon had moments where he was very affectionate, couldn't do enough for her, and wanted to sit next to her. She said she had met Ms. Forrester only twice, but both times, the mother was concerned about her son's education, asked about his classroom behavior, and wanted to be sure he was doing as well as he could.

The training program advisor said Ms. Forrester worked harder than anyone in the school, and was always afraid she wasn't doing well enough. She had moments when she would become very frustrated, and "have a tiff," but she always settled down, and tried again. The advisor said she was intermittently appreciative of support and assistance, and then appeared to become embarrassed and tried to manage on her own.

ASSESSMENT SUMMARY AND CONCLUSIONS

Who Is Included in the Family?

The Forrester family includes Ms. Forrester, and her two children, Jon and Wendy. Ms. Forrester's mother and older sister play an active part in her life. She has not mentioned other family members, a boyfriend, or other close friends. Jon's father does not appear to be involved with him at present. Carol needs to further explore other extended family resources.

Environmental Stressors and Resources

Ms. Forrester is living on limited income, but appears to manage fairly well. She is a skilled shopper, and had furnished her home nicely from garage sales and

Salvation Army stores. Her home is comfortable, her children are fed, and dressed cleanly and appropriately for the season. She is attending school to enable her to get a job that will help increase her income. Economic issues do not appear to be of serious immediate concern.

Psychological Factors of Parents

Ms. Forrester displays no evidence of mental illness, mental retardation, or serious personality disturbance. She does have a volatile and explosive temper, which she cannot always control. The violence against Jon is clearly related to this lack of emotional control. The intensity and volatility of her anger appear to be significant.

Ms. Forrester's anger is often precipitated by situations in which she perceives other people as hurting her. She is quick to find fault with people, and interprets their behavior as malicious or intended to harm her. Her perceptions of people are heavily influenced by her past experiences, in which she has felt herself victimized by many people. Her perceptions of other people's motivations may, at times, be distorted by her past experiences.

Ms. Forrester interprets the typical behaviors of a nine-year-old boy, such as selfishness, doing what he wants, occasionally lying, trying to get out of doing chores, etc., as comparable to the purposeful devious and hurtful behaviors of the adults she has known, and this is probably a significant contributor to the abuse.

Other than her explosive temper, she appears to have good ego strengths. She provides a stable home for her children. She is able to delay gratification, and she is not generally impulsive. She follows through with things she chooses to do. In general, she accepts responsibility. She has more strengths than she is aware of. Despite her lack of confidence, she makes autonomous, good choices, and is self-directed in managing her own life.

Ms. Forrester has low self-esteem, and often feels herself to have failed at everything she's tried. However, she continues to try to better herself, in spite of her lack of confidence in her own abilities. Her job training program is one example. Her ability to maintain a home and provide for her two children is another. These are strengths.

Ms. Forrester may have been abused as a child. She referred to her mother trying to "beat it out of her." She certainly seems to have been the victim of emotional abuse. This needs to be further explored.

Nature of Interpersonal Relationships

Ms. Forrester's interpersonal relationships are ambivalent at best. She openly acknowledges her distrust of people. During the three interviews, she mentioned one woman, in passing, whom she considered a friend because "she listens," apparently without criticism or censure. She is suspicious and hesitant to trust. Her worker will have to earn her trust by being sincerely supportive. It will be very important that Ms. Forrester's worker and other agency contacts be honest and realistic in their communications, and talk openly and acknowledge if, and when, they make a mistake.

Her relationships with family members are conflictual. Her one friend does not appear to play a significant role in her life. Yet, despite her initial strong protestations, suspiciousness, and considerable resistance, she was engaged into the casework relationship, suggesting that her relationship ability may well be intact. This is a significant strength. She may need help to learn who she can and cannot trust, and perhaps to help her rebuild a more positive relationship with her mother and sister.

Coping Skills and Strategies

Ms. Forrester has significant coping strengths. She has managed two children, school, and day care, and maintained a home with little external support. She appears to budget her money well, and provides well for herself and her children. She is self–directed, and acts successfully to meet her wants and needs.

Ms. Forrester has few dependable interpersonal support systems, and this probably contributes to her stress. Her family relationships are antagonistic and conflictual. Her suspiciousness of other people probably contributes to her isolation. However, the relationship with her sister is intact, albeit ambivalent. It appears that she is receptive to help, even though she may challenge and intermittently avoid a counselor. It will be important to help Ms. Forrester develop supportive and nurturing relationships. Linking her to services in her own community might open up other resources for her.

Ms. Forrester's sister could potentially be an ally in helping Ms. Forrester. So could her friend. Including these people in assessment and treatment planning might be a valuable intervention.

Parenting Skills

Ms. Forrester appears to have good general parenting skills with Wendy. Her relationship with Wendy appears warm and affectionate. Wendy seems bright, and her development is typical for a four year old. She shows no emotional or physical signs of maltreatment. Her day care provider reports no problems, and states that Wendy appears to be a happy, well–adjusted child.

Ms. Forrester appears to yell frequently and demand compliance from both children, but particularly from Jon. She says she spanks her children as a primary means of discipline. In the limited time the worker observed Ms. Forrester with her children, she was nurturing and warm with Wendy, and somewhat reserved, controlling, and edgy with Jon. However, additional information on the parent–child relationship is needed before conclusions can be drawn.

She does not appear to have a realistic perception of the normal, typical behaviors of a nine–year–old boy, particularly regarding oppositional behavior. Her expectations for Jon's behavior are more appropriate of an older child or adult than a nine–year–old. This contributes to her misinterpretation of Jon's behaviors as being deliberate attempts to get back at her.

Cognitive Ability

Ms. Forrester is at least of average intelligence. She is verbal and capable of insight. She correctly identifies her own feelings, and she can describe how other people feel. While she currently has limited insight into her own feelings about Jon and how they affect her care of him, this is probably due more to the emotional threat of such acknowledgment than to a lack of cognitive ability. With the proper supportive counseling, she may further explore and eventually understand this.

Child's Special Needs

Ms. Forrester's description of Jon suggests oppositional behavior. The teacher confirms this, but claims she can engage Jon to cooperate by using gentle reasoning and encouragement. It is not known how Jon has been affected by the family fighting, his father's abandonment, and his mother's abuse. The teacher's description of Jon suggests some early signs of emotional distress. A psychological assessment may be indicated, and depending upon the assessment findings, Jon may need counseling.

Summary of Strengths

Ms. Forrester's strengths include her intelligence; her motivation to continue to better herself; her warm and affectionate relationship with Wendy; her capacity for self-assessment and introspection; her ability to negotiate with service providers, such as the nurse at the hospital, the teachers at Jon's school, and the teachers in her own school program; and her willingness to participate in the helping relationship.

In spite of her vehement verbalized distrust of other people, and her initial resistance to meeting with Carol, she demonstrated a willingness to tell Carol a lot about herself in the first few interviews. While ambivalent, she appears able to take risks in new situations, even while expecting she may likely be hurt again. This is a strength. However, it further underscores the importance of not violating her trust, and also suggests that Ms. Forrester needs help in learning to assess who is trustworthy, and who is not.

Conclusions about Risk

Jon remains at considerable risk in the sole care of his mother. While Ms. Forrester has numerous strengths, and has begun to consider how Jon's behavior triggers her rage, she has not learned to control it. Until she does, Jon should not go home. However, since Carol's hope is to reunite Jon and his mother as soon as feasible, she believes leaving Jon with Ms. Forrester's sister, with unlimited visitation at the sister's home, is the best safety plan. This needs to be formally arranged with Ms. Forrester's sister.

Problem Areas to be Worked on in Case Plan

1) Ms. Forrester has an explosive, volatile, and violent temper, which, when triggered, results in physical injury to her son.

2) Ms. Forrester utilizes physical discipline almost exclusively, which increases the likelihood of physical injury to her son when she is angry.

3) Ms. Forrester has little understanding of normal oppositional behavior in nine-year-old children, and has unrealistic expectations for Jon. Her responses to oppositional behavior appear to escalate her struggle with him.

4) Ms. Forrester does not have adequate resources of emotional support. She is emotionally isolated. This greatly increases her stress level, and makes her more vulnerable to emotional distress and lability.

5) Regular visits between Ms. Forrester and Jon are necessary both to maintain the parent-child relationship, and to enable the worker to observe, more fully assess, and better understand their interactions.

SUMMARY

This dictation was designed to illustrate the following principles of relationship building and family assessment:

- Carol used relationship-building strategies to defuse Ms. Forrester's anger and hostility, and to develop the relationship necessary to conduct an accurate and comprehensive family assessment.

- At several times during the assessment process, Carol had to back up and reengage or reassure Ms. Forrester, before the assessment process could continue.

- Carol used open-ended questions to gather as much general information as possible about the Forresters before she became more directive and guided the interview to topic areas needed for a comprehensive assessment.

- Carol did not force Ms. Forrester to "confess" her involvement in the abuse; but, she used the casework process to help Ms. Forrester reveal considerable information about her relationship with her son. Carol did not confront Ms. Forrester with her failure to fully reveal the circumstances of the abuse. She positively reinforced any information Ms. Forrester was willing to share. She did not press for an explanation until their relationship was well-established, and Ms. Forrester had already disclosed considerable personal information in a supportive and safe environment. Even then, Carol was supportive and encouraging, rather than demanding or accusing.

- Carol used the assessment process as a way to help Ms. Forrester consider her own strengths, problems, and needs, and Carol reinforced Ms. Forrester for being an active and contributing partner in the assessment process. Throughout the interviews, Carol helped Ms. Forrester recognize her own strengths, and stressed their value in helping Ms. Forrester deal with the current situation.

- Carol used clarifying questions and responses to move Ms. Forrester from "content" issues to "process" issues, and supported and reinforced her willingness to explore the dynamics underlying her situation.

- Carol used gentle warmth and honesty in dealing with Ms. Forrester. She was consistently friendly, sincerely interested in Ms. Forrester as a person, and was willing to reveal information about herself, without compromising her professionalism, or forgetting her primary purpose for being there.

D. DEVELOPING THE CASE PLAN

1. Conceptual Framework

2. Application

3. Case Example

Conceptual Framework

Everyone plans. At times, planning is so automatic that it appears to be intuitive. For example, every morning, when we consult the weather report before we decide what to wear, we are planning. However, choosing clothing for the day to make sure we don't get wet in the rain is a straightforward process to solve a relatively simple problem. Complex problem solving and planning are generally not as easy. We need a formal and well–constructed planning technology to guide us if we are to effectively and efficiently solve our problem. Without a well–formulated plan, activities are often haphazard, poorly directed, uncoordinated, and unproductive, and we may expend considerable effort and resources without achieving our desired end.

In child welfare, careful planning is essential. Child welfare workers provide assistance to families in highly complex situations with multiple and interrelated contributing problems, often to achieve several desired ends. If we don't intervene quickly, children and their families can be seriously harmed. Yet, if we don't intervene appropriately, our interventions can be more harmful than helpful. A commitment to careful planning is, therefore, imperative to good child welfare practice.

Case planning is social work's application of planning technology to the process of helping children and families. Unfortunately, because the term "case plan" has been widely utilized to represent a written document that is completed to assure legal and fiscal accountability, the underlying planning process is frequently lost. Many workers never learn the complex technology of case planning, and as a result, their activities *are* often haphazard, lack clear direction, are poorly coordinated, may be unproductive, and may expend considerable effort and agency resources without ever achieving desired ends.

Planning is a cognitive process whereby we carefully think through the best course of action to achieve a goal or to solve a problem prior to taking any action. Effective planning requires a series of steps that must be executed in the proper order. They are:

1) Defining the problem or need to be addressed (problem identification);

2) Gathering and considering comprehensive information to be sure the nature and causes of the problem, or need, are fully understood, and to identify the resources and family strengths available to address the problem (assessment);

3) Clarifying what needs to be achieved, and defining the concrete desired ends toward which efforts will be directed (formulating goals and objectives);

4) Considering possible actions that could achieve desired ends, comparing approaches, and choosing the most appropriate actions;

5) Identifying who will do what, how they will do it, when, and where; and,

6) Determining whether the actions were successful in achieving the goals (evaluation of outcomes).

In child welfare situations, the "identified problem" is usually alleged physical or sexual abuse, neglect, or imminent risk of maltreatment. The dynamics and contributing factors to risk and maltreatment must be fully and carefully assessed. This enables us to design interventions that can meet each family's individual needs. After the family situation has been fully assessed, the necessary changes to reduce risk and protect the child must be determined. This includes setting case goals and objectives (desired ends), and delineating the activities and services that can best achieve these ends. All this occurs within a framework that assures that our interventions are family–centered, culturally relevant, and promote permanence for children.

In a casework model, the case planning process should always be implemented jointly by the worker and the family, and may often include other service providers as well. While in some cases this may not be possible, it should always be attempted. This helps to assure that all service interventions are relevant, well–coordinated, and integrated. The case plan document formally records the agreed–upon action plan, and ultimately serves as a contract that guides the worker, the family, and other providers in working together toward their common goals.

The technology of gathering and interpreting information during a case assessment has been fully discussed in other sections of this book. (See Section II–B, "Dynamics of Child Maltreatment," Section II–C, "Risk Assessment," and Section IV–C, "Conducting the Family Assessment.") In this section, we will consider application of the planning process to the development of an action plan to direct casework activities, thereby helping to assure a positive outcome for children and their families.

Application

GOALS

A goal is a statement of the desired outcome toward which all case activities are directed. To achieve a case goal often requires the coordinated implementation of many activities, and the resolution of a number of complicated problems.

Child welfare case goals are derived from child welfare's mission, which is to protect children from abuse or neglect by their caregivers, and to strengthen, preserve, and empower families to provide safe care for their children. The principal goals of child welfare practice are:

- To identify children who are at risk of abuse or neglect by their parents or caregivers;

- To assure children's safety and to prevent future harm from abuse or neglect;

- To enhance the ability of families whose children are at risk to provide proper care and nurturance for their children, within their own homes, communities, and culture, and to prevent separation of children from their families, whenever possible;

- To provide children who cannot be protected at home with the least restrictive, most family-focused, most culturally consistent substitute care placement that meets each child's needs;

- To reunify placed children with their families as quickly as possible; and

- To provide a stable, permanent, alternative placement as quickly as possible for every child who cannot return to his or her own home, or to emancipate the child to independent living.

At all times during the case planning process, we should be working toward one of these goals for each child and family we are serving. The identified case goal will influence the specific case objectives, activities, and services that should be included in the case plan.

The case goal may change during the time the case is open. Initially, the goal for a child at high risk might be to maintain the child in his or her own family, to be achieved by providing intensive in-home services. If this fails and we must provide immediate, safe placement to protect the child from harm, the goal may then change to reunification of the child and family when the situation that led to maltreatment is remedied. If it becomes clear that a child cannot be reunified with the family, the goal may again be changed to provision of an alternative permanent home.

Each time the case plan is developed and reviewed, the caseworker and the family should specify the current case goal. Objectives and activities should then be formulated to achieve this goal.

OBJECTIVES

An objective is also a statement that describes a specific desired outcome or end state. However, objectives are more specific and more limited in scope than are goals. Achievement of a goal generally requires the accomplishment of a series of more discrete objectives. Case objectives must be consistent with case goals, and achievement of an objective should represent a step toward that goal. For example, if the case goal is reunification of a child with her family, one objective could be to increase the length and frequency of visits in her own home.

Objectives should describe end-states that address one or more of the problems or needs identified during the case assessment. Achievement of an objective should, therefore, be synonymous with success in having met a need or resolved a problem. However, to accurately serve as criteria with which to determine success, objectives must be both observable and measurable. This enables the parties to the plan to reach consensus regarding whether the stated objectives have, in fact, been accomplished. Each objective must include some easily discernible criteria by which we can measure achievement.

Writing measurable objectives is one of the most difficult parts of the case planning process. Many of the expected outcomes in child welfare do not lend themselves to easy, precise quantification. Some criteria are easy to observe, but more difficult to measure. Mental illness is a good example. It may be evident from a person's behavior that she is mentally ill. But, how do we quantify or measure the degree of mental illness so we can assess risk or measure change? It is very difficult to devise a measurable criteria of mental illness. We may have to measure change in mental status using an associated change in behavior, or perhaps changes assessed by professional mental health assessment or psychological testing.

Measuring house cleanliness and sanitation is another example. At what point do dirt and clutter present a hazard to children? One three-day-old rancid egg in a skillet may not affect children's health, but a kitchen that is consistently strewn with decaying, bug-infested food will. How do we quantify home cleanliness to allow us to determine when neglect begins? While it is difficult to quantify all variables, we must develop objectives related to home cleanliness which are, in a real sense, measurable. It is not enough to simply say, "The house will be clean."

A practical solution is to develop objectives that include many observable criteria. As applied to the dirty kitchen, one objective might be, "The floor will be cleared of dirt, dust, debris, shredded paper, food, and garbage. Dirty dishes will be washed and put away immediately after use." Because the objective describes observable criteria, agreement regarding achievement of the objective is more likely, even though it is not as quantifiable as we might like.

Caseworkers may be accustomed to writing objectives that contain the word "improve," such as improved child care, improved housing conditions, or improved parenting. Objectives which contain the word "improve" are neither observable nor measurable. "Improve" can mean many different things to different people, depending both on underlying values and on personal criteria for measuring improvement. If observers have different cultural backgrounds or values, they may not agree on what can be considered an improvement. For example, self–assertive behavior by a child may be positively viewed as autonomy by one person, and seen as insubordination by another. In addition, since improvement cannot be measured until a criteria for success has been established, there may be conflict regarding just when the objective has been achieved; in other words, how much improvement is enough?

Just because it may be difficult to establish measurable criteria is not sufficient reason not to do so. Case plans are entirely dependent upon the establishment of identifiable measures of change. We cannot expect families to participate in a change process, nor can we help them measure their success at change, if we can't clearly communicate and agree upon the expected outcomes necessary to assure the safety of their children, and the criteria we will use to measure success or failure in achieving these outcomes.

To promote effective change, case objectives must be derived from the case assessment. This necessary characteristic of objectives appears deceptively self-evident. However, it is not uncommon for caseworkers to derive their objectives from a "laundry list" of potential outcomes which might improve parenting or care of the child. Let's consider the objective, "Mother will know and use nonviolent methods of disciplining the child, including time out and restriction of privileges." This would appear to be an intrinsically appropriate objective for any case. However, we are not interested in "intrinsically appropriate" objectives. We are only interested in objectives that are extrinsically determined by the individual case assessment. Therefore, if the primary factor contributing to maltreatment is that the mother is alcoholic and has blackouts, during which time the child receives no care, an objective related to nonviolent discipline is unrelated to the assessed problem. The proper objective, when accurately derived from the case assessment, would be, "Mother will remain sober and provide consistent care for the child at all times." If case objectives are not developed from our assessment and derived from case goals, they may very well be intrusive and nonproductive, regardless of their apparent intrinsic validity.

In a comprehensive case plan, objectives should be written to address all the significant factors or problems identified during the case assessment as contributing to risk. Objectives should also be formulated that address the development or enhancement of family strengths that can mitigate risk. This will assure that activities and services are properly directed toward eliminating the underlying or contributing problems to risk; that they are individualized to meet each family's needs; and that they build on family strengths.

Useful objectives are time–limited. A reasonable time frame for achievement of each objective should be specified. Time frames can provide an additional criteria by which achievement of the objective can be measured.

In a family–centered casework model, case objectives should be mutually agreed upon by the family and the worker. The more involved the family is in determining case objectives, the more committed family members will be to implementing them. Historically, workers using a "protective authority" model have written case objectives that are essentially descriptions of the agency's expectations for family members' behavior. While the expectations themselves may be appropriate to reduce risk, if they are formulated by the agency for the family, rather than jointly, they are much less likely to promote productive and lasting change.

ACTIVITIES

The activities section of the case plan is the step-by-step action plan that will guide the delivery of services. It must clearly delineate all the necessary activities to achieve each case objective. The final action plan should include: 1) what steps or actions must be performed, in what order, to achieve the objective; 2) who in the family will be involved or responsible for each activity; 3) what activities and services will be the responsibility of the caseworker or other community providers; 4) when the activity is to occur, including desired time frames for beginning and completing each activity; and, 5) where each activity is to take place.

Formulating activities that promote achievement of case objectives requires careful thought. A well-written case plan can specify the steps a parent and worker must take toward remedying the situation that led to child maltreatment. However, the reverse is also true. When activities are poorly or incompletely formulated, their successful completion may not result in achievement of the objective for which they were written.

Activities should be jointly formulated and agreed upon by the family and the caseworker. Disagreements should be negotiated before the action steps in the plan are finalized. The family's commitment to follow through with case plan activities is correlated with their degree of investment and involvement in developing the plan. When several service providers will be involved with the family, a case planning conference that includes the family and all key service providers will promote coordinated and effective service delivery.

Complex activities requiring multiple steps should be subdivided, with each step listed as a separate activity. For example, the activity, "Father will look for a job," may include a sequence of more discrete activities, including reading newspaper ads, going to the unemployment office, calling to get information from prospective employers, scheduling appointments, filling out written application forms, or attending job interviews. When activities consist of a series of small steps, they are easier to prioritize and to implement in a specified order. Limited, circumscribed tasks are more easily achieved, and provide better guidance and direction to families. Incremental completion of steps can also increase motivation to attempt additional activities.

When family members must learn new skills to achieve an objective, or when the family's capabilities are limited, activities should be simpler and easier to implement, and the time frames for accomplishment should be lengthened. In the above example, if the father lacks job-seeking skills, the activities may have to include, "Father will practice and rehearse job interviews with the caseworker," "Father and caseworker will read the newspaper to find possible job openings," and "Father will talk with a job counselor to discuss his skills and interests."

Case plan activities should be completed within a specified period of time. The average time frame for a case plan should be three to six months. A review of the goals, objectives, and progress in implementing activities should be conducted at least quarterly to assure their continued relevance. In very active case situations, the plan should be reviewed more frequently.

In situations where the family's ability to perform an activity is not in question, but their motivation or willingness to become involved in the change effort is, shorter but reasonable time frames should be identified to promote timely resolution. The caseworker must be cautioned, however, not to misinterpret a lack of ability or knowledge as resistance, particularly when family members may be embarrassed or ashamed to acknowledge their limitations or lack of confidence. The worker must also involve family members in discussion to identify the obstacles to completion of activities, and devise strategies to overcome these obstacles.

Finally, activities to achieve objectives should be culturally appropriate. Involving the family in a mutual process of case planning reduces the risk of assigning activities that family members either do not see as relevant, or that are not consistent with the family's culture or values. Suggesting that a father address his family's economic problems by applying for public assistance may be an unsatisfactory solution, if the family adheres to strong values of independence and self-sufficiency. Referral to a jobs program, where he could work for financial assistance while being trained for employment, might be more willingly accepted. Another example is referring a family to a local mental health center, when the family has strong values about not discussing family business with strangers. Utilization of a naturally occurring support network or church–affiliated counselors might be a more appropriate intervention.

When formulating activities to achieve case objectives, the caseworker should consider and utilize family strengths and resources identified during the assessment process. Building on and integrating strengths promotes success, provides positive reinforcement, and increases family members' confidence in addressing difficult problems.

PERIODIC CASE REVIEW AND REASSESSMENT

As a family's situation changes over time, the case plan must be revised and amended to assure that goals, objectives, and activities remain relevant and current. As casework services are delivered, the family's problems and needs will hopefully be addressed, and a case plan review can justify case closure.

Unfortunately, in many child welfare agencies, case plans are not routinely reviewed and amended. In fact, amending the plan is often perceived as unwanted additional work, particularly when changes require review by an attorney or the juvenile court. As a result, agencies develop case plans with predetermined "boilerplate" language that is broad enough to cover a variety of circumstances, and that will not require further revision.

The problems with this approach should be obvious. The case assessment and planning process, when conducted jointly with a family, is itself a casework intervention that teaches families a method of assessing and solving problems. The family's needs, and the service system's response to those needs must also be continually reconsidered, if we are to assure the ongoing quality and relevance of our interventions. Without this process, the case plan document is completed only because it is required; it will not promote constructive change.

All case plans must be reviewed and amended when necessary, at predetermined, regularly scheduled intervals. Case plan review should occur at least quarterly, and more often if there is a high level of case activity. All sections of the plan, including the assessment, goals, objectives, and activities, should be evaluated to assure that they are current, relevant, and accurate.

Case plan review also determines the relative success of the previously formulated action plan in achieving case objectives. The reassessment identifies where interventions have not been successful, and identifies obstacles that impede progress. These obstacles could include: a lack of service resources; psychological factors; lack of knowledge or skill; lack of clarity of case activities; lack of commitment; unrealistic time frames; or the absence of follow-through by the caseworker. Once obstacles have been properly identified, the case plan can be modified accordingly.

Formal case plan review by the supervisor and worker in supervisory conference promotes monitoring of case activities to assure that the plan continues to appropriately address the family's needs. The supervisor can then provide consultation to the worker to assure the quality of agency interventions.

Reviewing and discussing the plan with the family promotes their continued investment and involvement in the casework process, either by acknowledging and rewarding successes, or by identifying plan activities that have not been met and determining why. When multiple service providers are involved with the family, periodic case review conferences encourage teamwork, assure coordination of services, and clearly define the roles, responsibilities, and expectations of all involved parties. Representatives from other provider agencies, foster caregivers, and guardians ad litem or family advocates should meet with the worker, supervisor, and family members.

Good case planning requires a commitment by workers and supervisors, but they alone cannot assure this occurs. The agency must value and support case planning as a fundamental service intervention in all cases. Case planning should be identified as a priority by agency management, responsibility for case planning should be formalized in the job descriptions of caseworkers and their supervisors, and sufficient time must be allocated. A standardized model for case planning should also be adopted. The model should include policies and procedures for case review, instructions for the preparation of written case plans, and a format for the documentation of case plans in the family's case record.

In summary, the steps in the case planning process are:

Identifying the "Presenting" Problem

The referral concern or complaint that brings the case to the attention of the agency describes the conditions that place children at risk of harm from maltreatment, and provides the rationale for agency intervention.

Begin Establishment of the Casework Relationship

Engaging family members to be invested participants in the case planning process increases the reliability and validity of assessment information, assures the relevance and appropriateness of casework services, and increases the likelihood that family members will follow through with case plan activities.

Proceeding to case assessment without first establishing rapport and setting clear expectations for the relationship may result in an incomplete or inaccurate assessment. Without an established level of trust and rapport, family members may feel threatened, and will not be truthful or complete in disclosing relevant information.

Family Assessment

The family assessment process explores the validity of the referral concern; assesses risk and safety factors; establishes the level of risk to the child in the home; gathers comprehensive information about the family's needs, strengths, and problems; and summarizes this information to be used in developing the most appropriate goals, objectives, and intervention plan.

Formulate Case Goals and Objectives

The case goal states the desired end toward which all case activities will be directed. Measurable, observable objectives are then formulated to describe the expected outcomes of services to address and eliminate risk factors, problems, or needs, and to achieve the case goal. Both should be formulated from the information derived during the case assessment.

Formulate the Action Plan

The action plan should clearly and precisely describe the activities to be undertaken, the services to be delivered, the order in which action steps should be implemented, who is responsible for performance of each activity, and the expected time frames for completion.

Case Review and Reassessment

All case plans should be reviewed at least quarterly, and amended as necessary to assure the ongoing relevance and quality of services. Supervisory review assures that the agency is meeting its responsibilities; review with the family assures that the plan remains relevant and they remain involved; and review with other providers promotes continued coordination and integration.

CLARIFYING OBJECTIVES AND ACTIVITIES

It is not uncommon for caseworkers to confuse objectives with activities in case planning, since both are measurable, and both are derived from the case goals. The following is a commonly seen, but improper, formulation.

Problem:	Mother is schizophrenic, and when having a psychotic episode, mistreats children.
Case Goal:	To maintain children at home, and to eliminate risk of maltreatment.
Objective:	Mother will attend weekly counseling sessions at the community mental health agency.
Activity:	Caseworker will transport mother to the mental health center.

In the above example, it is communicated that attendance at counseling is an end in itself. As currently written, if mother goes to the mental health agency on a weekly basis, the case objective will have been met, whether or not the mother's mental illness or parenting capability have changed.

The easiest way to avoid confusion is to remember that an objective describes the desired end–state that reflects resolution of problems or needs; the activity is the means or process used to achieve that end. A more accurate formulation of the above situation would be:

Problem:	Mother is schizophrenic, and when having a psychotic episode, mistreats children.
Case Goal:	To maintain children at home, and to eliminate risk of maltreatment.
Objectives:	Mother's schizophrenia will be treated to allow her to function and care for her children independently.
	Mother will have ongoing professional mental health care and support.
Activities:	Caseworker will set up an appointment with the mental health psychiatrist for an evaluation of mother's mental illness.
	Caseworker will transport mother to the mental health center.
	Psychiatrist will develop and recommend a treatment plan for mother's schizophrenia.
	Mother will participate in the mental health assessment.
	Mother will attend weekly counseling sessions at the mental health agency.

In child welfare, many desired end states will reflect the elimination of harmful parenting behaviors and practices. If our goal is to retain the child at home or return the child to the family, many of our interventions will be directed toward helping parents alter their behaviors or lifestyles to eliminate risk to their children. In this situation, the objectives themselves often must clearly describe the specific behavioral changes parents will need to adopt. This can create confusion for caseworkers in distinguishing between descriptions of parental behaviors that represent objectives or end states; and descriptions of parental behaviors that represent activities as a means to some other desired end.

The differentiating factor is whether the change in the parent's behavior is considered the end in itself, or whether it is a means of achieving some other outcome. For example: "Sandra will be drug free and sober at all times," is a description of an end state, or an objective. "Sandra will attend counseling sessions at the drug rehabilitation center," is the means by which she will achieve sobriety.

In another example, "Sandra will use nonviolent strategies, such as time–out, and restriction of privileges, when disciplining her children," is our desired end state, or the objective. If Sandra uses nonviolent discipline, she will not be abusing her children, and we will have succeeded in eliminating maltreatment. The activities to accomplish this objective must include the specific action steps needed to learn and use nonviolent disciplinary measures.

SETTING PRIORITIES

In many families, abuse and neglect are the result of multiple, interrelated, often complicated factors. These factors may need to be addressed, and strengths may have to be developed before the family can competently care for their children. It is often not possible or feasible to address all the needed changes at once. The caseworker must help the family set priorities for objectives and services that can address the most critical needs or problem areas first; that is, those that are the most immediate and significant contributors to risk, and those that can most quickly promote safety for the child.

Setting priorities is a time management strategy. Prioritizing is a planning methodology in which an individual chooses which activities will be done first; and, if not all activities can be completed in the designated time period, which of them will be left undone.

In prioritizing objectives and activities in a child welfare case plan, two criteria must be weighed and balanced:

1) *How important is the objective or activity? Importance cannot be determined out of context; we must ask, "important toward what end?"*

   The importance of a particular objective will depend upon the degree to which it helps us achieve the case goal. Similarly, the importance of any case activity depends upon the degree to which it helps achieve a stated objective. For example: if an activity is central to achieving an objective, it is of high importance. Without it, the objective would likely not be met. If the objective could be partially reached without the activity, the activity is of moderate importance. If the activity will have little impact on the achievement of the objective, it is of low importance.

   To determine the degree of importance, it should be asked, "What would be the worst possible outcome if I never completed this at all?" If the answer is, "Not much," the activity can be rated very low on the priority rating scale. If the answer is, "A child will likely be seriously hurt," the importance rating is very high. If the answer is, "It would certainly help the family's situation, and would benefit the child in the long run, but it is not essential to immediate protection of the child," the importance rating would be moderate.

2) *How urgent is the activity? Urgency reflects the need to complete an activity, or meet an objective within a specified time frame to avoid a negative consequence.*

   To determine the degree of urgency of a case plan activity or objective, it should be asked, "What is the worst possible outcome if I do not complete this in our specified time frame?" Theoretically, the shorter the amount of time available, the greater the urgency. If a negative consequence is likely if we wait to perform the activity, it is of high urgency. For example, if delaying response to an abuse referral for several days may result in the death of a child, it is of high urgency. Conversely, if a family's application for housing can be submitted until the end of next month, we do not have to do it tomorrow. It is of low urgency. A week before the deadline, it will become higher in urgency.

In setting priorities, we cannot consider an activity urgent without also considering its level of importance, since an activity of little importance should never be performed, regardless of urgency. If a food pantry is providing free cheese to families today only, it would seem that a trip to the food pantry would be urgent. However, if the family has plenty of food and doesn't need cheese, the short time frame is irrelevant. Time would be better spent on more important interventions.

In child welfare, objectives and activities related to the determination or elimination of risk have, of course, the highest priority. They are, by definition, of extreme importance and urgency, and therefore require immediate attention. The importance and urgency of other potential case objectives and activities will vary from case to case, and must be prioritized by the worker and the family. Priorities should be regularly reassessed, and needed revisions made in the case plan.

In setting priorities, the following principles typically apply:

- Activities that are high in both importance and urgency are of the highest priority, and should be completed first.

- Activities that are moderately important and highly urgent, or highly important and moderately urgent, are at the second level of priority.

- Activities of high or moderate importance, but low in urgency, should be planned and scheduled for a later date.

- Activities of low importance, regardless of the degree of urgency, should not be performed at all.

Finally, workers should prioritize activities that can be more easily accomplished by family members. If early activities are smaller in scope, easier to achieve, and important to the family, family members are more likely to experience success, which strengthens their motivation and involvement. If, by contrast, the family experiences early frustration and failure in trying to fulfill case plan responsibilities that have little meaning to them, they are more likely to become resistive and withdrawn. The worker can increase the likelihood of case plan completion by subdividing large, complex tasks into their component steps; by prioritizing activities that are important to family members and achievable; and by providing sufficient reassurance and support to assure success.

SERVICE INTERVENTIONS

Once a family's problems, needs, and strengths have been fully assessed, and the case plan has been developed, the worker must help families access the most appropriate service resources to meet their needs.

In providing services to a family, the child welfare worker will assume one of two roles, and may, at times, perform both functions simultaneously. Child welfare workers generally serve as the primary case manager for families on their caseloads. The primary responsibilities of a case manager are:

- To work with the family to conduct a thorough, individualized family assessment to identify their needs, strengths, and problem areas, and to identify what needs to occur to make the home safe for the child. This information may be gathered directly by the worker with the family, and from other professionals;

- To work with the family to develop a plan for services that will meet the family's identified needs, enhance their strengths, and resolve the identified problems that have contributed to risk;

- To identify the most appropriate, accessible, culturally relevant services and resources in the local community that can address case plan objectives;

- To refer the family to service providers, to help prepare the family to access and utilize these services, and to remove barriers to accessing needed services;

- To educate the service provider regarding why the family is being referred, and to clarify the case objectives by forwarding relevant case assessment and case plan information;

- To follow up to assure that the family uses the services and follows through with case plan activities, and to assure that the service provider has delivered the agreed-upon services; and

- To regularly communicate with service providers, using a team approach to reevaluate the family's service needs and to determine the outcomes of the services, and to assist in negotiating issues between the provider and the family that may interfere with service delivery.

The child welfare caseworker can also provide direct services to the family. Home visits and other planful contacts can directly achieve therapeutic ends. For example, caseworkers might:

- Provide supportive counseling in regular meetings with the family to assess and identify problems and consider potential solutions, to explore strengths and resources, to access supportive and therapeutic resources, and to enable and empower the client;

- To help families learn different methods of child care, child management and discipline, and how to promote healthy child development, by describing and modeling new approaches; coaching parents as they practice; providing constructive feedback, and positively reinforcing more appropriate parenting behaviors;

- To help families learn and practice more effective ways of maintaining their home environment, managing on limited income, developing a budget, or accessing needed community services;

- To use play communication or therapeutic strategies to help a child understand the reasons for placement into foster or adoptive care, to elicit the child's feelings of anger, fear and sadness, and to prepare the child to move; and

- To accompany the parent and the child to appointments to provide support and advocacy. This might include a school conference, a visit to a hospital or doctor; an application for income assistance; to search for appropriate housing; or to meet the mental health worker. The caseworker often serves as an advocate for the family, while preparing and teaching families ways to access needed services and to advocate for themselves.

Most caseworkers will provide a combination of direct services and case management when serving the families on their caseload. Which intervention is used, and at what time it is utilized, depends upon several factors, including: the caseworker's own level of skill and expertise in a particular intervention; the availability of resources in the community; the amount of time available for the caseworker to devote to each case; and the agency's definition of the caseworker's job, and the types of activities which are expected of the caseworker.

Because the causes of child maltreatment encompass a wide variety of problem and need areas, child welfare agencies must have access to a variety of service providers. Workers must be familiar with their own community and its service resources. Additionally, workers and their supervisors should actively cultivate collaborative relationships with staff members of these provider agencies. Finally, if services are needed but not available, the child welfare agency may need to engage community professionals, and government and community leaders, to collaborate in identifying and developing additional service options for families and children.

The following categories of services should be developed within local communities to assure that families in the child welfare system can get the help they need.

Resources to Promote Environmental Change

- Referral to community providers for income maintenance or support, including supplemental income, disability, emergency assistance, and other financial aid programs.

- Linkage with resources such as the Salvation Army, local housing agencies, food pantries, and churches to access housing, food, clothing, home furnishings, transportation, and help with the cost of utilities.

- Advocacy to improve living arrangements: contacts with legal aid attorneys, landlords, and city or community regulatory bodies.

Resource Referral for Health and Mental Health Problems

- Referral to mental health agencies and other counselors for psychiatric or psychological assessment, individual or family therapy, group therapy, parent groups, and other supportive mental health services.

- Referral to drug and alcohol service providers for assessment and treatment of substance abuse problems.

- Referral to health and medical providers for proper health care services, prenatal care, immunization, and nutritional programs.

- Referral to specialized service providers for clients who have developmental disabilities such as mental retardation, epilepsy, cerebral palsy, and other disabling conditions.

- Referral to job training, work incentive programs, vocational rehabilitation, and to employment providers.

Education and Training

- Referral to community providers for parent education.

- Use of homemaker, parent aide, and other in-home supportive services to teach families in skills related to housekeeping, home management, budgeting, and child care.

- Use of foster caregivers to provide direct child care education to parents of children in foster homes.

- Direct involvement of caseworkers with parents to explain, train, and "model" proper child care, parenting, behavior management, and home management skills, and skills to properly access and use community resources.

Provision of Family Support Services

- Identification of, and access to, informal support networks within the client's community, including church groups, extended family, neighborhood community centers, and other community groups.

- Provision of support services including day care, protective day care, homemaker/home management, and other services to enhance the quality of care received by children in their own homes.

Direct Counseling by the Child Welfare Caseworker

- Regular in-home visits to provide therapeutic counseling, including problem solving, supportive counseling, reality-oriented therapy, insight therapy, and/or family therapy.

- Use of play therapy or specialized interviewing techniques for children to elicit children's feelings about separation and placement, and to prepare children to move to a substitute care setting, to adoption, or to return home after placement.

- Supportive counseling and problem solving with foster caregivers to help maintain children in substitute care placements.

Advocacy Services

- Contact with legal services and community agencies to advocate for clients' rights, to assure their receipt of proper services, and to prevent their "falling through the gaps" in the service system.

- Helping families access and link to service resources; completing applications, "negotiating the system."

Case Example

CASE PLAN DEVELOPMENT INTERVIEW

⅄ The Forrester Family

(Refer to prior case dictations for the Forrester family in Section IV–A, "Integrating Casework and Protective Authority," Section IV–B, "The Casework Relationship: The Foundation of Family–Centered Child Welfare," and Section IV–C, "Conducting the Family Assessment.")

Family:	Forrester, Susan, age 29
	Forrester, Jon, age nine
	Forrester, Wendy, age four
Worker:	Carol Johnson

Carol came to the Forrester home as scheduled to begin the process of reviewing the case assessment and developing the case plan. Ms. Forrester answered the door with her coat still on. Wendy was racing around the living room on a broom handle, pretending to be a witch. The phone was ringing, and the tea kettle was whistling. Ms. Forrester rolled her eyes and threw her hands up, but she was smiling as she ran to answer the phone. When she returned, Carol asked her, "Why are you so happy amidst such chaos?" She grinned and said, "I passed my make–up test. I just found out." Carol smiled and said, "Congratulations." Ms. Forrester said, "Thanks. I didn't think I'd be able to do it."

Ms. Forrester sent Wendy to her room to play, and asked Carol if she would like some tea. Carol said she would, and Ms. Forrester went to the kitchen to pour it. Carol called after her, "Ms. Forrester, I'd like some sugar, if you don't mind." Ms. Forrester returned with the tea and said, "You might as well call me Susan. Everyone else does."

> *Carol interpreted Ms. Forrester's behavior as evidence of success in establishing a relationship with Ms. Forrester. Offering Carol tea and asking Carol to call her by her first name suggest Ms. Forrester feels more comfortable with Carol. Carol knows the relationship is still new, however, and expects to revisit relationship issues repeatedly through their work together because of Ms. Forrester's history of suspiciousness and mistrust.*

When they were both sitting at the table, Carol began the interview by asking, "So, how are you feeling, in general?" Susan replied that she'd had a hard few days; she'd done a lot of thinking about their last meeting. She realized there was a problem, but had no idea what to do about it. Carol said that the point of their meeting today was to begin to sort through how the agency could help her and Jon. From their discussion, they would then develop a case plan together.

Carol then helped Susan organize her thinking. "Okay, here's how I suggest we do this. First, we should review the problems and needs we want to work on. We should decide which are the most important, and work on them first. Second, we should agree on what it will look like when the problems are solved. That's called setting our objectives. If we write our objectives so they're really clear to both of us, we'll know when we've succeeded. Are you with me so far?" Susan said, "I think so…." Carol said, "We'll go back through these one at a time. I just want you to get the big picture first." Susan nodded agreement. Carol continued.

"Third, we have to consider your strengths, and see how we can use them to help us solve the problems. We've already talked about some of your strengths. You might find, as we work together, that you already know how to resolve some of this, but just didn't think about it." Susan said, "That would be a change! Nothing's ever that easy." Carol said, "I'm not saying it's easy. I'm saying we're not starting with nothing. There's a lot to work with." Susan nodded.

Carol continued, "Finally, we'll choose the best activities and services to solve the problems. This last part is the work plan. It makes clear 'who does what, by when.' The case plan is like a contract between us. It makes sure we're working together to solve the most important problems in the most organized way. When we've agreed on everything, I'll write it all up on the proper form, and we'll both sign it. This way we both can be held accountable for what we agreed to do." Susan frowned and slowly shook her head. Carol asked, "What are you thinking?" Susan said, "Do you really think we can do this all today?" Carol said, "I don't know. We don't have to. We can always finish it next time. But it may be easier than you think. You ready?" Susan nodded.

Carol said, "First, we need to write down our goal. I think you and I have already agreed on that–that Jon will come home and stay home, and be safe from harm. Am I right? Is that what you want?" Susan said, "Absolutely." Carol wrote the goal statement at the top of her note pad.

"Okay, good. Let's review the problems we discussed the last time we talked. Why don't you tell me, in your words, what you think is the most important problem here." Susan thought and said, "I get angry at Jon and hit him too hard." Carol said, "I agree," and wrote it down under a heading "Summary of Problems."

Carol then said, "There may be several different things that together cause the larger problem. Let's try to identify all the things that contribute to the problem, and look at them one at a time. Let's start with your temper. Can we make a statement that describes the problem with your temper?" Susan said, "I get really mad, and when I'm mad, I do things I don't mean to do." Carol said, "Okay, let me write that down." Under Problem A, Carol wrote, "Susan gets angry easily and, when angry, can't always control her actions." She then asked, "Does that sound right to you?" Susan said, "Yeah…I hate to see it in writing though. It makes me out to be awful." Carol said, "This is all confidential. It stays inside our agency, unless we have to go to court at some point, or unless you give us permission to send it out. Besides, you already know how I feel about this; it's a problem, but it's not insurmountable, and it has a solution. Do you think it's okay the way I've written it?" Susan said it was, but asked what Carol meant about court. Carol explained that when parents refused to work jointly with the agency, and their children were at high risk of harm, the court was often involved to give the agency the authority to place the child without parental consent, and to protect the rights of the parents. Carol said she had no intention of involving the court, unless at some point Susan changed her mind about working together, or she failed to protect Jon. "Okay?" she asked Susan. "Anything else?" Susan shook her head.

> *Susan is again exhibiting her general concerns about the agency and the child welfare system. Carol responds in a supportive manner, once again reiterating the agency's role and responsibility, and explaining how the system works. Helping families understand the child protection system and how it may affect them is an ongoing part of child welfare casework.*

Carol then said, "Okay, next part. What happens when you're angry that creates a problem for Jon?" Susan said, "Jon gets hurt." Carol elaborated... "You hit him... with your hands, sometimes with objects?" She nodded. Carol said, "You told me you spanked or hit him to punish him." Susan said, "Yes, but the problem was hitting him too hard." Carol said, "Have you considered that there might be better ways to discipline Jon rather than hitting him?" Susan said, "Yeah, I've heard about sitting him in a corner and all that. But, hitting him is the only way to get through to Jon. He won't listen to anything else. If you've got any other ideas, I'd like to hear them. But I don't think they'll work."

Carol said, "Well, there are no magic solutions. But there are other ways to discipline children that are more effective than spanking or hitting. I think we can safely say that Problem B is, you don't know any other ways that work in managing Jon, other than yelling and hitting, and those are often hurtful to him. Would you agree?" Susan said her entire childhood she'd been whipped when she did something wrong. Carol asked how she'd felt about it. She said she hadn't much thought about it. Carol asked her to think about it. Susan said, "I may have been whipped too hard, and maybe too often, and I never liked it. But I probably deserved it." Carol said, "Well, regardless, we've already agreed it puts Jon at high risk of injury. So let's write that down as Problem B. "Susan uses only physical discipline, like spanking and hitting, to manage Jon's behavior."

Carol then said, "Let's think about the things that make you feel angry and upset." Susan said, "You mean like stress?" Carol nodded, and prompted, "And why you feel stressed." Susan looked at her blankly. Carol said, "Okay, let me tell you what I remember you saying. First, you told me that people had often disappointed you and let you down, and you were left to handle things on your own." Susan said, "Yes, that's surely true." Carol continued, "And you said that handling all the problems by yourself was really hard on you." Susan agreed. Carol said, "Do you think if you had more support, you'd feel less stressed, and maybe get less angry?" Susan said, "Yeah. It always makes me mad that I get left to manage everything alone. And when I ask people for help, like my family, they just criticize. I don't even bother to ask any more, unless I'm willing to put up with the sermon!" Carol said, "Okay, I think the problem is, 'Susan has no reliable support from other people. She must handle most stresses by herself.'" Susan nodded.

Carol then said, "Let's summarize here. Do you think if you learned other ways to discipline Jon, had good emotional support from other people, and could control your anger and temper, Jon would be at less risk?" Susan thought for a minute, and said, "I guess so." Carol said, "But...?" Susan said, "These are all my problems. What about Jon?" Carol said, "What about Jon?" She said, "Doesn't he need help in solving his problems too?" Carol said, "Tell me what you mean." Susan said, "Well, he's stubborn and selfish, and I don't deserve it. He's just mean sometimes. And he knows it, too. He gets that look in his eye like he's just going to get me, whatever it takes. I think he needs to learn to act better." Carol said, "How do you think that will happen?" Susan said, "I guess maybe he needs counseling or something. I don't know." Carol said, "You may be right. But I don't think we know right now, because children's behavior is often a reaction to the way their parents act with them, and if the parent changes, the child changes in response to the parent." Susan said forcefully, "Well, I don't agree. I think Jon has his own problems, if you ask me. Besides, I can't do all the changing myself. He has to meet me halfway."

> Carol recognizes a dilemma at this point in the process. Susan's belief that Jon should "meet her halfway" is an expression of her unrealistic expectations for his behavior. Her expectation of such reciprocity in relationships would be more appropriate if Jon were older. However, Jon is a child, and it is his mother's responsibility to create an environment in which he can grow and thrive. It is not Jon's responsibility to do things to make his mother happy. This is an issue that Susan will need to consider during counseling. However, even though Jon's behaviors do not make him responsible for his mother's abuse, he may indeed have intrinsic behavior problems which can, and should, be addressed. Also, if Carol negates Susan's suggestion about Jon needing help, the case plan will not be a mutually-developed document, and Susan will feel that her suggestions don't warrant inclusion in the case plan. Carol understands they must negotiate an objective related to Jon's behavior that is reasonable, yet still validates Susan's issue.

Carol said, "Well, Jon may be reacting to your actions, or he may have some underlying problems, or both. We could see if his behavior changes as you change. Or, we could request a psychological assessment of Jon, and that will tell us if he needs help and what kind of help. Would you agree to that strategy?" Susan said, "I suppose so. But I know he starts it sometimes, when I'm not doing anything to him. I'm not anywhere near him. He comes busting in the door, yelling and carrying on about something I did or didn't do, and throws things. He does that on his own. I'm just sitting there."

Carol said, "I know what you mean, and I agree, it might mean Jon has some problems. But looking at it another way, all children do that. No child is *always* satisfied with what his parents do. My own kids will whine,'You didn't do this for me. You didn't get that for me.' I just say, 'You're right, I didn't. Now go put your clothes away.' And I ignore it. In three minutes they're off doing something else and have forgotten about it."

Susan said, "Doesn't that make you mad?" Carol said, "Sometimes I find myself feeling a little unappreciated, but then I remind myself that children don't have the capacity to appreciate me in the same way I'd expect an adult to." Susan shook her head and said, "I can't let it go that easily. I think children should appreciate what their parents do for them." Carol said, "I agree. And I teach them to be appreciative. But I know, at times, they're going to forget, or be selfish and think of themselves first...they're going to act like kids. It doesn't mean they don't care about me or respect me." Susan frowned, as if she were thinking about this. Carol then asked, "Does Wendy always appreciate everything you do?" Susan frowned, then shook her head and said, "I guess not, but it doesn't bother me as much." Carol said, "That might be something we should talk about later on. It might help you better understand how things are between you and Jon."

Carol has used the case plan discussion as an opportunity to model a different way of thinking and perceiving. She has introduced the concept that parents cannot expect their children to behave like adults, yet she has neither lectured Susan nor acted as a teacher. She uses herself as an example to help make a very specific point. In doing so, she communicates that she relates to Susan's feelings, affirms that the feelings are valid, and then offers an alternative parental response to behavior. She also introduces the fundamental principle that parents can't expect their children to always behave as they would like. Susan may not relate this to her parenting of Jon at this point, but it brings the issue to her awareness to be dealt with later. It also helps her to become aware of her different feelings toward Wendy and Jon.

Carol then said, "Well, back to the plan. Would you agree that one problem is, 'Jon can be stubborn, obstinate, and difficult to manage'?" Susan agreed. Carol said, "We're not yet in agreement about what to do about it." Susan nodded. Carol said, "Perhaps we need more information about Jon to make that decision, and our objective for now should be to get that information. If it looks like Jon does need special services, we can add them later. Does that make sense to you?" Susan said it was okay, but that she wanted Jon to get counseling if he needed it. Carol agreed. Then she asked Susan if there were any other problems to work on. Carol reviewed what they had written, and Susan said she didn't think there was anything else. Carol reminded her if other things came up as they talked, they could always add them later.

Then Carol said, "We've already agreed on some of our objectives or outcomes. Let's see if I can write them down." She then wrote the following statements under "Objectives:"

1) Susan will learn and use nonphysical and nonviolent ways to discipline Jon and to manage his behavior.

2) Susan will control and express her anger in nonviolent ways that do not harm Jon.

3) Susan will have dependable sources of emotional and physical support to help reduce her feelings of stress.

4) Susan and Carol will better understand Jon's needs, and the causes of his obstinate and stubborn behavior; and use this information to develop the best ways to manage this behavior.

Carol then said, "We also need to write an objective about Jon's safety and placement. How about, 'Jon will remain in safe placement until Susan can par–

ent him without risk of future harm'?" Susan said, "Do you mean at my sister's?" Carol said, "That's how we've decided to protect him so far, and I see no reason to change that right now, unless you see a reason. Your sister is willing, and you seem comfortable with it. Are you?" Susan said she thought it would be the best way.

Susan looked at Carol's list of objectives and concurred that they were okay. Carol then said, "Now, time to consider your strengths. What do you already know or do well that might help you reach some of these objectives? Let's start with 1) *learning to use nonviolent and nonphysical discipline*. Can you tell me what strengths you have that might help?" Susan thought for a moment and then said, "I can learn." Carol agreed not only that she could learn, but that she was motivated to learn, and used her job training as an example. Carol wrote, "Susan is a good learner and is motivated to learn." Carol said, "What else." Susan said, "I really want to be a better parent to Jon." Carol wrote that down also. Susan then said she couldn't think of anything else.

Carol directed her to think about 2) *managing and controlling her anger*. She shook her head and said, "Wow, I don't know about that one." Carol waited. Susan shook her head. Carol said, "Okay, I'm going to put one in, if you don't mind. Remember when I told you that not everyone could understand their feelings and how their feelings affected their actions? Susan nodded, "I think so." Carol continued, "Well, it's called insight, and it's a real strength. It means you can probably learn how your feelings are connected with your angry outbursts. That will make it much easier to learn to handle them." Susan said, "Well, I'm not sure about that, but I guess you can put it down." Carol did. Carol also said, "You've solved a lot of problems on your own, and I think you have good problem-solving abilities." Susan shrugged and said, "I suppose you could say that's a strength."

Carol asked about her strengths related to objective 3) *having dependable sources of emotional support*. Again, Susan couldn't come up with any strengths, and Carol had to suggest one. "I think it's a strength that, despite all your bad experiences with people, you were still willing to let me help you." She said, "Well, you're different from any social worker I've ever met!" Carol grinned and said, "Well, I'm really not that unusual. There are a lot of trustworthy people in the world. Maybe you need to learn to evaluate who you can trust and who you can't." Susan thought about that, and Carol entered Susan's willingness to accept help into the "strengths" assessment.

Carol and Susan then looked at each objective and, together, negotiated the activities that would help them achieve their objectives. Susan said they had parenting classes through her church, and she agreed to find out more about them. Carol thought linking Susan with the church would be a good idea, as it could also be a possible source of support. They agreed to find out whether the church also had parent groups associated with the classes. Carol also suggested they visit the Children's Hospital clinic, where Jon had been seen, since they had a lot of programs and parent support groups. Susan seemed hesitant, and with considerable prompting explained that she was embarrassed to go to the hospital again. She thought she'd be labeled as a bad parent. Carol said most parents felt that way at first, and that if she would be willing to go once to check it out, she could decide afterward.

Carol stressed the importance of Susan working with a professional counselor, who would help her better understand the feelings behind her anger, and how those feelings might affect her treatment of Jon. Carol said that helping Susan learn to control her temper should be addressed first, since if she could accomplish that, Jon could come home safely, while they worked on other things. Susan agreed. Carol stressed she wanted Susan to work with somebody competent; she didn't want her to waste her time. Susan strongly agreed. Carol said she knew the clinic staff were competent, but she would also look for other counseling options for Susan beside the clinic, if Susan still felt uncomfortable with the clinic after they had visited.

They also discussed ways to get emotional support for Susan. Carol wondered if they should include Susan's mother and sister in the case plan so they could better understand how they could help her. Susan was very hesitant to do this, and Carol said they could talk more about it later, that she didn't have to decide just now. Carol also suggested Susan could talk with her counselor about this.

Susan asked why Carol couldn't work with her on these problems. Carol said she could help with some things, but other people had more training and experience in important areas, and could probably be of more help to her. Carol said she would want to know what Susan had been learning, both in counseling and in class; and, that she'd be happy to help Susan practice what she'd learned. Carol also said she could arrange for one of the agency's trained homemakers to come to the house and coach Susan to help her practice and use what she had learned. Susan said she might consider that, but she'd want to meet the person before she agreed to it.

They also discussed arrangements for Jon to stay with Susan's sister for a few additional weeks, while they linked Susan to counseling services. Carol and Susan agreed that they would evaluate Susan's progress weekly, and together with the counselor, they would develop a visitation plan which would include Jon coming home for short visits that increased in length as Susan became more able to manage him. Carol strongly advised that Susan visit Jon often at her sister's, and suggested that they meet jointly with her sister and with Jon to fully inform them of the case plan, and to enlist Susan's sister's help in accomplishing it.

The following is the case plan developed by Carol and Susan subsequent to the above discussion. The plan guides the delivery of services for a designated four-month period.

FORRESTER FAMILY CASE PLAN

Prepared By: Carol Johnson, Caseworker
                  Susan Forrester, Mother
Dates of Plan: 10-1-96 to 1-30-97

Goal: John will be returned to his mother's care, and will be safe from harm at home.

Summary of Problem: When Susan becomes angry with Jon, she hits him too hard, putting Jon at risk of serious and/or permanent harm.

Problem A: Susan gets angry easily, and when angry, cannot always control her behavior.

Problem B: Susan uses only physical punishment, such as spanking and hitting, to manage Jon's behavior. Physical punishment is harmful to Jon.

Problem C: Susan has no reliable support from other people. She must handle most stresses by herself.

Problem D: Jon is sometimes stubborn, obstinate, and very difficult to handle.

Susan's Strengths:

1)   Susan is a good learner and is motivated to learn.

2)   Susan really wants to be a better parent to Jon.

3)   Susan has insight and good problem–solving skills.

4)   Susan is willing to let people she trusts help her.

Case Objectives:

A.   Susan will learn and use nonphysical and nonviolent ways to discipline Jon and to manage his behavior.

Activities:

Susan will call her church and get information about parenting classes. Carol will locate other resources for parent training. Susan will choose classes to attend. By 10–7–96.

Susan will attend parenting classes according to the schedule set on 10–7. (Addendum will be made to case plan.)

Carol will arrange with agency homemaker to be present during Susan's visits with Jon in the home to help her practice what she has learned during parenting classes. (Will be scheduled.)

B.   Susan will control and express her anger in nonviolent ways that do not harm Jon or other people.

Activities:

Carol will call Children's Hospital abuse clinic and get information about counseling services. Carol will also identify other possible counseling resources. By 10–7–96.

Carol and Susan will visit Children's Hospital clinic. Susan will decide whether to attend the clinic; or Susan and Carol will choose another counselor. By 10–15–96.

Susan will attend all scheduled counseling sessions and work on issues related to anger management. Susan agrees not to miss sessions, except for illness or other emergency. Susan will reschedule all missed sessions with the counselor at the first opportunity.

Carol will help Susan arrange transportation to counseling, if she needs it. Susan must call Carol at least two days in advance if transportation will be needed.

Carol will talk with Susan's counselor weekly to determine Susan's progress. When Susan, the counselor, and Carol feel Susan has learned to understand and manage her anger, and can parent Jon without risk of harm, Jon can begin to visit at home. Susan, Carol, and the counselor will set the visitation schedule. (Will be attached when developed.)

C. Susan will have dependable sources of emotional and physical support to help reduce her feelings of stress.

Activities:

Carol will get information for Susan about parent support groups through Children's Hospital clinic. Susan will get information about parent support groups through church. Susan will choose a support group and will attend meetings. By 10–30.

Carol will meet with Susan at least once every two weeks. Carol will talk with Susan by phone as needed.

D. Susan and Carol will better understand Jon's needs, and the causes of his obstinate and stubborn behavior; and use this information to develop the best ways to manage this behavior.

Activities:

Carol will arrange for a psychological and developmental assessment of Jon to determine the extent and causes of his behavior. Carol will discuss results of assessment with Susan. By 11–1.

If counseling is necessary for Jon, Carol will help Susan choose a counselor. Susan will take Jon to appointments. By 11–30.

Susan and Carol will share information from Jon's psychological assessment with Susan's counselor and the homemaker to help in choosing the best parenting strategies to manage Jon's behavior.

E. Jon will remain in safe placement until Susan can parent him without risk of future harm.

Activities:

Carol, Susan, and Susan's sister will meet to arrange for Jon to stay at Susan's sister's home while the case plan is being implemented. By 10–7.

Susan, assisted by Carol, will help Jon understand why he is staying at his aunt's, and will explain the plan for services to help Susan. By 10–7.

Jon will remain in his own school while at Susan's sister's. Susan's sister will transport Jon to school. Ongoing.

Susan will visit with Jon at least twice during the week, and once on the weekend. Susan's sister must be present in the home during visits.

Jon may also visit at home when Carol or the homemaker are present. Carol will observe Susan and Jon together, and help Susan to assess and better understand their relationship. Begin immediately.

Unsupervised visits in Susan's home will be scheduled when Susan, Susan's counselor, and Carol all agree that Susan has better control of her anger and can parent Jon alone for limited periods without risk of harm to Jon. Date to be determined.

CASE PLANNING FLOW CHART

The Casework Process

Relationship*

A collaborative relationship wherein the caseworker enables and supports a family's efforts to make positive changes in behavior and life situation.

Casework is dependent upon the existence of a relationship. The family must be ENGAGED.

Assessment

A mutual process of gathering pertinent data about family needs, problems, resources, and strengths. Data are used to identify causal and/or contributing factors to family problems and to formulate conclusions about **WHY** problems exist.

Assessment provides rationale for all case goals and plans.

Goals /Objectives

Goals and objectives are statements of desired outcomes. **Goals** are broad statements of direction. **Objectives** are concrete, measurable, observable ends designed to reach a goal and eliminate the assessed problems or meet identified needs.

Goals and objectives describe **WHAT** should be done.

Intervention Activities

The intervention plan lists the necessary steps and activities to achieve goals and objectives. The plan identifies **WHO** should perform the activities, **WHERE, HOW,** and within what time frame (**WHEN**).

Gives direction to casework activities. The plan should be agreed upon by caseworker and family.

Implement Case Plan

Reassessment

Each component of the plan is reviewed to determine its current relevance and the success of interventions. Revisions are made as needed. Identification of needed changes prompts a return to the **assessment** stage, with resetting of goals and activities.

Resolution problems result in termination of casework activities.

* The relationship continues to develop throughout the casework process.

APPLICATIONS OF CASEWORK PROCESS TO CHILD PROTECTIVE SERVICES

Abuse/Neglect Referral: Child Served at Home

Relationship*

Worker engages parent into a cooperative relationship with agency to protect child and enable maintenance of child in own home. Caseworker uses strategies to develop trust and confidence of family.

Worker defines agency as supportive, helpful, and concerned with keeping family together. Worker also clarifies authority and mandate to protect child if parent is unwilling to work jointly to solve problems.

Assessment

Worker and family assess factors that have caused or contributed to risk, or the development and perpetuation of maltreatment of the child, and strengths/resources to resolve problems. Includes personal, interpersonal, and environmental problems/needs, and resources/strengths. Data should explain and validate **why** the child is at risk in the family.

Assessment data are used to 1) determine risk to the child if the child remains at home; 2) identify family strengths; and 3) define areas for which services should be planned.

Goals/Objectives

GOALS: Maintain the child in the home. Assure that the child will be protected.

OBJECTIVES: Includes statements of all necessary outcomes which will assure the child's safety within the child's own home, and which will strengthen the family and promote change to eliminate abusive or neglectful caregiving.

Intervention Activities

Includes activities and services to achieve the goals and objectives. May include activities representative of these services:
• Casework Support
• Crisis Intervention
• Counseling
• Intensive Home–Based Interventions
• Homemaker/Home Management
• Parent Education
• Protective Day Care
• Referral to Community
• Case Management
• Casework Monitoring

Intervention plan specifies **WHO** should perform the activities, **WHERE, HOW,** and **WHEN** (within what time frame?)

Implement Case Plan

Reassessment

Through formal case plan review, the following should be determined:
• If goals have been met and child is safe at home without casework intervention. If yes, **close case.**
• If family still needs agency intervention to assure protection of child. If yes, return to **assessment** phase and revise/update case plan. **BE AWARE:** If new or additional data indicates the child is at risk of harm at home and cannot be protected by agency intervention, consider placement in substitute care.

* The relationship continues throughout the casework process.

Child Cannot Be Protected at Home

Relationship*

Caseworker must:
- Clearly explain to parents why the child must be moved
  from the home
- Reaffirm commitment to reunify family as soon as possible
- Work through parents' anger and other feelings generated
  by removal
- Reinstate efforts to engage parents into cooperative relationship
  to enable return of child

Assessment

If the child is removed at intake, assessment is completed in a similar manner as noted above. If the child is removed despite prior services, most of the assessment should already have been conducted.

Additional assessment of critical risk factors may be necessary.

Goals/Objectives

GOALS:
- Reunify parent and child
- Maintain parent/child relationship
- Meet child's special needs

OBJECTIVES: All necessary outcomes to make the home safe for the child and to meet the child's special needs in preparation for reunification.

Intervention Activities

Identified steps and activities to:
1) Strengthen/empower family
2) Establish regular visits with child, siblings, and parents
3) Provide services to meet child's special needs
4) Reunify child with family

Implement Case Plan

Reassessment

Through case plan review, caseworker and family determine whether child can be safely returned and maintained at home. If yes, supervise at home, **close case.** If child can't be safely reunified, identify what else is needed to make the home safe. Return to **assessment** phase and revise/update all parts of plan.

If home cannot be made safe, consider permanent custody.

* The relationship continues
  throughout the casework process.

Reunification With Family Not Possible: Child Needs Permanent Home

Relationship*

Caseworker notifies parent that permanent plan will be made for child which may include termination of parents' rights. Caseworker strengthens relationship with child to provide support, stability, and guidance during permanent custody and placement activities.

Assessment

Information will be gathered regarding:
- Child's history, behavior, needs, problems, and strengths, formalized in a psychosocial assessment
- Child's placement needs; characteristics of family to meet physical, social, emotional, and any special needs
- Available placements/homes
- Document additional data to justify permanent custody action

Goals/Objectives

GOAL: Child will be placed in permanent home. (Preferably Adoption)

OBJECTIVES:
- Obtain permanent custody
- Identify best placement resources for permanency
- Prepare child for placement
- Child placed in home
- Family and child receive follow-up services to maintain placement

Intervention Activities

Identified steps and activities to:
- Facilitate court activity toward pursuit of custody
- Evaluate and identify the best home for the child
- Prepare and move the child into the new home
- Assist child and family in their adjustment
- Casework support, referral to community services, parent support groups, etc.

Implement Case Plan

Reassessment

If child successfully placed in adoptive home and placement legally finalized, **close case.**

If placement is not appropriate or disrupts, try again. Determine why it didn't work, (return to **assessment**) and make necessary revisions in goals and plan activities.

Continue in this mode until permanence is achieved.

* The relationship continues throughout the process.

E. CASE CLOSURE AND RECIDIVISM

Conceptual Framework

Without case plans to guide casework activities, decisions to close cases are often made using inappropriate or inconsistent criteria. As a result, some cases may be closed prematurely, while others may remain open for extended periods of time without intervention.

In many instances, the decision to close a case is unrelated to the service needs of the family, and is not the result of good case planning. For example, cases may be closed because of minimal case activity for a period of time. Workers may justify such closure, believing, "I haven't seen the family in quite a while, and I haven't had any referrals on them, so they must be doing okay." Caseworkers may also close cases because of agency pressure to reduce caseload size, or to adhere to the procedural requirements of a brief service or short–term intervention model.

Conversely, workers may keep inactive cases open, since closing them will reduce caseload size, which usually results in the assignment of new, perhaps more difficult cases. In some agencies, cases remain open while workers "wait and see if anything develops." This is more common when agencies are concerned about their liability if they close the case and the children are subsequently maltreated. However, this practice may actually increase liability, if a child is harmed in a family that is statistically open, but in which the worker has had little or no contact.

Some cases are kept open under a rubric of "preventive services." Preventive services can be misconstrued by both agencies and workers as a license, or even a responsibility, to remain involved in the lives of their cases indefinitely.

Some caseworkers keep cases open because they like a family and have been successful in working with them. Continued involvement with a family is reinforcing for the worker. Some families want the case to remain open, since they depend on agency supportive services, even when the risk of future maltreatment is low.

Improper case closure does increase liability. When cases are closed improperly, families in need of protective services may be prematurely closed, which can increase risk to the children. Or, families in which there is little risk may remain open, while the caseworker provides supportive interventions that utilize considerable worker time and agency resources. While income–related and family support services are often necessary to strengthen and preserve families, other service providers in the community should be identified or developed, and the family should be helped to access and properly use them. This enables child welfare staff to focus efforts on families and children at high risk of maltreatment.

The most valid criteria to justify case closure is the successful completion of a well-formulated case plan! Without such a plan, workers may not be able to say with reasonable surety that case goals and objectives were achieved, or that the risk to the children was reduced. When the caseworker can demonstrate that thorough planning was performed, that conscientious and planful delivery of services occurred, and that case objectives were met prior to case closure, the agency should generally not be considered culpable if further maltreatment occurs after the case has been closed.

RECIDIVISM

The reopening of a family case by the agency after the case has been served and closed is referred to as *recidivism*. Many factors can contribute to recidivism. Some of these are not within the control of the caseworker or the agency. However, several factors related to improper case closure or absent case planning can greatly increase the rate of recidivism. Cases are more likely to be reopened if:

- The case was insufficiently or improperly assessed;

- Services were not identified to properly address the contributing factors to maltreatment;

- The intervention strategies were not effective in significantly reducing risk before the case was closed;

- The family was not linked to permanent sources of support and assistance prior to case closure;

- The case was closed before the family was ready to function without ongoing casework assistance; or

- The caseworker did not terminate the casework relationship properly.

For the foreseeable future, human behavior will remain, to some degree, an enigma. In spite of our most conscientious and most professional efforts to achieve positive case outcomes, and in spite of our best clinical judgments, we will not always be able to reliably predict the future behaviors of clients. Some parents or caregivers will again abuse or neglect their children, in spite of our most professional efforts. We cannot be held accountable for every case of recidivism, or for every instance in which children in families whose cases have been closed are again abused or neglected. However, we should be held stringently accountable for the way we meet our responsibilities of risk assessment, case planning, and service delivery.

Application

DETERMINING WHEN TO CLOSE A CASE

A properly formulated case plan, regularly reviewed and amended when necessary, is the most legitimate means of determining when to close a case. The appropriate criteria for closing a case should be:

- The agency can demonstrate with reasonable surety that the children are no longer at risk and are not likely to be subjected to further maltreatment. The criteria on which to base the decision are: the contributing factors to risk or maltreatment were properly identified; services were delivered that effectively addressed and eliminated risk factors; and no new risk factors have been identified.

- The children have been placed into other, permanent family situations in which there is no risk of maltreatment.

- The family situation has been stabilized, and the family has been linked with other community resources to provide them with ongoing supportive services as needed.

- The family cannot be located, despite intensive efforts by the worker to find them; or, another worker or agency assumes responsibility for the family, such as when the family moves to another community.

ISSUES RELATED TO CASE CLOSURE

Caseworkers often believe that the families they serve are anxious to have the case closed. In reality, if a casework relationship has been established, and the casework method utilized, many families view the caseworker as a trusted source of support, even though they may never verbalize these feelings. As a result, there may be an increase in family stress when case closure is imminent. The family may view case closure as a threat to their stability, and they may not want to end casework involvement.

If, through casework intervention, a family can develop confidence in their own strengths and abilities, and can learn to use support from their families and communities, the stress associated with case closure can be reduced. This may include: establishing support networks within the family and extended family; pursuing membership in a church, or developing relationships with a minister and members of the congregation; establishing linkages with staff of local family service or community centers; attending parenting, support, or therapy groups; and becoming involved in community programs for their children, such as Head Start or other preschool programs. Helping families utilize these community-based supports should be a central objective of casework services. The most appropriate sources of support must be identified and individualized for each family.

When the caseworker and family have developed a positive relationship, family members may experience a significant loss when the case is closed. The caseworker may have been a consistently trustworthy and dependable person for family members, and through this relationship family members may have felt worthwhile, cared for, and valued by another person. Closing the case may reinforce some clients' beliefs that people come and go in their lives, that there are no permanent relationships, and that perhaps, the worker never really cared about them but was just doing a job. Case closure may be experienced as abandonment, which can precipitate a regression to previous ways of behaving and relating.

The caseworker can prevent this by ending the relationship properly. The following strategies facilitate a positive case closure and can help prevent recidivism:

- The worker must clearly state the purpose of the casework relationship early in its development. The worker should help family members understand that the worker is there to help them develop their own strengths and resources, and to learn ways to help themselves; and, that it will end when this purpose has been achieved. This will help prevent the family from feeling that the caseworker has somehow changed the agreement and abandoned them.

- The caseworker should involve the family in planning for closure through discussion and review of the case plan, and by setting time frames for case closure. The worker's direct involvement should be gradually decreased during this period. The caseworker should encourage and reinforce the family for managing problems themselves. Increased and successful management of their own problems will increase the family's self-confidence.

- The worker and family should acknowledge case closure as a kind of graduation, and should reflect on the family's successes, accomplishments, and growth. The worker's praise and support are reinforcing to the family's self-esteem. However, the worker must be honest in acknowledging both the family's gains, and the potential for continuing problems. Some clients respond to overstated praise by feeling the worker does not really understand their situation, and is glossing over the fact that they will continue to need assistance and support.

- The worker should encourage the transfer of attachments from the caseworker to other supportive relationships within the family's local community. Through the relationship with the caseworker, family members may have learned that other people can be trusted to help them. This may help them establish or strengthen other relationships available to them. The caseworker should reaffirm that, "I'm not the only person in the world who is trustworthy, who is helpful, or who can care about you." Linkage with naturally occurring support systems can provide the family with relationships that can survive over longer periods of time. The establishment of these linkages should be an objective of the case plan.

- Finally, the caseworker should reaffirm concern for the family, and reassure them that discontinuing services does not mean the worker no longer cares what happens to them. Some families may not verbally express their feelings of loss or abandonment unless given permission to talk about it. The worker can open discussion by saying, "You seem depressed and distant. Are you angry with me for closing the case? Many families feel abandoned and alone. Are you feeling that way?" The caseworker may need to talk about the permanence of positive feelings for other people, despite physical separation. When a relationship has been particularly strong, an occasional follow-up phone call or card may let the family know the caseworker is thinking of them.

- Finally, the worker should reassure the family that if they have additional problems and needs, they can always call. The worker will help them identify appropriate services, and can provide short-term support and guidance.

F. THE CASEWORK INTERVIEW: IMPLEMENTING THE HELPING PROCESS

1. Conceptual Framework

2. Application

Conceptual Framework

The term "interview" often brings to mind a formal process of targeted and pointed questioning designed to elicit specific information from a respondent about an identified topic. Our society's conception of interviewing is heavily influenced by frequent exposure to the media's investigative reporters, who conduct interviews to gather information for television news programs, documentaries, or published articles.

The dictionary definition of an interview, however, is "a meeting of people, face-to-face, to confer about something." The dictionary further defines *confer* as "to consult together, to compare opinions, to carry on a discussion or deliberation; to converse" [Webster's Unabridged Dictionary 1983].

The term "interview," as used in casework, is more consistent with the spirit of Webster's. A casework interview is a dialogue, a conversation, an interpersonal exchange of ideas and information, not an interrogation, a cross-examination, or a strategy of investigative reporting.

The casework interview is the means by which we implement the casework and case planning process. The purpose of casework distinguishes it from other types of interpersonal exchanges. Most social interactions develop to fulfill the social and affiliative needs of both participants. By contrast, the purpose of casework is to meet the needs of the client family. Therefore, the family's situation is the focus of dialogue in casework interviews, and it is the worker's responsibility to guide the interview to maintain this focus. In most other social relationships, if the needs and expectations of both parties are not met equitably, the interaction generally ceases.

The casework interview creates a safe environment in which family members can consider, develop, and implement strategies to change and improve their life situation. The worker's role is to utilize communication and intervention strategies that ultimately strengthen families and enable them to achieve this goal. We cannot minimize the interpersonal nature of this interaction. Casework can only be effective in the context of an interpersonal relationship characterized by trust, empathy, and honesty. Without the supportive environment of a trusting relationship, family members will be reticent to disclose personal and sensitive information, and will be cautious about investing themselves in a collaborative change process. Both communication and collaboration are essential for effective casework.

At times, workers equate interpersonal warmth, genuineness, and empathy with unprofessionalism. They see themselves becoming too familiar, personal, or "emotionally involved" with their clients, and believe this interferes with their ability to be "objective" professional enablers and problem solvers. They withdraw affect, and instead, become emotionally bland and impersonal in their relationships with families. Their behavior and questioning during interviews is stiff, stilted, and often artificial. Families interpret this demeanor as evidence of disinterest and disingenuousness. This interferes with the development of trust and confidence in the worker.

In casework, a primary determinant of professionalism is the worker's adherence to the clearly defined and agreed-upon purpose for the contact. The manner in which the worker achieves this purpose not only can be, but must be, in the context of a trusting relationship, characterized by empathy, honesty, and collaborative dialogue.

PURPOSE

In casework, purpose is considered at several levels. Initially, we as child welfare workers must define the purpose of our involvement with the family. This is always driven by our mission of protecting children from maltreatment. Involvement with any family is validated by this overriding purpose; unless a significant risk of serious harm to children is suspected, we have no right to intervene in the private lives of any family. In a casework model, defining the nature and purpose of agency intervention for a client family is an essential part of the engagement phase.

The effectiveness of casework depends upon the planned implementation of a series of discrete steps. We must first get to know a family and establish a positive rapport. We can then exchange and evaluate information to assess and understand the family's needs, strengths, and problems. Armed with this knowledge, we jointly set goals and objectives for services; we develop an intervention plan; we work together to implement change strategies; and finally, we evaluate our outcomes, and either recontract for additional services or close the case. Each contact with family members must, therefore, have a predetermined and explicit purpose that furthers the development of one or more of the steps in the casework process.

Finally, the topics to be discussed during an interview and the workers' interviewing strategies should both be selected to promote achievement of the purpose identified for the interview. For example, if we are in the early stages of relationship development, we will choose interviewing strategies that demonstrate our trustworthiness, our interest in the family, and our ability to understand. If we are conducting an assessment, we will choose strategies that elicit relevant information; we will listen and observe; we will ask clarifying questions when we don't understand; and we will provide support and reassurance to help the family feel more comfortable discussing personal or painful issues. If we are trying to engage a family member who has not participated fully in the change process, we may use planned confrontation, or probe to identify the barriers to his or her involvement. And, if we are helping families implement change, we may use constructive feedback and coaching strategies, we may model and demonstrate a new skill, or we may use praise and positive reinforcement to validate and support their efforts.

The skilled interviewer works with family members to set a clear purpose for each interview, and is an expert at guiding the communication to achieve that purpose. Family members must clearly understand the purpose of each interview in order to participate in it. Mutual agreement regarding the purpose of each interview also helps both worker and family remain focused and goal-directed as they talk.

WHERE TO BEGIN

Whenever we meet someone new, it is normal to begin an assessment of them. We try to determine if they are likeable, sincere, and of interest to us. If we feel appreciated and valued, we are likely to respond in kind. If we feel insulted, ignored, or otherwise treated badly, we are likely to withdraw or become defensive. If we cannot physically avoid an offensive person, we become emotionally remote, and we behave in a contrived manner that, while "appropriate" for the situation, reveals very little about ourselves. Our willingness to enter into a relationship is strongly determined by the way in which the other person responds to us.

An initial casework contact with a family sets the tone for all subsequent interactions. If the initial contact is positive and helpful, family members will be encouraged to work with us. If the initial contact is negative, family members will often withdraw, avoid subsequent contact, or act defensively. If they cannot avoid the worker, they may appear to cooperate, but will reveal very little of themselves, and will possibly sabotage change efforts. Therefore, the manner in which a caseworker approaches the family in the early stages of a relationship is critical to a successful outcome. (Refer to Section IV–B, "The Casework Relationship: The Foundation of Family–Centered Child Welfare.")

The first task in any casework relationship is to establish rapport with a family. To do this, we must act in ways that are consistent with child welfare values, even as we stress the necessity of protecting children. The child welfare profession adheres to principles of respecting families, supporting their right to self-determination, appreciating their strengths and individuality, believing in their desire to protect and care for their children, and expecting them to be partners in a change process. We cannot simply espouse these values. Our behavior, tone of voice, and body language must also communicate our adherence to these principles.

For example, if we enter a home without permission and demand that someone talk to us, we communicate profound disrespect for the family. We should, instead, ask permission to enter the home, and explain why it is in the family's best interests to discuss certain matters with us. Opening closets and cupboards to examine their contents is demeaning and intrusive; asking clients if they have sufficient food, and involving them in identifying what they need is a more respectful and collaborative way of obtaining this information. If we expect families to become invested in the change process, we must encourage and value their input. If we elicit their ideas, but always discard them in favor of our own, we do not have a legitimate collaboration, and our behavior negates our verbal message about collaboration.

Since involvement with families is often prompted by a referral from outside the family, as caseworkers we must clearly explain the purpose for agency involvement. We must communicate our intent to objectively assess risk and to respond with helpful, not punitive, interventions if we do determine the children to be at risk of harm. We must also share our expectations regarding the family's involvement. If we want family members to collaborate in problem solving, we must define child welfare as, first, a collaborative service process that helps families protect their own children, and explain that the agency will assume responsibility for a child's care and custody only if the parent can't, or won't.

Once we have explained our purpose, the most effective strategy to engage family members is to "start where they are." This fundamental social work principle affirms the importance of understanding a family's life circumstances, point of view, and feelings early in the casework process. We facilitate this by creating an environment in which families can feel less threatened disclosing personal information. We often must deal with anger and anxiety about the referral, suspiciousness and lack of trust in the worker or the agency, and embarrassment or shame. Validating these as expected responses to a child maltreatment complaint communicates acceptance of their point of view, and demonstrates we are capable of understanding their feelings. We can then implement the appropriate interviewing strategies to further the casework process.

Application

To effectively implement the casework process, the caseworker must be skilled at using a variety of interviewing methods, and must know how and when to use them appropriately.

There are several types of interviewing strategies and question formulations. Each has its preferred uses, benefits, and limitations. A skilled interviewer will use them all, usually several concurrently, and will select the best strategy to further the dialogue, to encourage family members' involvement, and to achieve the purpose of the interview.

The following are the general categories of interviewing methods, their purpose, and their benefits and limitations.

OBSERVATION

Observation refers to what we see while we are with a client family. As we interview, we should notice family members' body language, facial expressions, behaviors, and their interactions with each other and with us. These cues can provide us with considerable information that, at times, supports what the family is telling us, and at other times is inconsistent. When verbal and nonverbal messages are not congruent, the client's behaviors are often very important indicators of the more accurate message. For example, a father might verbalize his affection for his son, but may consistently ignore or dismiss his son's approaches. Similarly, a client may strongly verbalize her interest in job training, but may repeatedly fail to attend scheduled job interviews.

Attributing accurate meaning to nonverbal behavior can provide considerable insight into family members' personal and interpersonal dynamics. However, the operative word is "accurate." It is easy to misread nonverbal cues, particularly when the worker has preexisting biases about a family, or does not understand the cultural context of family members' behaviors. Garrett [1942] describes a social work class assignment in which pairs of students observed an individual or group of individuals in a public place, and documented what they saw, without comparing notes. Invariably, she reports, the write–ups were so different that the students could not believe they had been written about the same situation. For example, one student described a parent as "angry, callous to the pleas of his child for an ice–cream cone." The student's partner described the parent as "anxious, uncertain, indecisive, frustrated, and helpless in the face of a demanding offspring in a temper tantrum." The purpose of such an exercise is to "direct a student's attention to the limitations of his own capacity to see what is actually happening, and to his tendency to distort the objective facts with his own preconceived ideas of what he himself would feel or do in such a situation" [Garrett 1942].

While we should take note of certain behaviors, and can speculate on their possible meaning, we should seek supporting evidence from other observations and interview responses before making a judgment about the meaning of any particular behavior. Understanding cultural norms, values, and the meaning of culturally specific behaviors is also essential in properly interpreting what is observed. (See related discussion in Chapter V, Culture and Diversity in Child Welfare Practice.)

The following case example demonstrates how careful observation of family members can provide important information about family dynamics.

✵ The Wetherall Family

The Wetherall family had been referred by the school principal for suspected abuse of six-year-old Nicole. During the 30-minute interview with Nicole's mother, the caseworker noted that Nicole stood quietly by her mother and patted her softly on the shoulder, knee, and back while the mother cried and told the worker her story. Nicole brought her mother a box of tissues, threw the used tissues in the trash, and asked her mother if she would like a glass of water. When her mother began to look for her cigarettes and lighter, Nicole jumped to get them for her. Nicole repeatedly said, "It's okay Mommy, it will be okay." Nicole's mother sometimes ignored Nicole, and at other times rested her head against Nicole's shoulder. Nicole's face reflected serious concern. She did not smile or laugh. She intently watched her mother, scrutinized her mother's face and body language, and responded immediately when her mother seemed to want or need something. The worker noted that Nicole's behavior could potentially be interpreted as the "role reversal" that is typical of abused children. Further assessment substantiated that Nicole had, indeed, been abused by her mother for several years.

LISTENING

Listening is one of the most effective interviewing strategies. Listening involves not only hearing a client's communication, but also understanding its meaning. Workers can learn a lot by listening. They can infer affect, or feeling, by listening to a client's tone of voice. They may recognize that a family's use of certain words has special meaning. They can identify what a client chooses to tell them, and can infer what the client chooses not to discuss. They can listen for hints, prompts, and unfinished statements, and can infer that there are things a client wants to say, but cannot. They will recognize the potential importance of an issue when it is casually mentioned by a client for the third time in half an hour.

Listening can also help build the casework relationship. By listening without interruption or censure, the worker communicates interest in family members' viewpoints, and validates the legitimacy of their feelings. For some clients, they may feel "heard" for the first time.

Talking about an issue with a concerned and caring listener can also, at times, be therapeutic. This is called "ventilation" in social work terminology, and for some clients, simply talking about an issue reduces its threat and brings considerable relief. This is often a necessary intervention for persons who have been subjected to an exceptionally traumatic situation. Pam, age 14, is an example.

⚐ Pam Bellamy

Pam had gone to the garage to call her father for dinner and discovered that he had hanged himself from the rafters. Pam's mother had a severe reactive depression, and Pam was placed temporarily with her aunt. Pam went home a month later, but three months after her father's suicide, she was still experiencing debilitating anxiety attacks in class, and was referred to the school social worker. With encouragement, Pam told the social worker, in great detail, what had happened, what she had seen, what she had done, and how frightened she was that her mother would also commit suicide. The worker had talked to the mother's therapist, and was quite sure Pam's mother was not, nor had she ever been, suicidal. The worker was able to reassure Pam of this.

In the weeks that followed, Pam would ask to leave class and see the worker when she experienced her attacks. She would come to the social worker's office and say, "I'm seeing it all again." The worker would let her talk it through and tell the story again, always ending with reassurance that despite her loss and grief, life would one day again be more normal, and her mother would not also abandon her. Talking about the event appeared to give Pam some feeling of control over it, and her descriptions often began to include verbal reassurances to herself. For example, "I'm still scared my mom will go off the deep end again, especially when she starts crying about Dad…but I think she's pretty strong." Over the weeks, Pam's visits to the school social worker became more infrequent. After six months, Pam's visits were to talk about future plans. She was relieved that she only had her "visions" once in a while, and they weren't as scary. She could usually talk herself out of them.

Listening does not imply an absence of response by the worker. The worker who "sits like a bump on a log" and doesn't respond is often perceived as polite but disinterested, which discourages further communication. The worker must use strategies that encourage the client to continue, and that reinforce and support their continuing. These include nodding; maintaining appropriate eye contact; assuming a comfortable, listening posture; and using verbal confirmation and encouragement, such as "Yes, go on," or, "I see."

Conversely, a skilled interviewer is not compelled to fill all silences with comments or questions. Silences may mean the client is thinking, trying to decide what to say next, struggling for emotional control, or has run out of things to say. The worker can use nonverbal cues such as nodding, waiting, and continuing to listen to encourage the client to continue. When the client's verbal or nonverbal behavior signals that he or she is finished, the worker can then comment or begin another line of discussion.

QUESTION FORMULATIONS

Purposeful questions, comments, and other interjections are used by the worker to direct and guide the interview to achieve its purpose. The nature of a question or response, how it is phrased, the tone of voice used, and its placement in the conversation are all calculated to achieve a very specific goal. Each questioning strategy has its benefits and its limitations. The following describes the most often-used interviewing strategies, and exemplifies how and when they should be used.

Active Listening and Supportive Responses

Description   Active listening is listening combined with verbal and nonverbal responses that communicate the worker's involvement and interest in what the client is saying.

Supportive responses are purposeful interjections in the interview, where the caseworker's presence, actions, and responses have an enabling, soothing, and facilitating effect on family members.

Purpose   Active listening and supportive responses communicate and demonstrate that the caseworker is concerned, and understands family members' feelings and situation. These methods are important during the early stages of casework, when the caseworker is trying to establish a positive casework relationship.

Supportive responses have an enabling effect on a family, and should be used when the family has the ability, but needs assistance, to implement changes.

Examples

Mother: "I haven't had a good night's sleep in months. I lie awake all night wondering where Teddy is."

Worker: "I can tell you're awfully worried that something has happened to him." (Active listening.)

Mother: "You can say that again!"

Worker: (Nodding) "Mm, hmm."

Mother: "I don't know what to do."

Worker: "You must feel very frightened. I know how hard that must be." (Supportive response.)

Grandma: "It's been awful around here lately, especially with Jenny moving back in. The whole house is in chaos. I don't know where to begin."

Worker: "Your normal routine seems to have been disrupted lately." (Active listening.) "It would be hard to get everything done." (Supportive response.)

Dad: "I know that I should talk to John's teacher. But I just hate going to that school. They don't listen to you."

Worker: "It sounds like you'd rather not go to see John's teacher." (Active listening.) "You might be uncomfortable about it, since your last experience there was so bad. But if you like, we can decide together what you'll say, so you will feel more comfortable about it." (Supportive response.)

Benefits   Active listening and supportive responses build trust, communicate the worker's interest and willingness to listen and to help, and may have an enabling effect on the family.

Liabilities   The family has considerable control of the direction of the interview. The caseworker listens and responds to what the family chooses to say. Little change is generated, few goals are set, unless support by itself enables the family to take action.

Closed–Ended, Forced Choice/Yes–No, and Probing Questions

Description   Closed–ended or forced choice questions are questions for which there is only one appropriate answer, or which can be answered adequately with "yes" or "no." Probing questions ask directly for detailed information about a topic.

Purpose   To gather factual information and obtain answers to specific questions.

Examples   Where does your son go to school? (Closed–ended)

How many years have you been married? (Closed–ended)

Have you talked with the teacher lately?   (Yes/no)

How long has your boyfriend been living with you? (Closed–ended/probing)

Does your husband beat you? (Probing)

Are you going to go to work or apply for public assistance? (Forced choice)

Benefits   Forced choice and closed–ended questions are the fastest way to obtain direct, to–the–point, specific answers to very specific questions. They are an excellent way to obtain a lot of factual information in a short period of time about the topic in which we are interested.

Liabilities   Forced–choice questions limit the potential responses to those directed by the interviewer, and therefore may provide limited information.

Closed–ended and probing questions may be threatening to the family, and may encourage the respondent to be evasive, or to lie as a way of avoiding revealing personal information.

Open–Ended Questions

Description   An open–ended question is one in which the interviewer does not limit the content or scope of the response. As there are no restrictions placed upon the family to provide specific information, the open–ended question permits family members to answer in any way that they choose.

Purpose   Open–ended questions are best used when the caseworker wants to learn as much as possible about the family, and to become aware of the wide range of factors and occurrences which contributed to the family's situation. Open–ended questions also allow the family to reveal more spontaneously the dynamics of their situation by allowing and encouraging them to express their own views, feelings, and perceptions.

Examples   "Tell me about Katie. What kind of a child is she?" Compare with a yes/no formulation: "Is Katie shy?" "Is Katie friendly?" etc. By asking closed–ended questions, the worker leads the family to focus on specific issues which are determined by the caseworker. The open–ended format allows the respondent to answer with information he or she feels is most relevant to the situation; "She's stubborn as a mule."

"What kind of relationship do you have with your mother?" is an open–ended question. By contrast, "Are you and your mother on good terms?" which is a "yes/no" formulation, forces a choice without providing any information about the nature of their relationship. An open–ended format allows family members to provide what they perceive to be important information, and to elaborate on it, such as, "We generally get along pretty well, if we don't talk about my living with Joe. She doesn't approve of him at all."

Other examples of open–ended questions are:
"You said that the past two years have been especially hard. Can you tell me why?"
"What was it like for you when Dan was in the hospital?"
"You seem upset. Will you tell me about it?"
"I'm not sure I fully understand. Can you try to explain it to me?"

Benefits   Open–ended questions provide more extensive and elaborate information, and may help reveal family members' perceptions and feelings about the situation. Responses to open–ended questions may provide information about the "process" issues which are contributing to the problems.

A person's response to an open–ended question may provide new and unexpected information for the caseworker.

Liabilities   Open–ended questions take time. Once the question is asked, people must be given the freedom to respond in their own way and in their own time. If the caseworker cuts them off or refocuses them, they may feel the worker is not really interested.
The caseworker may need to sort through extraneous information to identify those issues which are most pertinent to the situation.
The open–ended question may be used by some people as an opportunity to digress, and to avoid discussing important and relevant, but potentially threatening, issues.

Clarification

Description   Clarification is the process whereby the caseworker, with insightful interjection, helps family members develop an understanding and appreciation of their own feelings, thoughts, and behaviors, while achieving a better understanding of the dynamics of the family's situation.

Purpose   Clarification is an integral part of the assessment process. It is used to guide the family to provide information which helps them and the caseworker identify the personal, interpersonal, and other factors which contribute to the presenting problems, and to determine needs and strengths.
Clarifying responses are also used to help the family attain insight into their own feelings and behaviors.

Examples

Mother:	"I get so angry at Alex. He won't take the trash out, he won't clean his room, he talks back, and he refuses to do anything I tell him. And his father lets him! I've asked my husband dozens of times to help me, and he tells me it's my job to raise Alex; he's worked hard all day and just wants to be left alone to read the paper!"
Worker:	"Sounds like you might be just as angry at your husband as you are at Alex."
Father:	"I don't think I'm going to apply for the job. I don't really have the qualifications. Besides which, I'm sure they won't hire me."
Worker:	"Well, you really are pretty qualified. Sounds to me like you

might be feeling nervous or scared about going, and are having second thoughts.

Mother: "I never realized how much work there is in caring for an infant. You're busy *all* the time! I never have a minute to myself. And when she screams, I think I'm going out of my mind. But when she started smiling and cooing at me, it's like the rest of this awful world doesn't matter. It's a wonderful feeling to know she's happy."

Worker: "Sounds to me like you really are enjoying her, in spite of all the work. It also sounds like it's very important to you to feel that you can comfort and satisfy her, and frustrating when you can't. Is that how it is?"

Benefits   Clarifying responses help the caseworker make an accurate assessment of the contributing or dynamic factors related to the presenting problems, and to accurately identify family strengths and nascent abilities.

Clarifying responses help the caseworker move family members from the content level to the process level in the interview, which facilitates a better understanding of the situation.

Clarifying responses may facilitate the development of family members' awareness and understanding of themselves and the nature of their needs and problems, which, by itself, can sometimes generate positive change.

Liabilities   Clarifying responses are often threatening to the family, because they bring into open discussion feelings, issues, and concerns that the family may either not be fully aware of, or may not want to talk about.

In the absence of a supportive, trusting relationship, clarifying responses may be perceived by the family as probing, and may increase resistance to talking with the caseworker.

Summarization, Redirection

Description   Summarization includes strategies to review what has been discussed, to restate conclusions that have been drawn, and to help a client organize information.

Redirection includes strategies that move discussion into content areas of greater importance, and avoid discussion of less relevant issues.

Purpose   l) Keeps interviews focused and on track; 2) helps family members organize their thinking and communication; and 3) creates order by identifying salient points and curtailing discussion of less important details or issues.

Examples

Worker:	"From what you've told me, there are three things that are really important to you–moving to a nicer apartment, getting coats for the children, and seeing that your son gets the help he needs." (Summarization.)
Worker:	"Before you tell me about Ted, will you finish what you were saying about the landlord? You said he had come out once and started to repair the roof, and then never came back. Then what happened? (Redirection.)

Benefits   Makes the most efficient use of interview time by keeping discussion focused on pertinent issues.

Helps family members organize their thinking, keep the important points in mind, and avoid becoming overwhelmed by multiple issues and details.

Liabilities   People may feel cut off when redirected by the caseworker. They may interpret the worker's directiveness as not wanting to listen to what they think. Also, if the caseworker redirects, summarizes, or closes discussion of an issue prematurely, important information may be missed.

Giving Options, Suggestions, and Advice

Description   Responses in which the caseworker provides an opinion or suggestion regarding what the family should do, and responses that direct the family into a particular course of action.

Purpose   By providing options and making suggestions, the worker may help a family identify possible solutions, and steps to achieve these solutions. Family members may be encouraged to try new ways to solve their problems.

Examples

Mother:	"I don't know what to do about this court order. "
Worker:	"Well, you should call the court to find out why you have been subpoenaed. You may have to get an attorney to represent you. Legal Aid is a place to start.
Grandma:	"Nothing I do to control Jenny has worked. It doesn't matter what I do. She still screams and throws herself on the floor. I can't stand it any more. I'm out of ideas!"
Worker:	"You might try 'time out.' I'll show you how it works, if you like."

Benefits   Gives the family options they hadn't thought of, or didn't know how to use. By providing the family with other perspectives, the caseworker can encourage action which the family may not have considered.

381

Keeps the interview goal directed by focusing discussion on "What do we want to do, and how should we do it?"

Liabilities   If the caseworker offers solutions too quickly, or provides most of the solutions, the family may be prevented from arriving at their own solution to the problem, may not learn how to solve their own problems, and may not become aware of their own skills and resources. The caseworker may be blamed for any failure the family experiences in implementing the recommended solution. The family may expect the caseworker to provide another, more successful solution, as in, "Okay, that didn't work. Now what?"

Confrontation

Description   An intervention, wherein the caseworker empathetically, but insistently, directs a family member to become aware of and consider issues, feelings, or processes which he or she has been avoiding. Most often this means disagreeing with the person, and pointing out defensive, avoidant, inadequate, or inappropriate thinking or behavior.

Purpose   Confrontation may be used to push family members to take steps toward solving problems when other interventions by the caseworker, including supportive and clarifying responses, have failed. Confrontation is an alternative to help family members face the reality of their situation, their feelings, or their behavior.

Examples

Bob: "It's my mother's fault. If she weren't so lazy, she would have helped me, and I wouldn't have failed the test."

Worker: "You failed the test because you didn't take the time to study, Bob. You didn't ask anyone for help. In fact, you went to a party the night before the test. That's not your mother's fault."

Aunt: "Well, if she wants to move out and get her own apartment, let her just go ahead. See if she can make it on her own. I don't care any more what she does. I really don't."

Worker: "If you didn't care you wouldn't be this upset. I think you care more than you're willing to let on. In fact, I believe you're very hurt that she doesn't want to live with you any more."

Benefits   Proper use of confrontation may facilitate insight on the part of family members when other, less directive interventions have failed.
Can help individuals become aware of their own defensiveness, including denial, as a means of coping with problems.

Liabilities   Confrontation, as an interviewing strategy, should not generally be attempted unless a strong casework relationship has been established between the family member and the caseworker. Confrontation can be very threatening to family members, and may greatly increase resistance. If overly threatened, people may refuse to talk further with the caseworker. This is less likely if the relationship between the caseworker and family members is well established, and family members perceive the caseworker as caring and helpful.

Confrontation will usually increase a person's anxiety and discomfort. Family members may require considerable follow-up support and assistance from the caseworker. Once confronted, their feelings and needs must be fully dealt with. This takes considerable time and commitment from the caseworker.

AVOIDING COMMON PITFALLS

In this section, we will examine common interviewing pitfalls, and provide more effective alternatives.

Leading Questions

A leading question is not really a question. It is generally a statement of the speaker's belief or opinion, phrased in a manner that seeks confirmation from the listener. For example, "Don't you think that John really likes his brother?" would be more accurately communicated if the speaker had said, "I think John really likes his brother. Do you agree?"

When a worker asks a leading question, a client has three options. The client may agree with the worker's statement. If he does not, he can directly express his own dissenting opinion: "No, John doesn't like his brother; he and his brother don't get along, never have." This, however, directly implies that the worker is wrong. To be this assertive, a client must feel secure with the worker, and comfortable with open disagreement. If he is not, his options are to avoid the question, make an equivocal response, or feign agreement. He might evade the question by saying, "Well, his brother certainly doesn't like him!" He may make a noncommittal remark such as, "Well, maybe, I'm not sure," or, "In a way, perhaps." Finally, if a client believes it important to maintain harmony, believes it impolite to contradict someone in authority, or wants to be conciliatory, he might verbalize agreement, even though he does not really agree. So, even if the client verbalizes agreement to a leading question, we may still not know what the client really thinks.

Other formulations should be used, depending on our reasons for asking. Open-ended questions, forced-choice, clarifying responses, or summarizing help us learn the client's opinion about the topic. Confrontation and direct statements should be used to communicate the worker's opinion. The following examples illustrate leading questions and more appropriate formulations:

"Wouldn't you be happier in a bigger apartment?" (Leading)
"What kind of apartment would you like?" (Open-ended—preferable in

that it allows the client to describe all the qualities desired in a living space)

"Do you prefer a larger or smaller place?" (Forced choice–appropriate if we are interested in learning our client's preferences regarding apartment size)

"Aren't you angry about your husband having left you?" (Leading–the worker presumes, from personal experience, that the client *should* feel angry)

"How do you feel about his having left you?" (Open–ended–preferable if we want the client to express the full range of her feelings)

"It sounds as if you're angry about your husband having left you." (Clarifying response–would only be used if we had heard anger in the client's tone of voice or choice of words, which makes it more likely to be an accurate statement. However, the client can still comfortably disagree, since the worker has phrased the response as an observation, not a foregone conclusion)

"Aren't his bruises evidence enough to conclude someone has been hitting him?" (Leading, and accusatory)

"Can you tell me how Billy got the bruises?" (Open–ended–preferable because it gives the client the opportunity to explain the circumstances around abuse)

"Billy has bruises all over his face, chest, and arms, and they are in various stages of healing. That kind of bruising is rarely, if ever, accidental. I have to consider that someone has been hitting him." (Confrontation – the statement clearly expresses the worker's opinion, and justifies his or her reasons for that position)

"You do want to go back to work, don't you?" (Leading)

"You told me last time we talked that you were looking for a job, and that you wanted to go back to work as quickly as possible, if you can find day care. Do I remember that correctly?" (Summarization, and requesting corrective feedback if summary is wrong)

Disclosing Personal Information

Casework requires both personal honesty and openness to foster the development of a trusting relationship; yet, the focus must remain on the family's situation. This may create confusion for workers regarding whether, and how much, personal information or points of view should be shared with a client. Some disclosure in the proper context is helpful, even constructive, especially in building a relationship. Other information is better left private.

In some contexts, it can be appropriate for the worker to disclose basic, factual personal information. This helps the client view the worker as a person. This can strengthen rapport and identify areas of commonality, both of which support relationship development. For example, the worker could appropriately disclose that he has three children of his own, and that raising teens was difficult.

He could disclose that his wife is an accountant; that he has been with the agency for three years; that he works on cars in his spare time; and that he loves Monday Night Football.

Consider the client's feelings if, when asked about himself, the worker were to respond, "I really can't talk about myself. We're here to talk about you and your family." The message to the client is that there is no reciprocity in the relationship, and that the client is expected to fully disclose very important information to a worker about whom he knows absolutely nothing.

It would not, however, be appropriate for the worker to engage in extended discussion about his own lifestyle, goals, needs, fears, or future plans, nor to talk about his own abuse as a child, recent divorce, or problems with his own children. This type of discussion draws the focus of attention away from the client to the worker. However, if asked directly, the worker should provide a short, factual response, and return the focus to the client. The worker may determine that the client is simply curious and trying to get to know the worker; or, that the client may be posing personal questions to the worker as an entry to discussing certain topics, albeit in a roundabout manner. For example:

Client #1:

Client:	"Are you married?"
Worker:	"No, I'm divorced."
Client:	"How long were you married, and why did you get divorced?"
Worker:	"I was divorced three years ago after a seven–year marriage. Why are you asking?"
Client:	"I guess if you've been divorced all this time, you know what it's like to live on your own."
Worker:	"Well, I know what my experience has been, but everyone doesn't see it the same way. What's it been like for you?"
Client:	"Very hard. Do you ever feel depressed?"
Worker:	"I did; more so at first, and now, every once in a while. Why, do you feel depressed?"
Client:	"I've never been so depressed and lonely in all my life."
Worker:	"Tell me about it."
Client:	"Have you ever felt angry about being alone?"
Worker:	"In moments. How about you?"
Client:	"I'm so mad that at this time of my life I have to do everything myself!"
Worker:	"Sounds like you don't have a lot of support or help from other people. Is that true?"

Client #2:

Client:	"What do you think about abortion?"
Worker:	"I think it's a pretty controversial topic, and people's feelings are pretty strong. Why do you ask?"

Client:	"I just wondered. I think it's wrong for anyone."
Worker:	"Well, you're not alone in thinking that. Why is it an issue for you just now?"
Client:	"Because my daughter is pregnant, and I don't know what we're going to do. I can't take care of another child, and she's too young, and yet I can't go along with an abortion. I don't know what we're going to do."

Client #3:

Client:	Have you been to college?
Worker:	Yes, I have.
Client:	Do you have a degree?
Worker:	Yes, two of them—a bachelor's degree and a master's. Why?
Client:	Well, you seemed so well educated. I've always admired that in people.
Worker:	Is that something you'd like for yourself?
Client:	Sure, but it'll never happen. I'm not smart enough.
Worker:	How do you know that?
Client:	I never did well in school. In fact, I quit. I've always regretted it.
Worker:	You're older now. Sometimes that makes a big difference. Had you ever considered going back?
Client:	You mean to get a GED (general education degree)? Yeah, I've thought about it. But I doubt I could do it. Do you think I could?
Worker:	Truthfully, I don't know you well enough to make a judgment about that. But you do express yourself very well, you read well, and you follow through with other things that you want. All that helps. We can get more information about it, if you like. It's something to think about, anyway.

Sometimes, the worker can use a personal experience as a model for a client of how to handle a similar situation. This can be presented as an option, with a clear expectation that the client has the right to choose whether to follow the worker's suggestion.

Client:	"I get so mad with Tessa. I know she's only three, but any time I try to correct her, she throws a screaming fit. Sometimes it lasts for hours. I can't tell you how that upsets me! Some days I'm ready to strangle her, or walk out that door and *never* come back. But I can't just let her do anything she wants…that's not right."
Worker:	"I know how you feel. My own daughter was a terror when she was three. There were days when I wanted to pack her in a shoe box and leave her on the closet shelf until she was five. She was a lot like Tessa; spirited and strong, but willful. I learned to use time-out with Laurie and it often worked. I can show you how to do it, if you like."

In the above example, the worker might have simply offered to teach the mother time-out without disclosing the information about her own daughter. However, the mother has expressed a strong negative feeling about her child, and in doing so, has placed herself at risk of being negatively perceived by the worker. The worker could also have offered blanket reassurance, such as, "Lots of people feel that way," but clients often experience this as a meaningless platitude, rather than as genuine support. The fact that the worker has had similar feelings, and was willing to acknowledge them, can be reassuring to the mother. It can communicate that the worker is not likely to think she's awful; that the worker has the capacity to understand; and, most important, that the worker has handled it in a way the mother might learn and model.

The worker's calculated self-disclosure provided the greatest amount of support possible, while still promoting growth. Yet, the mother still has the choice whether to follow through, since the worker made her offer as a simple statement and did not ask for confirmation of her interest.

If the mother does not express interest, but continues the discussion in another way, the worker should listen for another message. For example:

Client:	"Oh, they taught me that in parenting class. It works, sometimes. But not well enough."
Worker:	"Sounds like you're not sure what to do. Tell me more about what happens, and how you feel about it."
Client:	"I know three year olds are hard, and I should be more patient, but it just gets to me."
Worker:	"Tell me what you mean...how does it get to you?"
Client:	"It's like something shoots off inside me, and I can't stop it. I don't know what starts it. Well, Tessa starts it. But once it's started, I can't stop it. It's not good."
Worker:	"Sounds like you don't feel in control. Are you afraid you're going to hurt her?"
Client:	(quietly) "Yeah, it's awful to say it, but sometimes I think if I don't leave, I'm going to hurt her bad."

Handling Hostile or Accusatory Statements

There are many reasons clients make accusatory statements or behave in hostile ways toward a worker. The client may feel threatened and try to assert power or control; the client may be testing the worker to see what kind of response will be generated; the client may feel shame or embarrassment, and respond defensively; or the client may be legitimately angry about the perceived intrusion by the agency into his or her privacy.

In dealing with hostile and accusatory remarks, the worker must do two things. First, respond in a matter-of-fact and unemotional manner. The old adage, "It takes two to fight," is particularly relevant. If the worker becomes defensive or angry, the client often feels all the more justified in continuing to be hostile and defensive. However, if the worker cannot be engaged to argue, and is neither angry nor defensive, often the client's anger will diminish in intensity.

It is more difficult for a client to continue to be hostile in the face of calm, rational, and supportive responses from the worker.

The worker must also try to understand what feelings are generating the anger. It may be fear or anxiety; embarrassment or shame; threatened self-esteem; or hurt. If the worker can identify and acknowledge the client's other feelings, it may also help to defuse the client's anger.

The following examples demonstrate both inappropriate and appropriate worker responses to provocative statements or questions.

Client #1: "You have no right to come in here and accuse me of abusing my child! How dare you! I think you'd better leave."

Inappropriate Responses:

Worker: "I not only have a right, I have a responsibility to protect children from maltreatment. It's my job, and you need to cooperate, or else I'll involve the police." (Defensive, threatening)

Worker: "Sit down, let's discuss this, in a calm and pleasant manner, please. Let's not have any more yelling. We can behave like rational adults here." (Demeaning, sarcastic. Treats client like a child)

Worker: "Look, there's been a referral that Raymond was abused. I think it's important that we find out how it happened! (Accusatory)

Worker: "Well, maybe you're right. Sorry." (Self-deprecating)

Appropriate Responses:

Worker: "I understand why you're angry; you thought I was accusing you. I'm not here to make accusations. We do need to find out how Raymond was burned, however, to protect him from being hurt again. I was hoping you'd work with me to do that." (Matter-of-fact, validates feeling, clarifies intent, reengages)

Worker: "I expected you to feel angry. Most people in this situation are angry. But I'd like to talk with you further about how we can prevent this from happening again. Will you hear me out? (Acknowledges feelings, restates purpose for contact. Leaves client with a choice)

Client #1: "Why should I work with you, of all people!

Worker: "Whether you believe me or not, I really would rather work *with* you, not against you. Raymond's burns were very serious. How it happened is important, but only to help us prevent it from happening again. The choice is yours. But before you say no, I'd rather you ask me whatever you want, until you're satisfied that I mean what I say about working together. (Restates purpose and desire to be collaborative. Leaves choice with client, puts client in control)

Client #1: "Well, say what you have to say." (The client, while not yet convinced, has given the worker the opening to begin to dialogue)

Client #2: "Who do you think you are. You're 25 years old, have no children, and *you* are going to tell *me* how to raise my kids? (Laughs). Go on!"

Inappropriate Responses

Worker: "Just because I don't have children doesn't mean I can't help. I have studied a lot about child development. I've also worked with many other families. (Defensive)

Worker: "Yes, you're right. I can have my supervisor call you. She has children of her own. Or maybe she can assign a more experienced worker. (Self-deprecating)

Worker: "Well, it would seem you haven't done too good a job yourself, even after raising five of them. What does that say for experience?" (Accusatory)

Appropriate Responses

Worker: "Sounds like you're concerned that I don't have the ability to understand or to help you." (Active listening)

Client #2: "You're right on that one. It would be a waste of time! Meanwhile, Janna's still running the streets."

Worker: "Sounds like you think this is too important to entrust to someone who doesn't know what he's doing." (Clarification, support)

Client #2: "Yes."

Worker: "I don't blame you. I'd feel the same way. And you're right, I don't have all the answers, but then, raising kids can be pretty complicated, and I've never found anyone who had all the answers. I'd like to help, and I know of many other resources we can use if I can't help you directly. But I can't even help you find the best services, if I don't understand what's happening. Can you tell me?" (Confirms validity of feelings; restates intent; clarifies own abilities and limits; and reengages.)

Don't Make Promises You Can't Keep

The casework relationship is based on honesty. We expect families to be honest with us; we must also be honest with them. This means we must be truthful about what we can and cannot do, and about the possibility of negative as well as positive outcomes from the worker's involvement.

For example, while we can assure the client we will not unnecessarily divulge personal information, we cannot promise complete confidentiality, since certain information may be subpoenaed during court hearings. We should, however, reassure the family of our intent to retain confidentiality wherever we can, and explain the circumstances under which we cannot.

Another example: we cannot guarantee that we will never have to place a child. But we can reaffirm our intent to help maintain the child at home, and explain the circumstances when we would have to move the child. Here is an example of how a worker might handle this type of situation.

Shellie, age four, has been hospitalized with bronchial pneumonia. She is underweight, developmentally delayed, has had no medical care since birth, and was critically ill when admitted to the hospital. The caseworker has begun discussion with Shellie's mother to develop a safety plan for Shellie.

Mother:	"I have nothing to say to you."
Worker:	"It's important that we talk about this. Shellie is a very sick little girl. We have to talk about what will happen when she's ready to come home from the hospital."
Mother:	"I have nothing to say to you."
Worker:	"What are you trying to tell me?"
Mother:	"That I have nothing to say to you! Are you deaf or something? (pause) Don't keep looking at me. I won't talk to you. I know you people. You're going to put her into a foster home, regardless of what I say. So why should I even bother?"
Worker:	"Why would you think that?"
Mother:	"Don't give me that bull."
Worker:	"I'm quite serious about this. You're right. It's our job to protect children, and if we can't protect them at home, we will place them with someone who can protect them. But I haven't decided whether Shellie needs foster care. That all depends on you."
Mother:	"What do you mean? I have nothing to say about this."
Worker:	"As far as I'm concerned, you do have a lot to say about this. Whether Shellie comes home or not depends on whether we're both sure you can protect her and keep her from getting sick again. That's what we need to talk about. It's up to me to get you the help you need to take good care of her. It's up to you, first off, to convince me you're willing to try."
Mother:	"Of course I am. I'm her mother, aren't I?"
Worker:	"Good, I'm glad you want to try. The next step is to figure out why she got sick, before we can decide how to keep it from happening again."
Mother:	"I'll just take better care of her."
Worker:	"How do you mean?"
Mother:	"I'll just do better. Isn't that enough?"
Worker:	"You need to be more clear than that. I don't understand what you think you should change."
Mother:	"If I tell you, you'll call me unfit and you'll take her out. I know how you people operate."
Worker:	"Well, if I believe you're a serious danger to her, I may have to consider temporary placement. But even if you did

things really wrong before, if we understand what they were, and why it happened, we can develop a plan to help you. It's called a safety plan, and with it, we may be able to avoid placement. That's my hope. But I can't do it alone. I need you to help me understand everything that happened, so we can decide what has to change."

Mother: "What if you people still think I'm unfit?"

Worker: "Well, there are several options. Foster care is certainly one. But I'd see if anyone in your family could provide safe care for Shellie before I placed her with a stranger. We can also consider letting her come home from the hospital, if a homemaker came here and worked with you every day, or if Shellie went to day care during the day. We may find that parenting classes could help you, or counseling. And even if we do have to place her, I'll want to keep working with you to get her home as soon as possible. So, as I said, the most important thing now is to talk about what went wrong, and develop a safety plan. Shall we do that?"

Mother: "If you say so."

Worker: "I'd rather we both agreed...at least to start talking about it. What do you think?"

Mother: "I guess."

Worker: "Okay, good. I'd really like to be able to help you. Can you tell me what happened?"

If a worker is honest and straightforward with families early in the relationship, the family will be more likely to trust the worker, even if the worker's actions ultimately have negative repercussions for the family. The worker can then help the family deal with the realities of their situation and make necessary, hard choices. A lack of honesty by the worker, by contrast, will violate the family's trust, severely limiting the worker's ability to be helpful to the family in any situation.

INTERVIEWING CHILDREN AND YOUTHS

Caseworkers may directly interview children for several purposes: to establish a trusting, helping relationship; to gather relevant assessment information about the child and the situation; to explain and prepare the child for a change; to help the child deal with concerns or fears; to engage an older child or youth to participate in problem solving; to provide support and assistance in a traumatic situation; or to help the older child or youth plan and implement changes. In this regard, interviewing children is not dissimilar to interviewing adults; it is the means by which we implement casework.

There are differences, however. Children don't usually have the capacity to participate in the lengthy, verbal communication we usually refer to as an interview. Infants and toddlers lack the cognitive/linguistic capacity to understand, much less participate in, such a verbal exchange. We can usually converse with a preschooler for short periods of time, but the scope of information gained may be limited, and we may not always be sure of its accuracy or veracity. It is not until children reach late school-age that they can engage in focused, reciprocal, interpersonal verbal exchanges with adults. Even then, the degree to which an older child or youth can participate in a verbal interview will depend on his or her level of cognitive development, verbal fluency, comfort with verbal communication, and overall comfort with the worker.

Most workers are all too familiar with the behavior of a child or youth who doesn't want to talk. The more we question, the more reluctant the child is to divulge important information. Direct questions invite one-word answers. "How are you?" "Fine." "How was school?" "Okay." "What do you like best about it?" "Recess." "How do you get along with the kids?" "Good." "How do you feel about it?" (Shrug.) In addition, when forced to sit still in a face-to-face, formal conversation with an adult, most children and some youths will fidget, squirm in discomfort, avoid eye contact, and behave as if they are prisoners who can't wait to get free. Many workers avoid direct work with children because of their frustration and discomfort with this awkward, unproductive scenario.

The first step in learning to "interview" children is to change our focus. Our goal, after all, is to "communicate" with children–to learn important information from them, and to communicate things that may be helpful to them. Before beginning, we must first determine exactly what we want to communicate, and then select the communication strategies best suited to the child's age, developmental level, verbal and linguistic ability, and preferred communication style. We can then communicate with the child at his or her own level, and we will likely be much more successful.

In general, the basic principles of casework with adults apply equally to children. Children are likely to be suspicious, withdrawn, frightened, and resistive if they do not know us; don't understand who we are or why we are there; have misperceptions about our intent; or are worried that some harm will come to them from talking with us. We must engage children as we do adults by clearly communicating who we are, why we are there, and what will happen, before we can ask them to divulge information about themselves and things important to them. The first step with any child is to develop the casework relationship. Children must see us as dependable, kind, trustworthy, helpful, and genuinely interested before they will be comfortable relating to us.

Children also want to know all about us. They will ask a million questions: Where do you live? Do you have any children? Do you like ice cream? Do you have a mom too? Do you have a dog? Unlike adults, however, children usually do not have a hidden agenda for these questions. They are simply relating to you the way they relate to anyone new. Children know you by knowing things about you, and children appreciate it when there are things you have in common. The worker should answer with simple, but accurate, information. Adolescents, on the other hand, not only use personal questions to get to know the worker, but to test the worker, or to broach discussion about other issues. (See earlier discussion about disclosing personal information.)

Developing rapport and interacting with children happens most naturally if we involve our child clients in play or other activities while we get to know one another. This may also be true for many adolescents. Conversing casually while playing a game, throwing a ball, riding in a car, going for ice cream, or walking through the park is often more effective than trying to talk in a formal interviewing room. It is less intense, and children or youths are usually more comfortable. They can say things as they feel them, and they don't feel they are expected to answer on command. Workers can use open-ended questions, such as "Tell me about...," and then listen. Using gentle clarification and feedback can let a child know you're listening and understand. Using nonverbal feedback to communicate your continued interest will encourage the child to continue. Finally, when children are reticent to talk, we can let them know we're there to listen and help, whenever they're ready to talk.

The issue of authority, always present in casework, is also relevant when working with children. They will want to know your rules and how you will respond if they break them. They want to know if you'll punish them if they do something wrong. Some will have been told that the social worker moves children to different families. Some families may have threatened their children with, "If you're bad, I'm going to call the social worker and have him take you to the juvenile detention center." For some children, a social worker is akin to the devil's helper. The worker must clearly define his or her role, and deal with the child's fears before the child will feel like trusting.

Children, like adults, will test the worker to see if he or she can be trusted. They may act out and see how the worker will react. At times, they may contrive situations to test the worker's response. Ten-year-old Arthur had been very upset, and was asking his adoptive parents about his biological mother. He was at risk of disrupting his adoption. Yet, the social worker could not get him to talk about his feelings. After several sessions, the worker simply said, "I know you don't want to talk about it now, but I know it's important to you. So, whenever you're ready, I'm here to listen and help." Arthur appeared not to hear her. Three visits later, Arthur presented the worker with a "terrible problem at school" and asked for her opinion on what to do. It became quickly evident that the problem was not at all serious, and had probably been greatly exaggerated for effect. However, the worker recognized Arthur's problem as a test, listened intently, responded very seriously, and helped Arthur think through solutions. Two visits later, Arthur asked the worker what she knew about his mother.

Child welfare workers should become proficient at alternatives to verbal communication with children and youth. Workers can use art, dolls, stories, photographs, puppets, or other toys to help children communicate. They can use play techniques to prepare children for visits with their families; to change placements; to help them understand why they were placed; to rehearse different ways of handling stressful situations; and to learn how they are feeling. The worker might say, "I know it may be hard for you to say it in words. Maybe you could draw me a picture. Or show me with the puppets." Or, the worker could say, "Maybe you could tell me a story about a little boy just like you." Another strategy is: if a worker is trying to determine a child's feelings, he or she can ask the child to draw a "happy face," a "sad face," a "mad face," and a "scared face," and then ask the child to point to the face that most accurately expresses how the child feels: "Show me Dana's face when Mommy goes away?"

Acting out a scenario with dolls and photographs, accompanied by simple statements of explanation, also gives preverbal toddlers a visual representation of what is happening. This is an excellent means of preparing a toddler for adoption or a move to foster care.

Engaging children in play also has its own rewards; children readily relate to adults who are willing to play with them. A worker can do more to establish rapport with a child by playing a favorite game or reading a story than almost any other intervention. Workers must also remember how they appear from a child's perspective. We are larger, stronger, more powerful. The threatening aspects of this perception can be lessened if we approach a child in his or her own medium–play–and literally, at his or her own level. Children really like people who will sit on the floor with them, or who seat them so they are at eye level while they are talking. Interviewing rooms should be equipped with child–sized tables and chairs, and both the worker and the child should use them.

There will be times, of course, when we must ask children direct questions. The question formulations outlined earlier in this chapter are valid when conversing with children. However, we must consider the child's level of cognitive and linguistic development before we phrase our questions. We must be sure the child will understand what we are asking, and that the child has the ability to answer. For example, a caseworker would not ask a four year old, "Does your mommy do anything to hurt you when she's angry and upset?" Rather, we would ask, "Does Mommy ever get mad?" and then, "What does Mommy do when she's mad?" In general, the simpler the question, the more likely we are to get a valid response.

As with adults, leading questions directed to children are a sure–fire way to get misinformation, and will also guarantee that information gained during the interview will be inadmissable, if ever needed in court. Direct, uncomplicated questions are preferred. Rather than, "Your mommy hit you on the face, didn't she?" (a leading question), the caseworker would ask, "Did your mommy hit you?" If the child responds yes, ask, "Where did she hit you?" If the child answers no, then ask, "How did you get that bump (sore, boo boo…whatever word the child uses for bruise) on your cheek?" Open–ended questions are also effective. However, if they are too broad, they invite a barrage of extraneous and unrelated information, particularly from younger children. Rather than, "Tell me about it," the worker might narrow the scope and provide more direction by saying, "Tell me what happened next, after you watched cartoons."

Clarifying responses are particularly effective in helping children understand and share their feelings. One strategy is to label their feelings for them, using simple words–"mad," "scared," "happy," "worried," "sad." In response to a belligerent child, a clarifying response would be, "It looks like you're really mad today. Can you tell me what is making you so mad?" Clarifying children's feelings can also be supportive. "You look really sad. I wonder if it's because you miss your mommy." Workers can also encourage children to divulge their feelings by saying, "I know you've had a pretty hard time, and most children like you have lots of worries. I'm here to help you with your worries."

Workers must also recognize when children are uncomfortable talking about or divulging personal, or emotionally–laden information. The worker may need to prepare the child for such discussions by first identifying the child's feelings, and then providing considerable support. For example, "Lots of times children feel sad about this. You might too." "Lots of children cry when they talk about their mommies. I know how hard it is, and I know how sad you feel." "I can tell you're feeling mad right now. That's okay. Can you tell me what makes you mad?" "Does it make you scared when I come to see you? Are you afraid I'll take you to another house again?" While we want to help children deal with their feelings, if we push too hard, or allow them to become emotionally overwhelmed, they will often shut down and refuse to continue. However, providing opportunities to communicate their feelings in a supportive and nurturing environment can be extremely helpful to children in pain.

Finally, the worker should not underestimate his or her importance to a child. Termination of the relationship should be handled sensitively.

A worker should never simply disappear, or introduce a new worker, without helping the child with separation and termination issues. (Refer to Section IV-E, "Case Closure and Recidivism.")

PUTTING IT ALL TOGETHER

Interviewing is both a science and an art. It has been stressed in previous discussion that interviewing is much more than a means of gathering information from a family. It is the tool with which we implement the helping process, "where the rubber meets the road." Child welfare workers often wish there were an easy way to acquire and perfect interviewing skills. Unfortunately, skilled interviewing requires considerable training and practice.

When a caseworker is first learning to interview, it is common to become so preoccupied with our own performance–whether we're using the right questions or responses, whether our tone of voice is right, whether we're assertive enough, or supportive enough–that we often fail to hear what the client is saying, and we miss critical information. It is always important to take the few necessary seconds to choose the best interview option before responding. But, it is generally more important to observe and listen carefully than it is to say everything exactly right. Most workers, if tuned in to the client and focused toward a clear purpose, will be able to move the interview along well enough.

There is, therefore, legitimate concern about providing workers with a list of sample question formulations and responses. There is always a risk that the unskilled interviewer will consider this listing as the definitive "how to" of interviewing, and overuse them, or use them out of context. Our intent in providing a list of possible responses is simply to illustrate ways to achieve the various purposes of the casework process. These can serve as a model for workers in formulating their own questions and responses to meet the unique situation in each case.

Purpose: Opening The Interview, Developing Rapport

> "May I talk with you for a few minutes?" (Note the use of "with" rather than "to.")

"Where would you be most comfortable meeting with me?"

"I want to understand this from your point of view."

"Maybe you'd like to ask me some questions before I ask you mine?"

"Do you have any concerns about our agency? Or about me? I'd be glad to answer them."

"I'd like us to work together. You may not believe that. I understand you'll need to get to know me better before you feel confidence in me."

"I'd prefer not to do anything against your wishes. But you'll have to work with me; otherwise, we can't work out a solution that we can both agree on to protect Larry."

"I know this is hard for you. I'll try to make it as comfortable as I can."

"That's what we need to discuss. Where would you like to begin?"

"Please let me know if I say things you don't understand, or that bother you."

"Would you be willing to hear me out before you make a decision?

Purpose: Assessment

Two types of formulations are particularly well-suited for assessment. They are open-ended questions and clarifying questions. Generally, open-ended questions provide considerable information about a wide variety of topics. Clarifying responses help the worker and client focus on particular topics or issues to gain a more in-depth understanding.

Open-ended formulations might include:

"Tell me what you know about that."

"What do you mean?"

"Can you tell me more about it?"

"Can you help me understand what you're saying?"

"What would you like to see happen? If the world were perfect, what would it look like?"

"In your mind, what might the worst possible outcome be?"

"What do you think your strengths are?"

"What's most important to you?"

"What's the hardest for you to deal with?"

"What do you do when you're hurting?"

"Has it ever happened before? Tell me about it."

Clarifying responses could include:

"I think I understand why you're angry—but would you tell me again, so I can be sure?"

"Sounds like you're saying that your mother is a real problem for you. Can you tell me more about that?"

"You've mentioned your ex-husband three times. It sounds like he may still be important to you."

"I'm not sure I understand why you won't talk with her. I can't tell if you're afraid, or just angry at her. What do you think?"

"You keep referring to his temper. Can I assume you're saying he has a bad temper?"

"You seem afraid to trust anyone, including me."

"Seems like you don't have a lot of confidence that anything can change."

"Sounds like you'd like certain things to stay just as they are."

"Sounds like caring for your children may be more than you can handle. Is that how you feel?"

"You sound like you feel really defeated."

"I'm hearing that you might want to consider releasing your children for adoption. It's always an option. Would you like to talk more about it?"

"Sometimes people are afraid to fail. I'm hearing you express lots of concerns about trying this. Are you worried you won't be able do it?"

"I understand you want to protect him, and I understand you may also be afraid of him. But from what you've told me, I'm thinking perhaps he has hurt you and the children when he's angry."

Purpose: Introducing Change Strategies

"I have an idea about that...I'd like your opinion on it."

"What would you think about...?"

"What have you done in the past that's worked? I might be able to help you do it again."

"Well, it's going to take hard work. Let's start with something we know we can accomplish. What should that be?"

"You don't have to do this all by yourself, you know."

"The most important thing is to make sure Rita is healthy. Let's talk about how to do that."

"I know you want me to give you an answer. I can't guarantee that my suggestion is the best one for you. Let me tell you how I'd think it through. Then you can help make the decision."

Purpose: Confrontation

"I know this is hard to accept, but you can't avoid the fact that he has hurt Michael, more than once."

"I know you'd like to blame the foster mother...and maybe she did over-react. But you did go over there at midnight and create a scene in her front yard, and you were, by your own admission, very drunk. What else would you have expected her to do?"

"You keep telling me there's nothing wrong, but you have an eviction notice on your door–the third in as many months–you have no food in the house, and you're freezing here. That says to me that there are a lot of things wrong."

"I want to believe you, but I'm having trouble doing so. Everyone at the mental health center is telling me you took the wallet. They found it in your jacket pocket. I'm more interested in understanding why you took it."

"I know you're not happy. Every time I come by you've been crying."

"Just trying isn't enough. You told me last time that you could, and that you would. Can you tell me why you didn't? Did something get in the way? Did you change your mind?"

Purpose: Reassuring and Supporting

There are two supportive interventions that caseworkers should probably never use. The first is, "It must be really hard for you." The second is, "I'm sure everything will be all right." The first is so overused that it has become a trite phrase, rather than a genuine expression of understanding and concern. People use it when they don't know what else to say and want to appear supportive. The second is superficial and patronizing, and greatly minimizes the importance of the situation, particularly when we cannot say with any certainty that everything will be all right.

Support and reassurance must be situationally specific. They are not meant to gloss over or make light of problems. They must be honest, related to reality, and timed properly. They should be a natural extension of the conversation.

Examples are:

"You've been through quite a lot these past months. It's no wonder you're so tired!"

"I think you're doing fine, considering you just learned how to do it. You'll improve with practice. Maybe I can help you by giving you some feedback."

"I've talked with William. He still wants to come home, even with all that's happened. If we continue what we've been doing, I think we have a good chance of making it work."

"You may feel very alone at the moment, but I want you to know that we're here to help as you need us."

"You're not the only one who feels that way. I know of many people who have shared your experience. It might be helpful if you could talk to some of them directly."

"I know it feels overwhelming. Let's try it a little at a time. It'll be easier to handle that way."

"Yes, you messed it up, but I wouldn't call it a dismal failure. After all, you got the first half right. Let's work on the rest."

"Your anger doesn't frighten me. You can't scare me away just by being angry. If I understand why you're angry, I can handle it."

"In my opinion, I think it looks wonderful! It's obvious you've put a lot of work into it. Where did you find that chair?"

"How long has it been since you've had an hour to yourself?"

G. CASE RECORDING

1. Conceptual Framework

2. Application

Conceptual Framework

While many social workers verbalize that good case recording is important, it is often not given high priority in practice. Many workers view recording as an agency or legal expectation to assure accountability. However, properly completed case recording is an essential component of good casework practice, and can serve many beneficial purposes.

First, the written case plan is formal documentation of the outcomes of the case planning process. There are several reasons why this information should be documented in writing:

1) A written case plan assures that the caseworker and family members understand and agree on the case goals and objectives, and on the activities needed to achieve them. The case plan document becomes a working contract, which may be referred to during the intervention process to assure that activities are implemented as written. Each involved party should receive a copy of the plan to guide their activities.

2) The case plan document can organize the caseworker's thinking about planning. By following the plan's standardized written format, the caseworker can assure the thoughtful completion of each step in the planning process, in their proper order.

3) The written case plan can also be used as documentation to meet statutory case planning requirements. All child welfare agencies are subject to federal statutory mandates (P.L. 96–272) and, as a result, most agencies require that a standardized case plan be completed for each family served by the agency. Maintaining the written case plan in the case record provides documentation that a case plan has been formulated for the family, and also assures that the agency has met policy regulations.

4) A written plan can facilitate case review by supervisors. When a well-formulated case plan is included in the case record, the supervisor can assess case progress without relying on the caseworker to verbally communicate the information. This can save considerable staff time. Prior review of a written case plan also saves time for participants in formal case review sessions.

5) The case plan can serve as periodic summary case recording or dictation. A thorough, written case plan concisely documents all pertinent information regarding a family's strengths and needs, and the agency's response to those needs. Case plans and amendments should be filed chronologically in the family case record. This eliminates the recording of extraneous, random data, including "run on" descriptions of contacts, which are typical of process–style case recording. Using the plan as dictation consolidates paper work, and reduces the amount of time the caseworker must devote to documentation.

6) The case plan is also an effective way to transmit relevant case information to collaborating service agencies, such as the juvenile court. In cases where the court assumes custody of the child, the case plan is typically filed with the juvenile court. By reviewing the case plan, the court can more accurately review the agency's provision of services, and the family's involvement and progress. The case plan may also be used to justify reunification of a family and termination of court custody, or to support a request for temporary or permanent termination of parental rights.

7) When a family receives services from multiple providers, the case plan should be jointly formulated by the primary providers in collaboration with the family. This might include foster or kinship caregivers, or residential care staff, when children are in placement. All service providers should have copies of the most recent case plan to guide and coordinate their service delivery, thereby preventing service gaps, duplication of effort, or misunderstandings of roles and responsibilities by providers.

Caseworkers should not attempt to complete written case plans without first fully completing the proper planning process. Written case plan documents which are not preceded by thorough case planning are often sparse in content, and the designated goals, objectives, and activities often fail to properly address the family's needs. Unless the case plan has been properly formulated, the written plan document will serve none of the purposes listed above.

Application

Four principles are central to effective case recording. They are:

1) Record facts, not judgments.

2) Record only relevant information, and be concise.

3) Summarize activities in lists, not narrative.

4) Use summary dictation whenever possible, not process recording.

PRINCIPLE # 1: RECORD FACTS, NOT JUDGMENTS

The case record should record, as concisely as possible, what the worker sees, hears, and experiences while working with the family. The case record should document facts accompanied by dates and clear behavioral descriptions. A factual recording will also be more readily accepted by the legal and court system as legitimate documentation. Compare the following dictations describing the same home visit.

⚐ Lana and Ben

Lana is the 18-year-old mother of Ben, a six-month-old infant. The case was assigned to family services after Ben had been hospitalized for six weeks for severe malnutrition and failure to thrive. Family Services was assigned to protect Ben and assure he was being cared for properly.

DICTATION #1:

When I arrived at the home, Lana was disheveled and seemed drugged. She didn't seem happy to see me. I asked to see the baby. She resisted, and tried to change the subject. I finally convinced her I needed to see Ben. He was in his crib, and was filthy dirty and depressed. He looked like he hadn't been out of his crib for several days. I told Lana I didn't think he was getting proper care. She got angry and more resistive. I asked what she had been feeding him, and she assured me he was eating, even though it looked like he had lost weight again. I told Lana we needed to take Ben to the doctor immediately. She became belligerent and uncooperative. I took Ben to the emergency room myself.

DICTATION #2:

Lana answered the door dressed in a nightgown, her hair was uncombed, and she said she had been sleeping. Her speech was slurred, thick, and halting. She appeared to stare past me; her eyes were partially closed, and her face looked swollen. She asked why I was there. I reminded her we had an appointment, and I asked to see Ben. She said he was sleeping and couldn't be disturbed. I insisted, and followed Lana to the bedroom. Ben was in his crib, wearing only a soiled diaper. The crib sheets and blanket smelled of urine and feces. Ben had a serious diaper rash. He did not respond when I called his name. When I turned his face toward me, he stared beyond me. When I lifted him, he felt lighter than the last time I had seen him. I told Lana that we needed to take Ben to the doctor immediately. Lana swore at me, told me to leave her alone, and said she would not go anywhere with me. She stomped into her bedroom and slammed and locked the door. I bundled Ben into a blanket, called the police, and we took him to the emergency room at Children's Hospital.

Discussion

The first dictation relies on value–laden adjectives to describe Lana and Ben: disheveled, happy, filthy dirty, depressed, angry, resistive, belligerent, uncooperative. All are subject to question. How did the worker know Ben was depressed? What, in the worker's view, constitutes belligerence or uncooperativeness? We wonder just what the worker saw, and what her justification was for making these claims.

In the second dictation, the worker used nouns and verbs to describe behaviors, and gave more objective descriptions of what she saw. She does not use pejorative labels, nor make judgments about what she saw. The description speaks for itself. It is clear that Ben was in trouble, and Lana was not cooperative.

When appropriate, the worker can summarize the conclusions she has drawn. These are identified in the dictation as her own perceptions and judgments. For example, Lana's worker might conclude the dictation by saying:

It is my belief Lana was on drugs or alcohol, and possibly both, based on her slurred speech, erratic behavior, and her appearance. This has been typical during my home visits. This is also the third time I've visited and found Ben to be neglected, in spite of in–home services. His condition has deteriorated since we opened the case two months ago. He is lighter in weight, and much less responsive. and he seems to have lost muscle tone. I do not believe Lana is capable, at this time, of providing a safe environment for him.

PRINCIPLE #2: RECORD ONLY RELEVANT INFORMATION, AND BE CONCISE

Many workers report extensive, unnecessary, run–on information in their case recording. This adds paper to the case record, and makes it almost impossible for a reader to extract relevant information to determine what is really happening. Compare the following descriptions of a family interview.

🏃 Ricardo and Johnny Mendez

DICTATION #1:

On September 17th, I met with Ricardo at his house. When I got to the house, Johnny was playing on a tricycle in the yard. Ricardo was not yet home from work; he was late, so I played with Johnny and talked to the babysitter until Ricardo got there. Johnny looks healthy and happy. The babysitter said he had been eating and sleeping well, and didn't seem to be having any problems. When Ricardo arrived, we went into the house and met in the living room. He told me his ex-wife had called and threatened to take him back to court for custody of Johnny, if he didn't let her see him any time she wanted. He said she had been coming around at all hours of the night and waking the neighbors. He said he didn't want her to visit with Johnny, because nothing had changed for her, and he was afraid she would abuse Johnny again if she got the chance. He asked me whether I thought it would be a good idea to file a restraining order against her. He also assured me that his babysitting arrangements were set for the fall, when the sitter had to go back to school. Ricardo has arranged for his mother's aunt, an elderly woman who lives up the street from his mother, to care for Johnny during the day until Ricardo got home from work.

DICTATION #2:

Home visit, 9/17. I visited with Johnny and the babysitter in the yard until Ricardo arrived home from work. The sitter reported that Johnny had been eating and sleeping well, and she felt he was healthy and happy. Ricardo reported that his ex-wife has said she would file for custody of Johnny if she could not visit him when she wanted. She has frequently come to the house late at night to visit. Ricardo stated his concern about the possibility of her abusing Johnny during a visit, and asked about the validity of a restraining order. Ricardo has arranged for his mother's aunt to provide daytime care for Johnny in the fall.

PRINCIPLE #3: SUMMARIZE ACTIVITIES IN LISTS, NOT NARRATIVE

To document activities in a case, record the dates of the contact, who was seen, the purpose, and the outcomes in a list or chart. It is easier to understand the sequence of contacts, and the important outcomes of the visit than if they are buried in a paragraph of description. For example:

Date	Type	Who Present	Activities/Outcomes
10/1	Home Visit	Ann, Debra	Discussed Debra's returning to school. Arranged to transport Ann to clinic on 10/4 to be rechecked for antidepressant medication.
10/4	Home Visit	Ann	Transported Ann to doctor. Discussed her progress with Ann and psychiatrist. He is pleased with her progress. Reduced therapy to 2x/month. Set recheck of meds for 11/30.
10/5	Phone	Debra	Called me from school. She has been suspended. Asked me to intervene with principal.
	Phone	Ann	Called Ann. She met me at the school.
	Meeting At School	Ann, Debra, Counselor	Talked with guidance counselor. Agreed on plan to get Debra tutor to reduce her frustration. Debra agreed to seek out guidance counselor when upset; will not blow up in class. Counselor will inform Debra's teachers of arrangements.

PRINCIPLE # 4: USE SUMMARY DICTATION WHENEVER POSSIBLE, NOT PROCESS RECORDING

Process recording is the verbatim, detailed, often blow–by–blow description of what happened during a case contact. It is often called the "running record," which is an apt description, since it does tend to run on and on. It is wordy, redundant, and often confusing. It is impossible to glean important information quickly.

Summary recording is a concise, summarized description of the important facts and events in the case for a specified period of time. It enables the reader to quickly discern the family's needs, the services provided, and the outcomes of services. When combined with a record of activities, as illustrated above, the agency has complete documentation for court or other legal proceedings. When case activity is high, and explicit documentation is needed, occasional process entries may be added to the record.

Summary Dictation: Angela and Troy Dawson

Family:	Angela Dawson, age 24. Troy Dawson, age three. Mrs. Raelene Hunter, Angela's maternal grandmother.
Date of Dictation:	6/22/94
Dictation Covers Period From:	3/1/94 – 6/22/94
Contacts:	8 home visits, and weekly/bi-weekly phone calls. 2 meetings with protective day care provider. 1 meeting with psychiatrist at LMHC.

CASE SUMMARY:

Troy was returned to Angela's care on 1/1/94, after having lived with Mrs. Hunter since birth. Angela has been recovering from an addiction to crack cocaine, and is trying to maintain a home for herself and Troy. Mrs. Hunter continues to support Angela. Angela is still involved in individual and group therapy, and drug counseling at the Logan Mental Health Center. She enrolled in a job training program on 4/6/94.

Angela had considerable difficulty caring for Troy when he first returned home. (See previous dictation, dated 3/1/94). Troy was enrolled in protective day care to provide Angela with respite. He was retained in the day care program when Angela entered job training. Troy remains in protective day care during the day. Angela picks him up at 4:00, after her job training.

Angela reports no serious problems caring for Troy. Worker has made several dinner time home visits to observe Angela, and to provide support in feeding and bathing of Troy.

CURRENT ASSESSMENT:

Angela is managing school, therapy, and child care reasonably well. Each time I have visited the home, Troy has been clean, properly dressed for the weather, and he appears healthy. He approaches Angela often for affection, and she hugs or pats him. She talks to him, and looks at magazines with him, and she will occasionally playfully chase him around the apartment.

Day care provider says Troy's behavior is age-appropriate, and he gets along well with the other children. He has occasional "fits," but they seem to blow over quickly, and he can be reengaged into play.

Angela reports often feeling tired, stressed, and sometimes depressed. She says she calls her mental health therapist or her drug treatment "buddy" when she feels depressed. The mental health therapist has verified this. Angela also takes Troy to Mrs. Hunter's for anywhere from a night to a weekend when she feels overwhelmed. Mrs. Hunter has agreed to keep Troy whenever Angela needs help, but for no longer than a weekend. Angela says a weekend is long enough. She has always picked Troy up at the agreed-upon time.

Angela reports still having problems with Troy's tantrums. She claims she gets very angry with him, and even though she has learned time-out, she claims she can't always implement it. She says she can't help but yell at him to "shut up" while he's screaming. Mrs. Hunter received a call on 5/12 from Angela's neighbor, stating that Troy was alone in the house, and had been screaming violently for over an hour. Mrs. Hunter went to the house and found Angela at home, having put Troy in a "time-out" chair for having thrown his cereal bowl across the kitchen. Angela told Mrs. H. she was "letting him scream it out, like they taught me." I talked with her about considering other strategies that may prevent the lengthy bouts of screaming.

Angela has not been able to meet other case plan objectives. She has not talked with the employment counselor about jobs, and she has not looked for a place to live with two bedrooms. She claims she can't do everything at once, that it will "stress her out too much," and she's afraid of a relapse.

Drug counselor says she has attended all meetings but one, when she called in sick.

CASE GOAL AND OBJECTIVES

Case goal remains maintaining Troy at home with Angela.

Objectives from the case plan are still appropriate. Time frames have been adjusted to decrease stress to Angela. I negotiated an additional objective with Angela to increase her options for disciplining Troy. She agreed to work with a parent trainer in her home, or to let the day care provider help her, to assure she is properly implementing time-out, and to teach her other discipline strategies.

ACTIVITIES

Worker will continue to make regular home visits and communicate with mental health and drug counselors.

Worker will set up meeting with the job training counselor to help expedite Angela's job search, and will accompany Angela to the first meeting with the job counselor.

Worker will contact the housing authority to get Angela assistance in locating more appropriate housing.

Worker will refer Angela to a parent trainer, and will schedule meeting with Angela, parent trainer, and day care provider to arrange coaching on discipline strategies.

All other case plan activities will continue to be implemented as written.

V. CULTURE AND DIVERSITY IN CHILD WELFARE PRACTICE

1. Conceptual Framework
2. Application

Conceptual Framework

Culture and diversity have become important issues in the practice of child welfare. Child welfare values promote the provision of culturally relevant services to children and their families. To assure this, all staff in a child welfare agency must strive to become culturally competent.

Cultural competence is a complex faculty. It can be defined as the capacity to relate with persons from diverse cultures in a sensitive, respectful, and productive way. However, describing the elements of cultural competence can be more difficult. Cultural competence incorporates a complex and interrelated array of cognitive and psychological traits and behaviors. And, since it is virtually impossible for anyone to fully understand all the characteristics, nuances, and traits of all the world's cultures, achieving cultural competence requires a lifelong process of learning and development.

While child welfare caseworkers may never learn all aspects of the cultures of the families we serve, we should strive to be sensitive, respectful, and adaptive in our cross-cultural communications and interactions.

Cultural competence encompasses several components:

- Understanding that the world's cultures are social inventions of humankind, each with its own adaptive strategies for a life of meaning and worth;

- Recognizing and understanding the effect our own culture has on our values, beliefs, thoughts, communications, and actions;

- Understanding how our own "cultural lens" affects our world view, and can distort our interpretation of other cultures;

- Understanding how cultural differences may affect perception, communication, and our ability to interact with people whose cultural backgrounds are different from our own;

- Understanding how cultural "blindness" and bias contribute to racism, prejudice, and discrimination;

- Understanding that, to achieve cultural competence, we must be "lifelong learners." We should never become complacent and believe that we know all there is to know about culture;

- Being able to learn about other cultures from the people who know them best–the members of other cultural groups–and the willingness to be open to cultural differences;

- Being able to transcend cultural differences to establish trusting and meaningful relationships with persons from other cultures;

- Understanding that cultures are dynamic and continually changing, permitting continued successful adaptation to changing life circumstances; and

- Being able to integrate cultural concepts appropriately into child welfare casework to enhance and strengthen families within their own cultural context; and to provide families with opportunities to grow and develop in ways that might promote a better adaptation to their situations and environments.

DEFINING CULTURE

The first consideration in any discussion of culture is to define it, and to differentiate it from other related terms such as race, ethnicity, and nationality. While these terms are often used interchangeably, they have very different meanings.

Race refers to the classification of humans based upon biological and physical characteristics. Racial groups consist of people who share a genetic heritage, and as a result, have common morphological (physical and structural) characteristics. The characteristics that determine race include physical stature, the color and texture of hair, the color of skin and eyes, body proportions, bone structure, tooth formation, and many other less visible traits. Historically, the world's peoples were classified into three primary racial groups: Mongoloid, Negroid, and Caucasoid. However, many contemporary anthropologists and ethnologists are questioning the fundamental validity and utility of race as a system of classification, since diversity within groups has increased, and differences between groups are not always clear cut [Shreeve 1994]. Increased mobility, and the lessening of both geographic and social boundaries, have also increased intermarriage, resulting in an amalgam of physical characteristics that cannot be easily categorized. It should be kept in mind that the criteria for racial delineation is somewhat arbitrary, based more upon political utility and historical inertia than upon different genetic criteria.

Ethnicity generally refers to people's national or geographic origin. Ethnic groups could include German, Chinese, Lakota Sioux, or French–Canadian. The word "ethnic" is derived from a Greek word that means "foreign."

Culture is considerably more complex than ethnicity or race. It is a system of values, beliefs, standards for behavior, and rules of conduct. It governs the organization of people into social groups, and regulates personal and social behavior. A culture is an adaptive system. It is created by groups of people to assure the survival and well-being of the group's members.

Race is always determined by heredity. Ethnicity is generally determined by an individual's place of birth, or the birthplace of that individual's ancestors. Culture, however, is transmitted through learning. It is important to emphasize this point, since, once learned, so much of cultural behavior appears to be so "natural" that it can easily be perceived as "instinctive," or biologically determined [Hammond 1971]. In fact, many people remain unaware that their beliefs and actions are largely components of their culture, and have been learned over a lifetime.

Race and ethnicity are constants–unchanging circumstances of birth. Culture is not. For culture to remain viable, it must be sufficiently flexible to adapt to a changing environment. A person's individual values, beliefs, behaviors, and other cultural traits typically evolve throughout life. Yet, once we are conditioned by our culture to meet our needs in particular ways, we may become so set in these ways that change is perceived as a threat to personal, and interpersonal, stability and continuity. The capacity to change is essential for ongoing adaptation and optimal adjustment to a changing environment. In short, while cultural traditions sustain us, we must be open to learning new ways, and integrating change into our lives in order to survive in our changing world.

Throughout most of history, people were born, married, raised their families, and died within a limited geographic area and social group. Therefore, members of an ethnic group often had similar physical features, were usually of the same race, and they often shared a common history and cultural background. This cultural, racial, ethnic, and geographic continuity was ended with the colonization of the world by Western Europe, and the increasing emigration of Asian and African peoples, including the forced emigration brought about by the practice of slavery during the eighteenth and nineteenth centuries. Today, ethnicity, race, and culture are not interchangeable concepts. People of the same race, or from the same ethnic group, may be of very different cultures. Individuals of all races and varied ethnic groups are included among the members of many cultures around the world, and contribute and share in their common cultural development, traditions, and values.

The fact that culture is not synonymous with either race or ethnicity should in no way be construed to diminish the importance that race and ethnicity often play in both intercultural and intracultural relations. Fear and distrust of difference is an unfortunate, but often manifested, characteristic of human relations. Whether the difference is in the physical characteristics of racially or ethnically diverse individuals, or in the values, traditions, and beliefs of diverse cultures, prejudice and fear often breed distrust and discrimination. Such hostile and threatening responses to people's race or ethnicity can significantly affect their life experiences and world view. In turn, this can affect the evolution of a culture. For example, an ethnic group that is persecuted because of that ethnicity may develop self-protective strategies, which may then become cultural traits that enable survival and safety.

UNIVERSAL ASPECTS OF CULTURE

All humans share a set of fundamental needs derived from common, biologically determined requirements for survival. The need for food, shelter, and a means to assure reproduction and protection of the young are the most obvious examples. Less obvious, but equally important, are needs for some level of social and economic cooperation, communication, and organization of interpersonal activities. Therefore, however varied, cultures tend to resemble one another in that they all incorporate certain basic elements. These include:

1) *Language*, which promotes communication within the group;

2) *Technology*, which provides the tools and techniques to modify environmental conditions to meet basic material needs;

3) An *economic system*, which organizes the production of goods and services, and the distribution of products and resources among group members;

4) A *political system*, which regulates internal social order, governs relations with other societies, and provides a means of making decisions that affect group members' survival;

5) *Social organization*, which provides a framework for relating to others and relying upon them for cooperation;

6) *Art*, which reflects the distinctly human and apparently universal need for aesthetic expression and creativity; and

7) *Ideology*, a guiding set of beliefs that explain the nature of the world, people's relation to it, and people's functioning within it [Hammond 1971].

In short, all cultures serve a common purpose for all humans. What differs among cultures are the ways that people choose to achieve these common ends. The differences are largely the result of diverse environments and different historical experiences.

Culture can be better understood by examining its objective and its subjective elements [Stewart & Bennett 1991]. "Objective" culture refers to the visible institutions and artifacts of a culture, such as its language, economic system, social customs, political structures, and arts. "Subjective" culture refers to the psychological aspects of culture, such as assumptions, belief systems, values, and patterns of perception and thinking. Stewart and Bennett suggest that cultural diversity is more easily recognized when there are distinct and discernible differences in objective aspects of culture, as these are easier to recognize and observe. This may be why objective culture has more often been studied and documented.

By contrast, the subjective or psychological aspects of culture are often thought to be inaccessible to observers, since they consist of internal cognitive and emotional processes. Upon returning from a visit to a foreign culture, most travelers can provide detailed descriptions of "how they do things there," but are rarely as eloquent about "how they think, feel, or see the world." Yet, objective aspects of culture are, simply, the behavioral manifestations and expressions of more fundamental subjective values, attitudes, and beliefs. Therefore, understanding subjective features of culture is more important, if we are to fully understand cultural differences.

It is not surprising that we often fail to fully recognize cultural differences in this country, since the objective, observable expressions of our culture appear to be much the same. Most Americans do, in fact, share many aspects of a common culture. We live and work in a largely industrial/technical society and a capitalist/market economy. We are socialized in a national system of public education. We celebrate many common national and religious holidays. We are governed by a common political structure. And, most of us share a common principal food source in the very American institution of the "supermarket." We don't typically expect Americans to begin their day by placing small packets of rice or potatoes on the ground in the bushes around their houses to feed the spirit world, as do the Hindu people of Bali; nor do most American women dress to cover their faces when in public. The vast majority of Americans drive cars, eat hamburgers and french fries, and own a T-shirt and a pair of jeans.

Because of the many objective similarities of our culture, it is easy, if erroneous, to presume a common subjective culture as well. As such, when we are confronted with fundamental differences in values and attitudes, we often attribute them to the individual variability found in any cultural group. In doing so, we fail to realize the potential existence of very different subjective cultures in this country. In other words, we are more likely to recognize cultural variability when visiting a West African tribal village, the streets of Kyoto, or a farm in rural Mexico than in our interactions with American families of African, Japanese, or Mexican heritage.

The first step in understanding culture is to learn to identify and explore both the commonalities and the differences in both the objective and subjective cultures of different groups. To achieve this, further definition of each of the components of subjective culture is necessary.

DEFINITION OF VALUES

Values are the cornerstone of all cultures. They are the widely held principles or ideals, usually related to worth and conduct, that a culture holds to be important. Values describe strongly held beliefs regarding what life and people "should" be like, what is considered "good" or "bad" in life, and what is "right" or "wrong" about behavior. The values of any culture form the foundation for life within that culture.

The following statements could be considered expressions of cultural values:

- The needs of the group are more important than individual needs.

- Older persons are esteemed and respected.

- Being a kind and giving person is more important than attaining wealth.

- Shaming your parents is the worst thing a person can do.

- Providing children with an education is the most important thing a parent can do for a child.

- Each person should be as industrious and productive as possible.

- Enjoy today, because you may not have tomorrow.

- The sanctity of life itself is more important than the quality of life.

- Harmony in the group is the highest accomplishment and should be preserved.

- Personal worth is measured by success in a career.

- Successful people pull themselves up by their bootstraps.

- Living well is accepting what comes with equanimity, fortitude, and wisdom.

Values generally address common issues across cultures: what makes a person worthwhile, what constitutes success, and what are the desired qualities in interpersonal relationships. However, the specific content of values may be very different from culture to culture. For example, whereas individuality might be highly valued in one culture, group loyalty may be most valued in another. There might also be competing values within a culture, resulting from individual differences, acculturation, or adaptation to a changing environment. An example of competing cultural values can be seen in the difficulties some contemporary American women experience in deciding between pursuing a career and staying home to care for a family.

The values of a group evolve in response to the group's historical experiences. Values often express the group's perception of what is necessary for group survival and the well-being of its members. Loyal Jones [1983] provides an example of how historical experiences influenced the development of Appalachian cultural values.

> Our forefathers... came from England, Wales, and Scotland...Most came seeking freedom–freedom from religious and economic restraints, and freedom to do much as they pleased...Our forebears were individualistic from the beginning, else they would not have gone to such trouble and danger to get away from the encroachments on their freedom. This led them to take to the wilderness when they got to the New World. Once in the wilderness they had to be self-reliant or else they perished. Thus, individualism and self-reliance became traits to be admired on the frontier. The person who could not look after himself and his family was to be pitied...The pride of the mountaineer is mostly a feeling of not wanting to be beholden to other people...We don't like to ask others for help. Mountain people find it very hard to seek various sources of welfare aid when they are in need...I have known Appalachian persons who were in dire economic straits but who pretended that all was well. The value of self-reliance is stronger than the desire to get help." [Jones 1983]

Other Appalachian values can be traced to the group's adaptation to its new environment. The general trait of independence was tempered by a fundamental neighborliness, hospitality, and cooperation, since survival on the frontier depended upon people looking out for one another. Loyalty and a sense of responsibility to family are highly valued, and this commitment extends to a broad kinship network that persists, even when family members are separated by hundreds of miles. An ability to "get along" with others and avoid offending them, even if it meant hiding feelings, promoted group cohesion when extended families occupied cramped quarters with little or no privacy and few diversions during long mountain winters. And economic uncertainty prompted an understanding that hard work did not bring a sure reward; that while a person could see what needed to be done, failure was still possible; and, while life on earth was hard, a person could look forward to a better life in the hereafter. These values and religious beliefs, says Jones, have sustained Appalachian families, given meaning to their lives, and enabled them to survive for generations in the often unforgiving wilderness environment [Jones 1983].

TRANSLATING VALUES INTO BEHAVIOR

Codes of rules and standards for conduct, referred to as "norms" in sociology, delineate "right" and "wrong" behaviors in all cultures. These rules of conduct assure that the behavior of group members is consistent with the group's values. The code of conduct defines what constitutes proper or improper behavior in all life situations, particularly in social interactions.

All cultures also have systems of rewards and punishments, or sanctions, that reinforce what is considered "proper" behavior. Positive and negative sanctions are developed into a complex system of rewards and punishments that insures adherence to normative rules of conduct. Some examples of such rules and standards of conduct are:

- Don't talk when other people are talking.

- Children should not talk back to adults.

- Assert yourself. Don't let people take advantage of you.

- Killing is not permitted, unless it is in self–defense.

- Never hurt another person.

- Don't discuss personal business with strangers.

- Don't show your emotions in public.

- Never start a fight, but always finish one.

To fully understand the meaning of a behavior, we must understand how it relates to underlying values. For example, "Don't talk when other people are talking," may reflect respect for others, which is communicated by deference. "Killing is not permitted, unless it is in self–defense" reflects a value of nonviolence in interpersonal relationships, with an exception in situations when a person's own life is threatened. "Never start a fight, but always finish one," reflects two values; a value of nonviolence, and defining personal integrity as standing up for your rights if confronted by someone else.

VARIATIONS IN THE MEANING OF COMMON BEHAVIORS

While cultures hold many common values, different cultures may attribute widely different meanings to the same overt behaviors. Much cross–cultural miscommunication results from an incorrect interpretation of the meaning of a particular behavior, rather than from any significant differences in basic values.

This can be illustrated by examining cultural rules that govern interpersonal relationships. All cultures adhere to standards of respect and deference in some relationships, and promote familiarity and intimacy in others. However, the behavioral expressions of deference and friendliness may be quite different, as are the degrees of deference or familiarity appropriate for different types of relationships. As an example, to look a person in the eye in some cultures communicates sincerity, an interest in the other person, and a desire for increased familiarity. In some cultures, eye contact may also communicate that you see another person as an equal. Direct eye contact in other cultures may be interpreted as a challenge; suggests aggressiveness; may communicate an intent to fight another person for position or status; or may communicate disrespect, or a lack of appropriate deference to someone in a position of authority.

The avoidance of eye contact can also have varying meaning. It may communicate shyness or discomfort. It may also reflect a desire to ignore another person, discount his or her importance, or avoid a relationship with the person, and may, therefore, be viewed as "unfriendly." Avoiding eye contact is sometimes interpreted as a sign of deceit, of not being truthful (consider, "Look me in the eye and tell me the truth.") Conversely, it may be a sign of respect and deference in the presence of someone in an esteemed or honored position.

Among the rules that guide interpersonal relationships are those that communicate the status, position, or worth of people, and that define a person's position and intent within a relationship. For example, in some cultures, being on a first-name basis with another person may denote friendliness, by dropping "artificial barriers" to permit free and easy discourse. Using formal titles may be interpreted as a wish to maintain interpersonal distance. Where titles reflect differences in status and position, dropping the use of titles denotes equality in the relationship.

However, in other cultures, the use of a first name may be perceived as disrespectful and ill-mannered. It may communicate that a person does not hold another in high regard, or believes that person to be of lower status. In some cultures, to use first names or nicknames may imply a degree of intimacy that is reserved for very few relationships, and the use of titles connotes deference and respect.

Particular words and phrases may have very different meanings in different cultures and geographic areas. If someone does not understand these idiomatic uses of common words, it can lead to miscommunication. One child welfare caseworker asked a mother if she would accompany the worker to a school conference to plan for the child's special educational needs. The mother answered, "I don't care." In the worker's culture, "I don't care," was often a noncommittal, polite way of expressing disagreement or avoiding conflict. The caseworker decided, based upon her interpretation of the message, that the mother didn't really want to go to the school, and she dropped the subject.

However, in the client's culture, the assertive expression of personal opinions was considered impolite. The mother was expressing agreement, while leaving room for consideration of the worker's feelings. As such, "I don't care," was equivalent to, "Sure, it's fine with me, if you want to." Consequently, when the caseworker never followed through with the meeting, the mother decided the caseworker was unreliable and didn't really care about her opinions.

Another potential area of cultural miscommunication is failure to recognize differences in the belief systems that underlie behavior. For example, one mother was devoutly religious, and believed that the Lord would look after her, and that all was in His hands; whatever happened was within His plan, and she needed only to trust in His wisdom. Her behavioral responses to problems included patience, tolerance, and quiet acceptance of her situation. By contrast, the caseworker's culture stressed a value of self-reliance and independence. She had been taught that the only way to survive was to "pull yourself up by your bootstraps," and to pursue a path that you determined, through reason and rational consideration, to be the best for you. The resulting behaviors were action–oriented. Subsequently, the caseworker interpreted the mother's behavior as "passive," reflecting an absence of motivation or initiative, avoidance of the real issues, and a lack of interest in changing her life. The mother interpreted the caseworker's desire to "teach her to help herself," as pushy, intrusive, short–sighted, and critical of her.

In child welfare, we serve families from a wide variety of ethnic, racial, social, cultural, and class backgrounds, and caseworkers often have very different cultural backgrounds than their clients. As we have seen, failure to understand and properly interpret differences can interfere with a caseworker's ability to make fair and informed judgments about families and their situations.

Our personal view of the world is always shaped by our cultural background, but it is often difficult for us to view our own culture objectively. Most people take culture for granted, or remain largely unaware of its effects, because it is such an integrated part of our lives. However, a lack of insight regarding our own culture creates blinders that prevent us from recognizing and understanding the effects of culture on other people's thinking and behavior. To develop cultural competence, we must first understand the role of culture in our own lives, and become aware of our own potential cultural biases.

COMMON ERRORS IN ASSESSING CULTURE

There are several possible perspectives in viewing cultural diversity. The majority of people in all cultures have an ethnocentric perspective, particularly when they have had little exposure to other cultures or cross–cultural training. The word "ethnocentrism" is derived from the root words "ethnic," and "center." Essentially, people who are ethnocentric place their own culture at the center of their universe, typically resulting in an "emotional attitude that one's own race, nation, or culture is superior to all others" [Webster 1983].

An opposite position to ethnocentrism is "cultural relativism." A cultural relativist believes that any value, trait, or behavior is valid, as long as it is condoned within a culture or subculture. Cultural acceptance is the sole criteria for validity. No cultural trait or component is considered to have intrinsic worth. Since a cultural relativist uncritically accepts all cultural traits as equally valid, an objective assessment of the strengths and shortcomings present in all cultures is never made. The cultural relativist may be blind to inherent adaptive limitations of some cultural attributes. This may promote adherence to traits that may no longer be adaptive or valid.

A position sometimes referred to as "cultural pluralism" is a more valid way of viewing cultural diversity. Cultural pluralism is based on the premise that all groups develop culturally specific ways of achieving their goals; and, that differences in cultural expression result from differences in the physical, social, and emotional environments in which the group must survive. Cultural traits have validity if they promote survival, enhance social integration and organization, and assure the well–being of group members, both individually and collectively. The validity of a component of culture is its functional value, or usefulness, for a group of people or individual members.

Ethnocentrism

Since most people are ethnocentric by nature, understanding and modifying ethnocentrism is the essential first step in developing cultural competence.

Ethnocentrism is one of the most common causes of cultural misunderstanding, and it can contribute to bias and prejudice. Ethnocentrism is typically characterized by a lack of exposure to persons from other cultures, an unwillingness to objectively consider alternative ways to live, and a naiveté about a person's own beliefs and values. The ethnocentric person's own world view is defended as the "best one," the "right one," or even the "only one," and the person's own values and standards are assumed to be an immutable and intrinsically valid criteria against which other people and their behaviors are measured. Differences in behavior and lifestyle are typically thought to be strange or deviant. Such an uncritical acceptance and valuation of a person's own culture prevents recognizing that culture's shortcomings and limitations, or a need to change. At worst, an extreme and uncritical idealization of a person's own culture and accompanying self-pride can be exhibited in prejudice against anyone or anything that is different.

Ethnocentrism prevents us from communicating effectively with people from other cultural backgrounds, from benefiting from the experiences and successes of other cultures, or from recognizing the commonalities in values and beliefs that underlie different cultural expressions. An ethnocentric perspective, at the very least, creates a profound lack of understanding of others. At worst, it creates a pervasive disrespect and disregard for other people.

Despite the obvious detrimental effects of ethnocentrism on human relationships, it would appear to be a "naturally occurring" condition. According to Stewart and Bennett

> People typically have a strong sense of what the world is really like, so it is with surprise that they discover that reality is built up out of certain assumptions commonly shared among members of the same culture. Cultural assumptions may be defined as abstract, organized, general concepts which pervade a person's outlook and behavior. They...define what is "real"...for members of a culture...Additionally, cultural assumptions exist, by definition, outside of awareness. That is, we cannot readily imagine alternatives to them. In this sense, assumptions are like primitive or zero-order beliefs, defined by Daryl Bern as "so taken for granted that we are apt not to notice that we hold them at all; we remain unaware of them until they are called to our attention or are brought into question by some bizarre circumstance in which they appear to be violated [Stewart & Bennett 1991].

Stewart and Bennett contend that retreat to ethnocentrism is a common reaction to cultural diversity, because people often experience discomfort and ambiguity when they are initially confronted with cultural differences. Immersion in a foreign culture results in the "disappearance of the familiar guideposts that allow [people] to act without thinking in their own culture." The loss of these cultural anchors makes it necessary to consciously think and plan our actions and responses, actions that "come naturally" in our home environment. Simple activities like greeting people, knowing how to address them, and knowing what is expected of us become difficult problems with potentially risky outcomes.

Most people have similar reactions to the ambiguity generated by exposure to a foreign culture.

> Faced with these cross-cultural uncertainties, people tend to impose their own perspectives in an effort to dispel the ambiguity created by the unusual behavior of [people in other cultures]. They are unlikely to suspend judgment about differences in behavior because they assume unconsciously that their own ways are normal, natural, and right. Those of the other culture, therefore, must be abnormal, unnatural, and wrong. This presumption of superiority of one's own culture is, of course, characteristic...of most peoples of the world [Stewart & Bennett 1991].

It is important to recognize that ethnocentric behavior is not always intentionally directed to demean persons of another culture. It is often a response to cognitive dissonance. Ethnocentrism can, of course, be exacerbated by a pathological need to increase our own esteem and feeling of power by presuming superiority over other people. But in its purest form, ethnocentric behavior is the product of a need to reconcile competing and potentially disconcerting information, accompanied by the natural emotional reaction of discomfort when faced with the strange and unfamiliar.

Piagetian psychology suggests that people strive to maintain cognitive equilibrium, constancy, and balance. To be comfortable, we must find ways to "fit" new knowledge or information into what we already know and strongly believe to be true. When new information is consistent with, corroborates, expands upon, or enlarges what we already believe, we are likely to view the information as valid, and we easily incorporate it into our existing belief system. By contrast, information that is not consistent with what we believe to be true, or that conflicts with our previous experiences creates a cognitive tension, or dissonance, that is uncomfortable. People typically try to resolve this discrepancy and eliminate the tension, thereby reestablishing a sense of cognitive equilibrium...a "peace of mind" where everything fits comfortably together. This is most quickly and easily accomplished by rejecting the incompatible information as untrue, flawed, deviant, or eccentric. Thus, when we confront a value system that is in significant conflict with our own, it is not unusual to initially dismiss the other values as "abnormal, strange, or wrong," while retaining our own conception of what is "normal, best, and right." This, in cultural terms, is a description of the ethnocentric perspective. The more potentially threatening the new information, the more forcefully people will tend to reject it in order to maintain their own psychological comfort.

Piaget's concept of "accommodation" provides a second option for dealing with conflicting new information. When confronted with dissonance, we can evaluate and weigh the new information and seek evidence of its validity. We may then alter some aspect of our preexisting cognitive system to incorporate the new information. We can do this in several ways; by discarding or modifying previously held beliefs, now recognized as less valid or simply wrong; by discovering similarities in information that at first appeared to be discordant; or by acknowledging, without feeling personally threatened, that people can, and do, have competing perspectives with relatively equal validity. This seemingly complicated process is called, in simple language, learning. This is the goal of cultural education. To the degree that we succeed, we will increase our cultural competence.

The first step to becoming culturally competent is, therefore, to be open to examination and discourse, allowing our own world views to be challenged by others whose beliefs and views are different from ours. While our socialization as children into a culture was judged by our families and ancestors to serve our best interests, as adults and professionals we must accommodate to the information that not everyone sees the world as we do. As the proverb so aptly states, "There's more than one way to skin a cat." However, without first understanding the processes underlying the development and transmission of culture, we are likely to experience dissonance and emotional discomfort when confronted with behaviors and values that appear to challenge some of our most deeply held beliefs.

The first step in developing out of ethnocentrism is to explore and understand the assumptions and values of our own culture, and the impact of our culture on our lives. Objectively assessing our own culture allows us to then explore the cultures of others, and to discover cultural commonalities and differences. Armed with this understanding, we can transcend cultural barriers and establish meaningful communication and relationships with people from other cultural backgrounds.

Stereotyping

Stereotypes are generalized statements about the presumed characteristics of a group of people and its members. The greatest danger of stereotypes is that they often communicate misinformation and promote misjudgments about people.

It is interesting to note that a stereotype was originally a metal plate made from a mold and used on a printing press. The dictionary definition of "stereotype" is a "fixed, unvarying form or pattern, having no individuality, as though cast from a mold" [Webster 1983].

The following statements could all be considered stereotypes:

- Persons who are mentally retarded are happy, carefree, childlike individuals.

- Latino men are "macho," and make the major decisions for their families.

- African American women are very strong and capable, and tend to be the heads of their families.

- Caucasian people are emotionally constricted and unable to express feelings.

- First Nation peoples strongly believe in the spirit world.

- African American and Latino people are likely to be on welfare.

- Women have a lower status than men in Islamic groups.

- Gay men are highly creative and artistic.

- People with disabilities want to be treated exactly like anyone else.

- Puerto Ricans love music and dancing.

- Asians are docile, polite, and easygoing people.

- Native Americans are often alcoholic.

- Jewish mothers are very controlling and try to manipulate their children with guilt.

- Unemployed people are not motivated to work.

- The homeless are drifters who prefer to live on the streets.

- African Americans are superb athletes and entertainers.

- Catholic people don't believe in birth control.

- Caucasian people are racists.

- Middle class families only care about making money and collecting possessions.

- Jewish people are high achievers; they strive to be well-educated, and choose careers as doctors and lawyers.

- Sibling incest is common among rural Appalachian families.

- Latino families have strong extended family ties, and they are loyal.

- African American men avoid parenting responsibility.

- Native Americans are recluses who don't want to be involved in mainstream society.

- Asian people won't tell you what they are really thinking.

- Appalachian families are strong and independent.

- Working class families are flexible and adaptable.

Some of these statements may be patently false. Others may be accurate when applied to some members of a cultural group. Still others may be essentially valid descriptions of common traits for a majority of group members. Yet, all are stereotypes.

While it is true that members of a cultural group share many common values, traits, and characteristics, it is not true that all members of a cultural group are alike in all ways. In fact, we can always finds a range of differences in values, attitudes, and behaviors among persons of any cultural or ethnic group. These individual variations result from several factors:

- The genetic makeup of individuals, including aspects of temperament, personality, and cognition, will vary within a culture. Inherited differences will contribute to different propensities for a variety of attitudes and behaviors.

- Often, people who consider themselves part of the same culture have very different life experiences. They may be raised in different parts of the country, some in urban settings, some in rural. Their family composition, structure, and relationships may vary. And unique personal experiences may significantly affect their development.

- Some members of a culture may have more exposure to the values and beliefs of persons from other cultures, and they may modify their own values and beliefs in response to this exposure. This can occur in any situation that results in cross-cultural experiences.

- Sociocultural factors, such as level of education, income, or social class identification, affect individual values and behavior. Some people contend that intergroup differences are more a factor of social and economic group identification than ethnic or cultural identification.

- The presence of psychopathology or personal dysfunction of an individual or a family, including the presence of mental illness and clinical emotional disorders, results in characteristics that often deviate from the norms of the cultural group.

- Many identified "cultural" groups are not actually made up of people who share the same culture! For example, "Latino" refers to Spanish speaking people of many different nationalities, including Mexican, Spanish, Puerto Rican, Cuban, and many groups in Latin America and South America. While these groups may have some common cultural elements, they also differ in important ways. Similarly, "Asian" refers to people whose national origins are in Asia, and can include people from Korea, China, Vietnam, Japan, Cambodia, and Nepal, to name only a few. Similarly, the term "African American" refers to people with an often-shared racial heritage and geographic origin, but not necessarily the same ethnic or cultural background. And the backgrounds of "Caucasian Americans" represent dozens of countries and cultures from several continents.

The problem with stereotyping is a common mistake of logic; we make generalizations when such conclusions are not logically warranted. As a result, we can be sure that our conclusions will often be wrong!

Stereotypes take many forms. At times they may be derived from an accurate description of general traits that are observed in a majority of members of an identified group. A statement that, "Religion is important to people of Latino descent," accurately reflects a common trait in this group. Similarly, "Jewish families highly value education," is a generally accurate statement about members of this cultural group. However, we can never assume that all persons of Latino heritage value religion, or that all Jewish people promote higher education. Nor can we assume that an individual will possess a trait that is typical to members of his or her culture. To do either is stereotyping.

At other times, stereotypes are formed when we draw conclusions about an entire group from our experiences with a small and not always representative sample. In other words, we may form general ideas about a culture or group based upon only a few experiences with a very limited number of people. For example, when people are challenged about their stereotypic remarks, they often retort, "Well, all the _(label)_ people I've ever met are like that!" The "all" referred to may be a handful of people, or a small subgroup in a larger community, but they are rarely representative of the culture as a whole. At times, special circumstances may cause certain group members who exhibit particular characteristics to achieve a high degree of visibility. They are then mistakenly assumed to be representative of the group as a whole. For example, a significant number of African American athletes participating in professional basketball leads many people to conclude that, "African American males are good basketball players." Similarly, media publicity about youth gangs perpetuates a stereotype of African American youth as prone to violent, aggressive behavior. It is possible to draw such conclusions only when we have limited contact with members of the cultural group. Without broad exposure, we cannot sort the myth from reality, the exception from the rule.

The above examples also suggest that stereotypes can communicate misinformation that may be both positive or negative. Stereotypes that communicate negative information can promote censure, mistrust, and fear. Such stereotypes engender strong emotional reactions, as when an African American person in confrontation with a Caucasian person automatically assumes the Caucasian person is racist; or, when a Caucasian person assumes the African American youth walking toward him on the street is likely to assault him.

If a stereotype describes a trait that is normally valued as positive, it is less likely to be recognized as a stereotype. For example, the statement that, "Appalachian people are strong, independent, and prefer to help themselves," could be an accurate description of many persons with Appalachian heritage, and might even be perceived as a compliment. However, a caseworker who believed the stereotype might presume, without asking, that her Appalachian clients always preferred to manage themselves. This would be a serious disservice to the families who would welcome her assistance. A stereotypic statement about a positive attribute is still a stereotype and, therefore, has the potential to misinform.

Finally, ethnocentrism can contribute to the development of stereotypes, and can seriously interfere with our ability to understand persons from other cultures. Stereotypes can result when we draw conclusions about the behavior of others from our own, ethnocentric perspective. For example, Mrs. A. was raised in a culture that valued a neat, orderly environment. She observed that the homes of her neighbors in an ethnic community were always cluttered. Objects in their homes, many old and worn, were stacked high, and crowded each other on every conceivable surface. Mrs. A. interpreted her neighbors' behavior using her own values as the standard, and she concluded that members of her neighbors' culture were poor housekeepers. In truth, her neighbors belonged to a culture that saved everything because they believed you should never throw out anything you might need later. To them, good housekeeping was, "Waste not, want not," and, "You can make a lot out of very little, if you try." Most objects had value. Old objects, particularly, were revered. To throw them out was wasteful and destructive. Therefore, the observation of clutter was accurate; the meaning assigned to the observed behavior was inaccurate. Mrs. A's statement that members of her neighbors' culture were "poor housekeepers" was a stereotype that communicated misinformation.

Once a stereotype is accepted, it can affect all further judgments about a group, and it is often very difficult to change. When a person with a stereotypic perception about another culture is presented with ample evidence of persons who do not fit the stereotype, these are often thought to be "exceptions" to the rule identified in the stereotype. The presentation of accurate information, unfortunately, may not alter the stereotypic belief.

To understand another culture, we must be fully familiar with the characteristics and traits that are prevalent in that culture, and know their accurate meaning. Yet, such attempts to understand other cultures have too often resulted in the development of a "laundry list" of characteristics thought to exemplify a particular group. This places us in a dilemma. To be culturally competent, we need accurate and relevant information about that culture. However, making generalized statements about the traits or behaviors of that culture's members can easily become stereotyping.

For descriptive information about a culture to be "culturally relevant" rather than stereotypic, the following characteristics must be present:

The descriptive information must be accurate.

> This means the sample on which the conclusion is based must be large enough, and representative enough, to identify and describe traits that are present in a majority of group members. Therefore, the likelihood of a trait occurring in any individual is greatly increased, although by no means guaranteed. To get accurate information, we must have multiple and varied sources of information. It is a fallacy to expect that any member of a cultural group will be able to accurately describe the common traits of his or her own culture. Ethnocentrism occurs in all cultures, and people may mistakenly consider their own, or their immediate social group's, unique traits to be more universal than they really are.
>
> Child welfare caseworkers are also more likely to develop or perpetuate stereotypes if they draw conclusions about a culture from a sample that includes only client families. Families who become involved in the child welfare system may not always accurately represent the norms and values of their larger culture. Yet, we can make such generalizations without thinking. Getting to know and learning from many representatives of any cultural group will help us to understand the common elements of a culture, as well as help us identify idiosyncratic beliefs and behaviors in individual members of a cultural group. Accurate generalizations can be made only by someone who understands culture, and who has had broad exposure to a wide variety of persons from a particular cultural group.

Like stereotypes, accurate descriptive statements about a culture can reflect either positive or negative traits.

> Many people are quick to suggest that any description of a negative cultural trait is a stereotype. In fact, all cultures have their

highly valued attributes, as well as those that are not so highly valued, and those that are maladaptive or even destructive. Culturally relevant information must include a balanced description of all aspects of the culture, and cultural competence requires a willingness to be objective and accept both positive and negative attributes in all cultures, including our own.

An accurate general statement about a group trait or characteristic cannot be particularized to any individual member of that group.

If we automatically presume the presence of any cultural trait in an individual or family, we are likely to be wrong. Knowledge of the general cultural traits should help us recognize and understand a trait, if it is present. However, we must always "check it out" before drawing any conclusions.

Any cultural trait common to members of a group may be present in any individual member of that culture to varying degrees.

Individual differences, cultural assimilation, generational differences, and variations in historical and family background can modify the presence and expression of any cultural trait.

We must recognize when someone has accurately observed and described a cultural trait, but has misinterpreted its meaning.

Cultural competence requires that we clarify the meaning and intent of any culturally specific trait, behavior, or communication before we make a judgment about or respond to it.

Having defined some ethnocentrism as a naturally occurring cognitive state of uninformed people, and being aware of the dangers of stereotyping, we can see the potential risks of a professional education that defines cultural competence as knowledge of the "typical" traits and characteristics of various cultural or ethnic groups. We cannot simply provide a listing of "dos and don'ts" for the caseworker to follow in working with certain populations, such as, "Don't ever look an Asian client directly in the eye," "Always address the man first in Latino families," or, "Don't ever discuss public assistance with an Appalachian family." Clearly, it would be impossible to draw up a list of appropriate and inappropriate behaviors for each cultural group served by our agencies. Nor, can we define rules for our own behavior that always apply in cross–cultural situations, since the same behavior may have very different meanings for the same people in different situations. We must always appreciate the context and contingencies of a cross–cultural encounter, as well as the individuality of the participants, before being able to decide on appropriate responses. Cultural competence requires, that while we recognize and understand general cultural traits, we must always thoughtfully and carefully assess them with family members before we make any assumptions about their culture. Stewart and Bennett suggest that we delude ourselves if we think we can identify behaviors that are categorically "desirable" or "taboo." Rather, this practice "invites inflexibility, and falls short of equipping [us] for effective interaction" [Stewart & Bennett 1991].

This caution is of particular importance as we examine how to apply cultur-ally specific information to the tasks and activities of child welfare practice. We must realize that understanding the typical traits of cultural groups cannot sup-plant a thorough, individualized assessment of each client family, by a case-worker who is open to learning about each family's culture from the sources with the most accurate information–the family and the community in which they live.

THE DYNAMICS OF PREJUDICE AND DISCRIMINATION

Prejudice is, literally, the disposition to draw conclusions without any data or information that would support such conclusions. In most cases, prejudice involves unfounded negative prejudgments, beliefs, and attitudes about individ-uals or groups of people. These can become powerful, unchallenged generaliza-tions and negative stereotypes, which interfere with cross-cultural interactions. Prejudices, once formed, usually become rigid, and they are maintained without regard to subsequent contradicting information. This is especially true if our family, peers, and cultural group maintain similar beliefs and attitudes.

Discrimination against races, cultures, or groups of people based upon nega-tive prejudice is a maladaptive and highly destructive social dynamic. If we believe people are different, and if we believe those differences are profound and threatening, then we treat those people differently. We act to separate ourselves from people who are different, and we congregate with persons we perceive to be similar. If we are in a position of power, discrimination can result in political and social hegemony. Differences are avoided, and privileges are protected. If we are not in a position of overt power, discrimination can be manifested in actions of subversion and obstruction.

Racism, sexism, ageism, and the other "isms" are a combination of prejudicial attitudes and discriminatory behaviors against others because of their race, gen-der, age, or other attributes. Religious persecution, homophobia, and other types of discrimination fit this category, even though there are no "ism" words to iden-tify these particular types of prejudice and discrimination.

Discrimination is not, however, a simple dynamic. The personal, interperson-al, environmental, and social factors that promote the formation of prejudicial attitudes, and support discriminatory behaviors, are complicated. And, the foun-dations of prejudice and discrimination may vary greatly in different individu-als. It is essential that we recognize and differentiate these various psychological and social dynamics, in order to respond in the most appropriate and effective manner.

A person may exhibit inaccurate prejudgments (prejudices), and may act on those prejudices, for several reasons. They include:

- Many people are ethnocentric. They are usually ignorant about diversi-ty, may know little or nothing about people from other cultures, and may not recognize the impact of their own culture on their lives. They interpret other people's behavior through their own cultural lens; and, since they are unaware of their own culture and its biases, they interpret "difference" as "deviant" or "strange," and sometimes "frightening" or "threatening." They often respond accordingly. They may genuinely harbor no ill–will toward people who are different, and they may be totally baffled, and hurt, when accused of displaying prejudicial attitudes or discriminatory behavior.

- Some people lack accurate knowledge about a person or group, and instead, rely on information gained from stereotypes to organize their thoughts and beliefs. They may have had limited personal contact with persons of a particular group. Their judgments are based on what they have heard from others, or what they themselves have observed in a few situations. They are, therefore, prone to believe and act upon stereotypes and misinformation.

- Some people are sensitive to cultural differences, but they may not know enough about more subtle components of a culture to accurately interpret a person's affect and behavior. They may misinterpret both verbal and nonverbal communications, may become offended, hurt, or angry, and may respond in defensive or other inappropriate ways.

- Some people may have accurate information about a cultural group, but they may wrongly presume that all individuals in the group share common characteristics. They may make inaccurate judgments about an individual, because they automatically attribute a specific cultural trait to a person without "checking it out" first. They do not understand why a person does not act or respond the way that person "should," which promotes a misinterpretation of the other person's actions.

- Some people with low self–esteem and a strong psychological need to increase their own status may develop attitudes that demean others. This is often an attempt to elevate themselves in their own eyes, and in the eyes of their peers. The distorted logic is something like, "If they're worse off than I am, then I must not be so bad." By making others inferior, the person can presume himself or herself to be superior. This dynamic may be prevalent in individuals who do not meet their own or their cultural reference group's standards for "success," and who must demean others to cope with their loss of self–esteem. It may also exist among groups of people who are in competition for very limited resources.

- Some persons with personality disorders derive pleasure and satisfaction from demeaning and harming others. Their behavior is motivated by malice and ill–intent. They enjoy feeling powerful, they like controlling others, and they often justify their behavior by claiming their victims "deserved it," either because of their behavior, or simply, because of whom they are. They may assume a dominant position by forcing others to submit to their will. These people are psychologically ill.

It is important that we accurately assess these dynamics in any cross–cultural situation. Otherwise, our responses to the situation may be inappropriate, and may promote increased divisiveness. If prejudicial attitudes and discriminatory behaviors result from ignorance, ethnocentrism, or reliance on stereotypes, being open to new learning can often change these attitudes and behaviors. If people maintain prejudicial attitudes or demean others as a result of psychopathological strategies, such as enhancing their own psychological status, it is less likely that education will change either their attitudes or their behavior. However, if these people can be helped to achieve status and worth in other ways, they may, at times, be able to relinquish the need to demean others to protect their own self-worth. Finally, people who derive pleasure from demeaning others are dangerous. They must be identified so protective strategies can be developed.

Cultural competence requires that we learn to differentiate among the possible dynamics behind fear of differences, and to approach the phenomena in a constructive and individualized manner. If we engage in open communication and dialogue about our perceptions, assumptions, and beliefs with people from different cultures, we are likely to promote mutual growth, increase mutual understanding, and prevent the perpetuation of prejudice and discrimination.

A WORD ABOUT ASSIMILATION

In today's increasingly pluralistic society, with newly attainable and acceptable cultural pride in history and difference, cultural assimilation is a dirty word. Assimilation has become the "bogey man." To the degree that assimilation means the ethnocentric homogenation of subcultures, it fits the epithet. But, the opposite of assimilation is not the static continuation of a culture's ways of being and doing. Healthy cultures, like the individuals within them, change. This change is not without reasons, nor is it haphazard. It is a methodological and adaptive evolution of a vital organization. The life of a culture is a life of developmental change, a slow evolution toward more and more adaptive social systems. We speak of the history of a culture precisely because cultures change over time, in response to both internal and external pressures.

When two healthy cultures come in contact, there is a new opportunity for learning, accommodating, and adapting. Both cultures should benefit from the voluntary exchange of adaptive strategies and experiences as manifested in cultural values and traditions. Through intercultural exchange, we can find valuable opportunities for growth and enrichment. However, to benefit from such contact, we must be open to such cultural change.

Culturally competent people, unfettered by the biases and self-aggrandizing beliefs of ethnocentrism, are constructively critical learners, always open to learning new and better ways of being and doing that can enrich their lives, and are always willing to share the benefits of their own culture with others, enabling them to enrich their own.

Application

Cultural knowledge is very important in all phases of child welfare practice. The following briefly summarizes some of the ways that cultural information must be directly applied, if we are to conduct effective, culturally competent child welfare casework.

THE DEVELOPMENT OF THE CASEWORK RELATIONSHIP

The casework relationship is the cornerstone of family–centered casework. Knowledge of common cultural norms regarding family structure and interpersonal relationships will help caseworkers approach families in ways that enhance, rather than interfere with, this relationship.

In the initial contacts with a family, the caseworker should determine the family composition, and the position and roles of family members. This will help the caseworker discern who should be approached and engaged into the helping process, and when. For example, in a two–parent family where the husband makes the major decisions, he should be involved in the casework process very early, perhaps first, unless there are specific case–related reasons not to do so. In some families, elders or extended family members are often sought out for advice, and to make decisions. Casework will not be as effective unless these members are engaged and involved early in the casework process. Not adhering to such cultural norms may communicate disrespect, and can create major barriers to the development of trust.

A caseworker can also inadvertently offend a client if the social rules of the client's culture are not known. Examples would be addressing some elderly African American women by their first names, or looking some Asian clients directly in the eye while questioning them. The disrespect communicated by lack of adherence to the culture's social rules can interfere with the development of a mutually respectful casework relationship. The caseworker should become familiar with the norms and practices of the cultural groups served by the agency. The caseworker should also carefully observe a family's behavior and follow their lead until she better understands the meaning of their communications and behavior. Caseworkers can also ask family members for guidance when in doubt. For example, a caseworker might ask family members what they would prefer to be called, and invite them to address her in whatever way they feel comfortable; allow them to direct her where to sit; and ask who the family would like to have involved in the interview.

If the caseworker does not understand the meaning of a particular behavior or communication, misinterpretation and miscommunication often result. Since clear communication and acceptance form the foundation of the casework relationship, cultural misunderstandings can prevent such a relationship from ever developing. The caseworker should acknowledge with families that cultural differences may lead to miscommunication, and that it is important for family members to help identify when miscommunication has occurred. The caseworker should also routinely clarify her own and family members' communications by using open-ended and clarifying questions, such as, "Help me understand what you mean," or "Are you saying (restate what was heard)?" The caseworker must also invite the family to let her know when she may have inadvertently done or said something that they don't understand or find offensive.

It is not only caseworkers who may have stereotypes. Clients often maintain stereotypes about caseworkers as well. Rather than be offended, we should use the casework relationship to educate others about our culture and values. Enhancing such communication can strengthen the casework relationship, particularly when we can identify commonly held values and beliefs that underlie behaviors that would appear, on the surface, to be very different.

Finally, trust is essential to the development of the casework relationship. People are often hesitant to trust someone who is different from them, and the caseworker may have to work harder to engage a client of a different cultural background. We must also understand that many persons from minority cultural groups do not trust governmental agencies and many other organizations to be helpful or concerned about their best interests. The caseworker who understands this will be less defensive, and better able to engage her the family by proving her trustworthiness through her behavior, thus dispelling the client's stereotypes about agency personnel and interventions.

THE ASSESSMENT OF RISK OF ABUSE OR NEGLECT AND FAMILY STRENGTHS

"Strengths" and "dysfunction" are culturally defined terms. If we define strengths as behaviors that promote successful adaptation to life's changing circumstances, and we define dysfunction as less adaptive or unproductive responses, we can better evaluate the legitimacy of any particular cultural trait or behavior. Since the assessment of risk and maltreatment are dependent upon an accurate appraisal of "dysfunctional" and "adaptive" parenting behaviors, understanding the meaning of these behaviors in their cultural context is essential to a fair and balanced family assessment.

Individual characteristics identified as strengths, or as dysfunctional, must be assessed within their relevant cultural context. If we value individuality and self-assertion, then the ability to "take charge" would be considered a strength. In cultures that value group harmony, the ability to negotiate and come to consensus would be considered a strength. In a group in which only certain members of the family make major decisions, the capacity to gracefully accept such decisions without protest may be considered a strength.

Any cultural trait must be measured by its efficacy within a specific cultural context. What may not appear to a caseworker as a strength in a particular case situation may have considerable adaptive integrity within the client's cultural context. Unless the caseworker recognizes this, a behavior may be interpreted as a lack of adaptability or personal dysfunction. In fact, it may indicate the person has adapted well within his or her subculture, even though his or her behavior may be situationally problematic. This does not imply, however, that the client's adaptation is the best or only one. Helping families identify alternative ways to meet their children's needs is the hallmark of effective child welfare casework.

Identifying and enabling clients to use their strengths to achieve such positive adaptation is the goal of strengths–based interventions.

Dysfunction must also be viewed within a cultural context. Dysfunction literally means that something doesn't work in a particular situation. Dysfunctional behavior refers to behavior that creates problems, rather than solves them. Feeding a child a diet of beans and rice is a resourceful way to provide good nutrition and eliminate hunger on a very limited budget. Out of context, the trait could be viewed as parental laziness, lack of knowledge about good nutrition, or unwillingness to prepare creative and well–balanced meals. A mother's failure to spend a full day with her child at a clinic waiting for a "well baby" check because her sister needed her to babysit might be viewed as a strength in a culture that depends upon help from extended family in stressful situations. Within a different cultural context, it could be viewed as failure to provide what her infant needs.

There are wide differences among cultures in child–rearing practices, particularly if we are working with families who have recently immigrated to this country. They can be expected to retain, in large measure, the traits and characteristics that were typical in their home cultures. However, parenting values have commonalities across all cultures–no legitimate culture promotes the abuse or neglect of its children, and as a rule, culturally sanctioned parenting practices are adopted because they promote the safety and best interests of children.

However, the ways a culture evolves to meet its children's safety and developmental needs may vary greatly. For this reason, parenting behaviors must be viewed in context to be understood. For example, one South American hunting and warring culture, renowned for its propensity for violence, was known to purposefully goad and tease infants until they screamed with rage. This cultural group believed that learning to tolerate frustration and diverting energy into rage gave their children a strength and fortitude that would make them better warriors and hunters as adults. This parenting behavior, at first glance seeming to be punitive and insensitive, within its own cultural context could be understood as adaptive, in that it promoted the development of qualities necessary for survival in a hostile and challenging environment.

In "gray areas" of abuse or neglect, assessing the risk to the child must occur within the context of the family's culture. For example, a situation of moderate physical discipline, which leaves bruises on the buttocks and legs of a 10 year old, may represent a varying degree of risk or potential harm, depending on the context in which the discipline occurred. The same degree of physical discipline might inflict less harm, when the child is disciplined for a clearly defined infraction, in a culture where many other children are disciplined using the same methods, and where all other parenting practices in the family promote healthy development. By contrast, equivalent physical discipline could have a greater negative impact when unpredictably applied, by an irrational parent, in an emotionally sterile and punitive environment, and where the child is singled out to receive the punishment. While the child–rearing practices of most American families have much in common, the fact remains, if caseworkers try to interpret parenting behaviors out of context, at times they may misinterpret the parent's behavior or intent, as well as the potential risk to the child.

Caseworkers must also understand cultural practices related to survival in situations of extreme poverty. If we do not understand the function of these practices, they might be misinterpreted. For example, depending upon young children to assume considerable responsibility for supervising even younger children may be considered an unfortunate necessity by a parent in poverty attempting to work for subsistence wages, rather than a result of the parent's lack of interest and concern, dysfunctional "role reversal," or insensitivity to the children's needs. The young child may, in fact, be subjected to a high risk of harm in any case, but the interventions should be situationally determined and culturally legitimate.

Finally, some cultural practices that create situations of risk for children may be defended and justified by members of that culture as "culturally relevant." When these practices place children at high risk of harm, the child welfare agency has a responsibility to clearly identify the potential risks to the child, and assist the family to develop other ways of behaving. Failure to challenge dangerous parenting practices because they are defined by the family as "culturally valid" is an abdication of our protective responsibilities.

THE PROVISION OF SERVICES

A caseworker should expect resistance when asking clients to use services or resources that are not compatible with their values or cultural standards. For example, when a client's cultural norms suggest that disclosing information about family problems to outsiders is shameful, the caseworker should expect that the family might be reticent to attend counseling sessions at a community mental health agency. Similarly, a caseworker may have difficulty convincing a family who places a high value on self-sufficiency of the need to consider applying for public assistance. Other ways of accessing supportive counseling or assuring subsistence should be considered.

The caseworker should develop intervention plans that consider culturally appropriate methods for handling problems. This means involving people that the members of a culture normally turn to for assistance, such as elders, extended family, the minister of their church, or close friends. Linking a client to these "naturally occurring" resources can also increase the likelihood that the client will use the resources after the case has been closed.

The caseworker should understand how to balance the functions of casework with case management. Often, the service itself is not as important as the family's relationship with the service provider. In many cultures, personal contact with a caring individual can have much greater impact than more comprehensive or sophisticated services provided by a large and/or threatening community service agency. Many families are more comfortable using neighborhood and community-based agencies and providers. Caseworkers might also refer families to a particular person within an agency, and facilitate the transfer by working jointly with the new service provider until a relationship with the family has been established.

Intervention plans are often complicated by what appear to be the benefits assimilating different cultural values and traits. For example, a caseworker may want to explain the advantages of individuality and self-reliance for survival in our competitive social and economic environment. The caseworker must realize that a client's "feet" may simultaneously be in more than one culture, and must accept the client's right and need to behave accordingly. For clients to feel that a trait or an attribute is a strength, it must be valued within their culture. For clients to change, they need to feel confident that adopting a different way will benefit them more than their current approach. Cultural competence requires that caseworkers develop the ability to help people grow and learn more adaptive ways of coping, but in a manner that does not undermine or compromise their clients' strongly held cultural values, unless clients themselves choose to explore, and perhaps adopt, a different personal perspective.

FOSTER CARE AND ADOPTION

Cultural differences between children and their foster or adoptive families can create extreme stress for the child, and frustration for the caregivers. The child might not understand the "rules" in the new home, and the caregivers might misinterpret the child's actions, and chastise the child for behavior that was, perhaps, valued and supported in the child's own culture. Foster and adoptive parents should be trained in issues related to culture so they, too, can be culturally competent with children placed in their homes. Similarly, a caseworker who knows and understands the norms and standards of a child's culture can also better prepare a caregiver for what to expect from the child. This will reduce the likelihood of placement stress and disruption.

Shared parenting is a strength in many cultural groups. Understanding this should help caseworkers to recruit such placement resources for a child. This not only expands our resource base, but helps to preserve cultural continuity for the child coming into care.

Understanding a group's perceptions of the child welfare agency can help a caseworker identify strategies to overcome resistance, and to use "grass roots" contacts to facilitate recruitment of foster and adoptive families from that culture. A caseworker who understands a cultural group will be better able to recruit and identify qualified families as foster and adoptive homes for children. An awareness of our own biases can also prevent us as caseworkers from misjudging the qualifications and capabilities of families from different cultural groups. A worker's cultural knowledge can also help to properly "match" a child to a home which will best meet his or her needs.

An important and very controversial issue in adoption practice is the appropriateness of transracial or cross-cultural placements. Some believe children should not be placed transracially or cross culturally because of the negative impact on the child's adjustment and identity. Others believe that while the potential negative cultural effects of transracial and cross-cultural placement are important considerations, culture is only one of several variables that must be considered when selecting the best placement for an individual child. A caseworker must be thoroughly knowledgeable of cultural issues in order to make judgments about the validity of such placements for an individual child and family. (See Section XI-B, "Selecting and Matching Families and Children," for a more detailed discussion of transracial and transcultural adoption.)